The Economics of Enough

THE ECONOMICS OF ENOUGH

HOW TO RUN THE ECONOMY AS IF THE FUTURE MATTERS

DIANE COYLE

PRINCETON UNIVERSITY PRESS   PRINCETON AND OXFORD

Requests for permission to reproduce material from this work should
be sent to Permissions, Princeton University Press

Published by Princeton University Press, 41 William Street,
Princeton, New Jersey 08540

In the United Kingdom: Princeton University Press, 6 Oxford Street,
Woodstock, Oxfordshire OX20 1TW

press.princeton.edu

Jacket art: Julee Holcombe, *Babel Revisited*, copyright © 2004.

Library of Congress Cataloging-in-Publication Data

Coyle, Diane.
The economics of enough : how to run the economy as if the
future matters / Diane Coyle.
p.   cm.
Includes bibliographical references and index.

ISBN 978-0-691-14518-1 (hardcover : alk. paper)
1. Economic policy. 2. Values. 3. Happiness. I. Title.
HD87.C69 2011
330—dc22   2010041654

British Library Cataloging-in-Publication Data is available

This book has been composed in Sabon and Futura

Printed on acid-free paper. ∞

Printed in the United States of America

10 9 8 7 6 5 4 3 2 1

CONTENTS

The Economics of Enough

OVERVIEW

In mid-September 2007 my sister phoned me to ask whether she should withdraw her savings from the bank and put the money somewhere else—and if so, where would be safe. She was with Northern Rock, and there was an old-fashioned run on the bank. It was unable to meet customers' demand for withdrawals and had to ask the Bank of England to lend it the cash. The television news showed lines of anxious depositors hoping to take out all their funds. It was the first full-fledged bank run in living memory in the United Kingdom. I told her that the government would bail out all the depositors, as it would be political suicide to do anything else. My sister ignored my advice (although it ultimately turned out to be right) and joined the line outside her local branch. As for Northern Rock, it had to be taken over by the British government.

A year later, in September 2008, the investment bank Lehman Brothers collapsed. Within a day or two, as financial markets around the world plunged, it was clear that this bankruptcy threatened to bring down the entire global financial system like a house of cards. The banks didn't know if they would get repaid for transactions they had engaged in, which through a massively complex series of links, might end up at Lehmans. They stopped trusting each other, literally overnight. The interbank market, the engine room of the financial system, came to a halt. For a whole week, I went to the cash machine and withdrew my daily limit. It seemed entirely possible that if the interbank market had stopped working, so might the clearing and settlements systems between banks which make possible everyday payments with credit and debit cards or checks. Going to the store, ordering online, paying bills would have become impossible. Companies wouldn't have been able to pay each other for goods they ordered. Salaries would not have come through into people's bank accounts. The economy would have ground to a halt. A year later, the Bank of England confirmed that this catastrophe had been horrifically close. The financial system is the pinnacle of the trust on which all economies and all societies have to operate—and that trust almost evaporated.

This is not a book about the financial crisis. But that crisis has proven a catalyst for many people to ask fundamental questions about the way the economy is organized, and about the links between the economy and the kind of society we'd like. *The Economics of Enough* looks at this wider question, or rather set of questions. It is about how to ensure that government policy and the actions of individuals and private businesses serve all of us better in the long term, and how to make sure what we achieve in the present doesn't come at the expense of the future. It's about how to run the economy as if the future matters.

This certainly hasn't been the case for at least a generation. Western economies face a staggering set of problems, all politically difficult to tackle. We face them in the context, too, of global uncertainty—of an unstable world where the balance of power is shifting and in every direction there seem to be new threats. At present we lack the analysis and the institutions needed for addressing the seemingly intractable economic and social challenges, and even more fundamentally the political framework for debating what to do. While majorities in many countries report in opinion polls that they don't trust politicians and establishment institutions, there is no obvious political process or vision that will allow us to reach a democratic agreement about what to do. Politics seems to either reduce to questions of managerial competence—which party or leader will be most efficient?—or to bitter partisanship—where each party attacks the other regardless of practical matters. So I also address the *politics* of Enough, the kind of debate we'll have to hold about the economic challenges and how to respond to them.

This is in some ways even more urgent than the economic issues, because past experience in times of great change and uncertainty suggests that irrational and violent responses can hold sway if everyday politics do not seem to offer a path out of current difficulties. The economic parallels between the post-crisis downturn and the Great Depression are not encouraging if they're an indicator of political parallels too. It has become a truism to say that the old left-right division in politics has become outdated. I'm not sure that's wholly true, but it is certainly the case that neither left nor right has a clear map of the new political terrain. However, by the end of this book some of the profound political choices ahead of us will be a bit clearer.

THE ECONOMIC CHALLENGES

Although, as I write, there are tentative (and perhaps temporary) signs that a recovery is under way, the banking system is still being propped up by massive government help schemes and partial state ownership. Indeed the financial crisis might have further to go, depending for instance on whether European governments such as Greece can repay their debts, or how high unemployment stays and for how long. To say the economy is in a mess is an understatement. Any recession is unwelcome because people lose their jobs, and this has been no ordinary recession. The banking crisis made it the deepest since the Great Depression. The recovery will be a long, slow haul, and there will be a legacy of spending cuts, tax increases, *and* a huge government debt burden in many countries. The debate about public spending is not whether it will have to be cut, but rather how much and how quickly. It is hard to see where jobs will come from for the next few years.

Financial crises have happened frequently throughout the history of capitalism. Many are relatively brief and small in scale, but a few do go down in the history books as major catastrophes, from the South Sea Bubble to the Great Crash of 1929, to our own recent experience.[1] Part of the continuing debate about the merits of capitalism concerns precisely this constant vulnerability to crises, and to boom and bust. Market economies are unstable. The price of increasing prosperity is uncertainty about what the future holds. But even though the financial crisis has prompted many people to revisit this longstanding issue of instability, there are many other deep problems facing all the world's richest economies at present.

For, as if the fallout from the financial crisis were not enough, the developed world has a rapidly aging population, people whose pensions and health care will also add to the financial burden on those in employment. The proportion of the population still working is declining in many countries. Regardless of the specific financial structure, and whether or not pensions and health care are privately or publicly funded, all the people not working at any one time need to be supported by the efforts of those who are working. In every OECD country the aging of the population will inexorably increase government spending because state support of the elderly through one route or another is universal, whether it takes the form of pensions, subsidized health care, or other forms of social care. The generation of people who fought in the Second World War were rightly rewarded for their sacrifices, and these rewards included many publicly provided services. Their children, the baby boom generation, extended those pension and health schemes and are benefiting on a huge scale from them now, as they pass through the age structure of the population like a mouse through a snake. The benefits they are enjoying are being paid for by mounting government debt, some of it acknowledged, but much of it simply implicit in the promises of what services the government will pay for. Those promises will almost certainly be broken.

In some countries, particularly the United States and United Kingdom, the political friction that will undoubtedly be caused by these fiscal pressures will overlay the fractures caused by great and growing inequalities of income and wealth. In both those countries, inequality during the past twenty-five years has increased to levels not seen since the early twentieth century, although the pattern differs in details between the two countries. Some other rich economies have not experienced such a rapid increase in recent decades and yet also have high levels of inequality. There are subtle and complicated differences between countries. But overall, there is a contrast between the postwar era of convergence in incomes due to an emphasis on more equal social and economic outcomes and the early twenty-first-century pattern of more extreme inequality. This has led to a loss of social identification between different groups of people and a weakening of the social ties that make for a healthy society and a dynamic economy.

Whether related to greater inequality or not, there has been a dramatic erosion of trust, or cohesion, "social capital" as it's sometimes known, in many of the rich countries. The evidence for this takes many forms, which points to it being quite a widespread phenomenon. There is evidence from politics, the downward trend in turnout at elections, or what people say in opinion polls about their view of political institutions. There is evidence from opinion surveys showing declines over time in the status of formerly esteemed institutions, ranging from journalists to the police, local authorities to big businesses. There is also a similar downward trend in the proportion of survey respondents in almost all the rich countries who say that generally speaking they think people can be trusted. Although the picture in terms of actual social outcomes varies greatly between countries—say in crime rates, teen pregnancies, or social mobility—it is a fair generalization to say that people in the West broadly speaking feel decreasingly inclined to trust their fellow citizens.

And then, of course, there's the small matter of climate change and the debate about the extent to which every economy needs to adapt to avert catastrophic changes in the weather and environment. In this book I can only touch on some aspects of the debate about climate change, which is growing increasingly ill-tempered and controversial. Some people, growing in numbers, organization, and confidence, deny that man-made climate change is occurring at all. Others debate the extent to which the threat of climate change means we should curtail our lifestyles or invest in new energy technologies. This isn't a book about the environment and climate so I try to avoid specific conclusions about environmental controversies. Different readers will bring their own opinions, but I think all would agree that it is an important part of the debate about the structure of the economy and how well it serves us.

THE CURRENT CRISIS OF CAPITALISM

These immense challenges are all linked.

Once a generation there is a crisis of capitalism, an array of problems that are driven by profound changes in technology and society. The institutions, the rules for governing how we organize the large and complicated societies of the modern world, lag behind people's behavior as they go about their day-to-day activities—working, spending, investing, saving. The sense of crisis will come to a head due to some trigger—in the mid-1970s it was the OPEC oil price rise, in 2008 the near-collapse of the global financial system.

The current structural fragility revealed by the banking crisis has deeper causes. These lie in a dramatic series of technological innovations since the late 1970s, the information and communication technology (ICT) revolution. The financial sector is the most dramatic example of the way ICTs have revolutionized ways of organizing business and relationships in the economy. Technical change has been redrawing long-standing relationships throughout the economy, destroying and creating jobs and businesses. Much of this turmoil has been intermediated through the financial system. What's more, modern communications and computer technology have transformed finance itself, making it a lightning-fast amplifier of shocks around the entire global economy.[2] There is no previous example of a new technology whose price has fallen so rapidly, or which has diffused through the economy as quickly, as innovations such as computers and mobile phones. It is impossible to predict what their ultimate impact on the world will be, just as it would have been impossible in the early days of Gutenberg's printing press to foresee the Renaissance and the Enlightenment. However, the declines in the prices of the new technologies—a marker of the pace of innovation—and estimates of their impact on economic growth show them to be much more significant than any previous disruptive technologies such as steam or railways.[3]

What's more, ICTs are special because they fundamentally affect the way the economy is organized, as well as what it produces and the goods and services people can buy. For example, much cheaper access to information makes a centralized hierarchy an inefficient way to run a business, or a public service. It becomes more efficient instead to decentralize decisions so people can tailor outcomes more closely to their needs, taking advantage of their greater access to the information needed to decide well. This is why in so much of the corporate sector the hierarchies of the 1960s and 1970s have given way to matrix and network organizations. Other institutions, however, lag far behind, especially in the public sector.[4] The new technologies also drive globalization. Although there was also a political impetus behind deregulation and more open borders, especially in finance, the moving of production and people around the world in the past twenty-five years could not have taken place without ICTs. The impacts of globalization and ICTs have become powerful and entwined, while national policy responses to them are inadequate, and there are as yet few international political or institutional bodies that can address these problems either. Just think of the hurdles to getting international climate change agreements or coordination between countries on how to regulate the banks.

More fundamentally, the new technologies mean more weight than ever is placed on *trust* for the economy to function well. Any transaction that's more than just a face-to-face barter of goods depends on trust, as the goods and services being exchanged will be separated in time and place. But those distances and chains of connections have been stretched ever further. Trust is both more essential and more fragile in the modern economy. Political and economic institutions haven't adapted to the new technological basis of the economy, and building appropriate institutions will be essential to strengthening trust—both the trust we have in each other, in large and complex societies, and the confidence any of us can have about future prospects.

In sum, the developed economies, which are the focus of this book, face a series of enormous challenges without any response so far in the institutional framework. The policymaking process no longer functions adequately. The standard economic policies have been directed toward fending off the moment when the unsustainable can't be sustained any longer. This has been possible only by borrowing from the future on a massive scale, whether through the accumulation of debt in order to finance continuing spending now, or through the depletion of natural resources or social capital. The limits to the continuing scope for maintaining our own well-being at the expense of people in the future are becoming all too apparent. What to do about it is less obvious. It requires both solving the economic challenges and building a process that will allow solutions to be implemented. Finding a process is all the more important given that social trust has been corroded by the conditions that paved the way for the economic crisis.

The economic crisis is therefore also fundamentally a political crisis. It cannot be addressed without reform of the policymaking process so as to make the necessary difficult choices widely acceptable—to give them legitimacy. It is quite striking that there is a sense of near-despair about politics in every country—there is apathy, cynicism, distrust, contempt. These public attitudes are corroding the willingness of the many talented and public-spirited people who do go into politics—yes, there really are some—to stay there. It's hard to build political institutions and policymaking processes that command a consensus, as required in democracies, and therefore hard to change them. Attempts at reform tend to add complexity on top of existing structures. Looking at the political institutions and policy processes of any of the leading democracies always reminds me of the gothic realm of Gormenghast in the novels by Mervyn Peake, a place fossilized to the point of paralysis by its old traditions piling up on each other like a mass of stalagmites. This institutional sclerosis gets in the way of effective policies.

The severity of the crisis and subsequent recession was expected in some quarters to pave the way for a definitive political shift, a crisis of capitalism bringing about a left-wing moment. That hasn't happened, not least because left-wing politicians have lacked a clear alternative. However, there has been a system failure. As Benjamin Barber put it: "There are epic moments in history, often catalyzed by catastrophe, that permit fundamental political change. . . . Today we find ourselves in another such seminal moment. Will we use it to rethink the meaning of capitalism?"[5]

HAPPINESS, SOCIAL WELFARE, AND ECONOMIC GROWTH

One reaction to the crisis has been the argument that we should turn our backs on economic growth. It's growth that puts pressure on the climate and natural resources, it's growth that lures people into debt. What's more, many people have been persuaded by evidence apparently showing that in the rich countries at any rate, economic growth doesn't make people happier. If this were true, it would offer a way out of at least some of our problems. Only wean people off the idea that economic growth is needed for their well-being, this line of argument goes, and the environmental pressures or the social and cultural pressures arising from the drive for economic efficiency would abate.

One might have thought that seeing the impact of a recession (when there is no growth, by definition) on people's well-being would have given "happiness" advocates pause for thought. The absence of growth seems to make many people unhappy, so perhaps we should be a bit cautious about the reverse proposition that growth doesn't make people happy. There is a growing body of research about what does make for happiness. The "positive psychology" movement points to the importance of factors such as active social engagement, absorbing work, and freedom for human happiness. This is consistent with empirical economic research indicating that employment, marriage, religious participation, and political liberties as well as income are important indicators of reported happiness. This all seems highly sensible and plausible, and points toward policies such as avoiding unemployment, safeguarding political freedoms, and facilitating people's natural inclinations to settle down with a — life partner and take part in collective worship.

However, there is a large question mark over the claim that because reported happiness doesn't rise in line with GDP over time, growth in GDP doesn't make people any happier. This is a big claim based on treating GDP, constructed data that can grow without limit over time, as having the same statistical character as surveys in which people rank their happiness on a scale of one to three. This scoring has an upper limit, reached when everyone scores a 3 (and countries such as the United States and United Kingdom are currently well above 2 on average). Expecting surveyed "happiness" to carry on growing on a par with GDP is like expecting people to get ever taller as the economy grows. There is an indirect link between the economy and average height, via nutrition; nobody would deny it exists just because we're not yet twenty feet tall after two centuries of capitalism.

Actually, the links between growth and happiness are more direct than the links between height, or life expectancy, and growth. We tend to think of "growth" in an abstract way, but what it means in practice is access to an ever-increasing array of goods and services, and ever-greater command for each individual over how they want to lead their life. The "happiness" movement is dismissive of the freedom and scope for self-definition this implies. Do we really need the freedom to choose one more variety of designer jeans, asks Professor Barry Schwartz in his book *The Paradox of Choice*.[6] He argues that too much choice makes people unhappier. Chairman Mao too was against choice: he thought everyone in China should wear the same style of clothes. Having professors or bureaucrats decide what items we should be able to buy doesn't seem like a prescription for a happy society. The increase in consumers' well-being from the availability of new goods and more varieties over the years—from economic growth, in other words—has been enormous. That includes everything from new flavors of breakfast cereal to the variety of books and music available to us to enrich our lives or the introduction of new medicines improving health.[7]

So unfortunately just stopping the economy from growing isn't an easy answer to the multiple economic challenges of our time. Downgrading the status of consumption might, perhaps, address the problems arising from great inequality and all the social tensions that brings, on the assumption that it's "conspicuous consumption" that keeps people in the rat race or makes them incur debts they can't afford in order to acquire consumer goods. There are clearly many people for whom the vision of a kinder, gentler economy, with less work, more leisure for family and friends and fulfilling nonwork activities, is hugely appealing. The recession has given the sharp edge of necessity to trends such as downshifting and handcrafting, but these strike an emotional chord as well. However, I suspect this appeal is very limited—indeed, that it's a view most likely to be found among people who are pretty comfortably off; the pursuit of "happiness" through ostentatious abstemiousness is just as much of a lifestyle choice as "conspicuous consumption." Retreat into an imaginary arcadia of precapitalist homesteading is not a sensible proposal, no matter how strong its emotional appeal.

So the need to keep the economy growing in order to improve the well-being of citizens makes addressing the challenges set out here all the harder. As I go on to explain, there will need to be more saving and less consumption out of current resources than has been the case for at least the past two decades. This will slow down growth unless the economy's potential improves thanks to productivity increases. What's more, faster growth is going to be essential in order to repay much of the mountain of debt incurred by governments on behalf of their citizens. In most OECD countries, long-term economic potential did improve during the 1990s and early 2000s, thanks to the technological revolution. However, that wasn't enough to prevent overconsumption, the depletion of natural resources, and a massive buildup of debt to be repaid by future taxpayers. So somehow policies that are likely to limit economic growth in the short term must be implemented even though voters will continue to expect a growing economy, not one that is contracting or stagnant as it has been throughout the recent recession.

BUILDING BLOCKS FOR THE ECONOMY OF ENOUGH

How can a better balance between the present and the future be brought about? There are three elements needed to answer the challenge: measurement, values, and institutions.

The first of these is an acknowledgment that all economies lack the kinds of statistics needed to ensure that policies take due account of their legacy for future generations. A number of recent initiatives have emphasized the need to supplement GDP with an array of other indicators of the current state of the economy, and some countries—notably Australia—do this already. In addition, better measures of economic wealth, in its widest sense, are needed: the economy's natural resources, and the human and social capital available to it. Looking at the wealth or stock of assets in an economy as well as the flow of income each year is vital to lengthening the time horizon over which policies are aimed. However, initiatives of this kind only address one kind of statistical shortfall. Harder challenges arise from the way the structure of the leading economies is changing. The impact of the new technologies, and increasing affluence, mean that the great majority of the additional growth in economies such as the United States is *intangible*. Services account for a rising share of output, and so do servicelike aspects of manufactured goods, such as the research and design that went into them or the customization of after-sales care. Conventional statistics have not kept up with the challenge of measuring an intangible economy, although there are some interesting innovations.

There is a particular problem in not having an adequate statistical framework for measuring intangible value, which is that much of it consequently gets undervalued. There are large and growing swaths of the economy where productivity as it is conventionally measured simply cannot grow. In fact it's not clear what "productivity" means when there is no tangible product. In an intangible service-based economy, we need to be measuring something else entirely. But because an inappropriate definition of productivity is what gets measured, and doesn't in fact increase, large and increasing parts of the economy are systematically undervalued, as are the people who work in those jobs. For example, performing artists only have a maximum of 365 nights a year on which they can do a show, and can't become more "productive." Nurses become arguably less, not more, productive in a meaningful sense if they treat more patients but the statistics work the opposite way. In the online economy, digital products can show infinite productivity—they can be duplicated essentially for free—but if they're priced for free, they will perhaps not be produced in the desirable quantities. In these varied examples, the conceptual framework of measurement isn't up to assessing the things we value (in a noneconomic sense), which in turn actually makes it hard to value them in the monetary sense.

This leads directly to a second requirement, which is clarity about the values and aims of economic policy and political choices. There is a fundamental set of trade-offs—a "trilemma," or three-way dilemma—in the management of the economy—using resources as *efficiently* as possible, sharing them *fairly* between people, and allowing people as much *freedom* and self-determination as possible—and it is only possible to hit two of these three aims at any one time. Thus tilting toward markets for efficiency and higher growth, and toward greater liberty at the same time, will set back equality. Emphasizing equality as well as efficiency requires downplaying individuality and self-realization; instead of looking out for themselves and their own standard of living, people will need to develop for themselves a sense of self-discipline, much as the "Protestant work ethic" drove the achievements of early capitalism and allowed these to be widely shared. During the past generation, the shared values that allow a capitalist economy to function well have eroded. Our current sense of malaise reflects the absence of meaning in the institutions and arrangements that make up the economy. They've tilted too far in favor of individualism and the gratification of immediate wishes. Mutuality and patience will be more important values in the Economy of Enough.

At different times, and in different societies, people will collectively make different choices about which aims matter most. Up to a point the trade-offs of the trilemma will not bite—for example some efficiency improvements might be possible within the prevailing standards of individuality and equality—but ultimately doing better on one or two of these fronts will involve doing worse on another. The existence of the trilemma is why so often there seems to be an innate dynamic to capitalist economies. Marx and Engels thought that capitalism contained the seeds of its own destruction. Others, notably Joseph Schumpeter, have seen the process as a continual reinvention driven by technology and enterprise. My take on the dynamic is that depending on the circumstances (including technology), the policies and the institutional framework of the economy must change in order to restore a balance between the three aims of efficiency, equity, and liberty.

Clarity about the trade-offs between values often plays out in the way people typically think about the role of "the government" and "the market," especially now that the crisis in the financial markets has tarnished the reputation of markets in general. As any applied economist knows, there is no such thing as a "free" market. In any context where people or firms are trading goods or services, they do so within a framework of laws and government regulations, and also the expectations and cultural norms of their society. There's nothing "free" about this, although certainly the regulations can be more or less restrictive in specific cases. Markets are one of the many types of economic institutions—along with households and families, businesses, not-for-profits, unions, and indeed different bodies and branches of the state. In many circumstances, organizing the many and varied transactions people want to undertake is most effectively done via a market. There's no better way of coordinating the vast amount of information needed to match supplies and materials with the things people want to buy— government planning turned out to be a terrible way to do this. Other times, markets do not achieve very desirable outcomes.

This is no surprise to economists, who have an ample catalogue of "market failures." Unfortunately, the circumstances in which markets fail make it just as hard for governments to achieve desirable results. Take the classic example of pollution caused by a factory, an external "bad" that is imposed on the environment by the factory. The price charged for its products will not reflect the side-effect of the pollution, and the factory will have no incentive to curb its emissions. In theory the government can offset the externality by imposing a tax on the factory's output. But usually it won't have enough information to work out what level the tax needs to be. In practice, governments are more likely to set caps on the amount of pollutants allowed. They are quite vulnerable to lobbying about it. It's hard to monitor the outcome. They're unlikely to take firm action if there are pollution spills. In short, the existence of an externality makes it difficult for either government or market to get to the ideal outcome. This is why so many other types of institution emerge to address situations where there are externalities, or shortages of information. Effective institutions manage to align everyone's interests in the same way. Traffic lights are a good example: it's in almost everyone's interest to obey a red light most of the time, otherwise they'll likely be involved in an accident, so they are largely self-policing.[8]

This takes us on to the third building block, the need to adapt institutions in general to the structure of the economy as it is emerging in the ICT age, and particularly the institutions of government and the processes by which collective decisions are made. *Government* is the name we give to the framework that enables us to live in large, complicated societies. *Governance* is the word social scientists use to include in addition other institutions around the periphery of politics and the official bureaucracy. In no country have the institutions of governance kept pace with the speed and ease with which information can now be accessed.

Nowhere are there processes for implementing policies that command real legitimacy any longer, and this makes it next to impossible to envision the achievement of something like a consensus for taking difficult decisions. Instead, some Western democracies have a bitter, partisan politics, which doesn't seem to stem from large differences in practical policies, whatever the apparent ideological or philosophical differences between politicians. The rhetoric of parties might differ greatly, but the differences between specific measures typically are matters of nuance. The United States is probably the clearest example, so great are the cultural and philosophical differences between core Republican and core Democrat supporters. Elsewhere, there are bitter yet meaningless debates over questions of the managerial competence of different parties, with little or no difference between them in terms of their political philosophies or ideologies. So alongside the institutional challenge there is a political challenge too, the need to find an appropriate political debate about shared priorities and beliefs.

In time, the technological tools could transform the way politicians engage with voters. There's certainly plenty of experimentation under way. Finding appropriate institutional structures—using the new technologies—will be important if decisions about today's choices and activities are to give proper weight to the needs of the future. The right structures will take decisions out of the hands of centralized hierarchies. They will involve a more productive and thoughtful interplay between markets and governments than we've typically had in the past, one taking account of the dramatic technological and structural change in the economy. Markets and governments need each other to function well, and indeed often "fail" in the same contexts. The existence of transactions costs and information asymmetries present a challenge to any institutional framework. The work of the 2009 Nobel laureates Elinor Ostrom and Oliver Williamson focuses precisely on the way these aspects of reality shape different kinds of institutional response. The utterly transformed world of information, due to ICTs, is revolutionizing the governance of every economy, and we're only partway through the revolution.

THE STRUCTURE OF THIS BOOK

This book is divided into three parts. The first sets out the interrelated challenges forming the Economics of Enough, and the common theme of the need for economic decisions and policies to address a much longer time frame. The first chapter addresses the myths and realities of happiness, to make the scale of the challenge clear, and it demonstrates that there is no "easy" option of simply reeducating people in order to make them truly happy. The succeeding chapters look at the challenges of climate change, high debt, inequality, and deteriorating social capital in the context of an economy whose deep structure is being transformed by the new technologies. These seemingly disparate areas are my focus because they are where prospects for the future have sustained the greatest damage, and where individual interests are most interconnected. The common thread is the importance of a sense of responsibility for others, and particularly for posterity. Our failure to say enough is enough means our children and grandchildren will pay a high price to repair the damage inflicted by the current generation.

The second part of the book sets out some of the obstacles that make it hard to address those difficult challenges. How can we measure the economy appropriately and in particular make sure measurement tallies with value in an increasingly intangible economy? How should we try to reconcile or weight underlying values that are perhaps mutually incompatible? And in what ways do the institutions governing our economies, in the widest sense of governance, need to change in order to carry the majority of citizens and therefore deliver effective change?

The third part, the final chapter, sketches out a Manifesto of Enough. It would be possible to get depressed about the chasm between the policies and governance we have and where we need to get to within a decade at the outside, so this chapter sets out some first steps along the path. Once we start walking, further steps will become easier and clearer. There has been a serious collapse in trust in the rich Western societies, and that makes it impossible to safeguard the future.

This book attempts two things: a description of the huge and linked economic challenges we face, and the outline of a pathway to more effective politics and policies. More important, it describes the terrain of a much-needed new politics, which will be crucial if there's to be any hope of shaping economies and societies that will serve people better in future. Amartya Sen, the Nobel Prize–winning economist, has written that "profit-oriented capitalism has always drawn on support from other institutional values."[9] The policies of the past thirty years have lost their anchor in values outside the market. I hope by the end of this book to have set out some of the initial, practical steps that will be needed to build a future economy based on a true sense of value.

PART ONE   Challenges

ONE Happiness

AN IMAGE OF HAPPINESS will prompt a warm glow of emotion, a recognisable mental or even physical reaction. If a picture of a dollar bill or credit card, or of the earning or spending of money, stimulated any emotional reaction it would most likely be a negative one.

For many centuries, philosophers have considered the nature of happiness. During the past hundred years, psychologists have accumulated experimental results about the reality rather than the theory of happiness. In just the past decade or so, economists have muscled into the happiness debate.

Figure 1. Happiness.

What on earth can economics contribute and why is happiness the starting point for a book about how to improve the running of modern economies?

The reason is that virtually every society in the modern world has come to be focused on the achievement of economic growth, although with different degrees of success. The purpose of governments is taken to be making their citizens richer. The assumption underlying this focus has always been that greater wealth is good for people and brings greater contentment, or at least enough contentment to help keep governments in power. But some people have started to challenge this presumption. In the richest countries the relevance of growth as the central aim of policy has increasingly come to be questioned. The consumerism of the boom era has generated something of a sense of revulsion; as the economic and financial dust settles after the banking crisis, a sort of existential introspection questioning the moral basis of the economic order has set in. Don't Western consumers have *enough*? And even though growth is agreed to be vital still for poor countries, it is often thought to come at a high cost—for example, in terms of its effects on traditional culture or urban squalor.

The challenge to the central importance of growth as a policy goal dates back some years but has been strongly reinforced by the recent financial and economic crisis. This prompted many commentators—including many economists—to criticize the presumption that as long as real GDP (gross domestic product, the standard measure of the size of an economy) is growing, other things people might want will follow, including even ephemeral states of mind like happiness. The cause of anticonsumerism has become for some people either a moral campaign or—depending how cynical you are—a fashion. What's more, the flaunting of wealth by the superrich has become politically charged now that so many taxpayers count the costs of recession. The recession has fed into a deep-rooted suspicion of conspicuous consumption.

That phrase was coined by the maverick economist Thorsten Veblen in his 1899 book *The Theory of the Leisure Class*. In many cultures, including my own Western cultural tradition, it's a commonplace that money at best does not bring happiness and at worst causes great misery. As the Beatles put it: "I don't care too much for money, for money can't buy me love." The King James Bible warns: "For the love of money is the root of all evil: which while some coveted after, they have erred from the faith, and pierced themselves through with many sorrows." King Midas bitterly regretted his golden touch and in Ovid's telling: "Rich and unhappy, he tries to flee his riches, and hates what he wished for a moment ago. No abundance can relieve his famine: his throat is parched with burning thirst, and, justly, he is tortured by the hateful gold."[1] Economists themselves, drawing on research by psychologists, are now asking: Do the higher incomes created by economic growth make people happy? If not, what will increase people's happiness, and what economic policies will help? Should economics continue to insist that governments should always aim to increase GDP growth?

There is a happiness bandwagon which says not. It's widely taken as a fact by media commentators and many academics that GDP has gone up but happiness hasn't increased. Consequently, some prominent economists and psychologists even advocate policies that trade off growth for happiness, including taxes on luxury goods to stop consumers indulging in wasteful spending.[2] Their call for governments to force people out of the rat race has gathered quite a lot of support on the center-left of politics, enough to grab significant media attention although not always enough to win votes in elections. The underlying idea that economic growth does not increase happiness (at least in the rich West) has become increasingly commonplace.

This view has the additional attraction of making it seem much easier to reconcile concerns about the pressure of human activity on the natural environment with our own interests. If a halt to growth would make us happy as well as reducing greenhouse gas emissions, so much the easier for policymakers.

In this chapter, I will argue that unfortunately it is not so easy to escape the horns of this dilemma. The new conventional wisdom about happiness and growth is mistaken. Growth *does* make us happier, easily seen perhaps as the mirror of the unhappiness caused by economic recession. The policy challenge for governments is to deliver economic growth while ensuring it does not undermine other important goals, or indeed the health of the economy further into the future. Often this is described as "sustainability," although that is a narrower concept than the Economics of Enough. Figuring out policies that can achieve a better balance between the present and the future is what the rest of this book is about. I draw on a long, if overlooked, tradition in economics, dating back to Frank Ramsey and revisited recently by Partha Dasgupta, which emphasizes that the optimum or desirable rate of growth is unlikely to be the maximum possible growth, once due account is taken of the future. This will be a central point of this chapter.[3]

Sustainability includes our impact on the natural world but it has other dimensions too. The threat of disruptive climate change is not the only problem with economic growth as we experience it now. Our political and social arrangements haven't adjusted to the fundamental changes in the structure of the economy that have occurred in the past two or three decades. Information and communication technologies have radically reshaped how goods and services are produced in the leading economies, leading to phenomena such as globalization, changing patterns of skills and work, the demise of some businesses and restructuring of others. These effects are bigger than those of steam or electricity, reflected in the fastest declines in price and increases in quality ever recorded for a new technology.[4] The impact of the technologies has been and continues to be profound. Their potential benefit to our prosperity and welfare is enormous, but so too is the disruption to jobs, businesses, and the institutions which govern us. Political and social arrangements and institutions have not kept up with the economic changes.

This gap between the underlying technology and economic events and the capacity of governments and others to deal with them was brought into focus by the financial and economic crisis that began in 2008. It has been one of those periodic upheavals that are a feature of modern economies, recurring with every new generation of fundamental technologies, just as in the 1930s and 1970s. Every time, crises rightly raise questions about how to ensure that fundamental structural change will benefit the whole population. These questions have not been adequately addressed since the impacts of ICTs began to be widely felt in the 1990s, which explains the widespread sense of unease and discontent in so many countries.[5] The institutions and social conventions with which we organize collective life have not kept up with the radical technological changes, which are overturning established business and social relationships. For example, in the second half of the twentieth century governments used big companies to administer much of the tax and pension system, but now too few people stay in a stable large company for years for this to be a viable structure. Or to take another example, the global community is struggling to find the rules to govern trade between countries with entirely different social and ethical frameworks.

What this means is that as well as environmental sustainability, we need answers as to how governments are to bring their citizens financial, political, and social "sustainability" too. Whether it is the massive government and personal debt burdens, inequality, or the corrosion of social trust, many countries are suffering a largely unacknowledged and yet pervasive crisis in their organization and policies. These different aspects are addressed in subsequent chapters.

In this chapter I start with the prior question of what's the appropriate *goal* of government policy, or for that matter personal effort. Not surprisingly, the recent crises have led many people to believe the time has come to reevaluate the pursuit of material wealth, both for themselves and by governments on behalf of society as a whole. So this chapter starts with questions of social welfare.

There is a tradition of anxiety about whether the social and cultural effects of capitalism corrode welfare and make us worse off. I ask whether social welfare should instead be defined as the pursuit of happiness and argue that this is too narrow a definition, just as narrow in its way as the presumption that economic growth alone is enough. Then I explain why the antigrowth bandwagon is misguided in which case growing prosperity is still a valid and important policy goal. In other words, I argue that economic growth does increase happiness and also contributes to other important aspects of welfare, especially freedom. Finally, I turn to what governments need to do to address the varied challenges of our times and increase social welfare. I conclude that we still have a serious policy dilemma in trying to identify and achieve the best balance between growth now and the needs of people in future.

THE CULTURAL SUSPICION OF CAPITALIST GROWTH

In recent times in the richest economies, the pendulum has swung away from economic growth, and what's seen as its moral consequence, greed. There is a widespread sense that the Western economies during the financial bubble went from enough to excess. This has manifested itself in countless magazine articles and books, analysing and commenting on the financial crisis. It is hard to single out some examples from the crowd but one title makes the point: *All Consuming: How Shopping Got Us into This Mess and How We Can Find Our Way Out*, by Neal Lawson, is a typical example. Others are more thoughtful. The writer James Meek, in a British newspaper feature on the economic crisis, put it this way:

> The worst enemy most of us are being presented with by politicians and the media is the loss of a prosperity few of us believed we had. . . . We feel we've fallen from something and it hurts; but the rise to whatever that something was was not as pleasurable as the fall has been painful. . . . The struggle we are engaged on now seems to be the struggle for Britain to be prosperous enough. But until we decide what "enough" means, we'll never know whether we've won or not; we'll never be happy.[6]

There have been significant social reactions to the widespread sense of excess. One example is the Slow Movement. This began as Slow Food, an Italian protest against the fast food exemplified by, of course, McDonalds, already the target of other protests like those led by farm activist José Bové in France. Over time an array of dispersed "slow" organizations have emerged, described by writer Carl André in his book *In Praise of Slowness*. André describes the Slow Movement as a cultural revolution, a philosophy, and places it in the tradition of the nineteenth-century Romantics or the 1960s hippie movement. Slow means a rejection not of all that is modern—its adherents have no hesitation in using the web and mobiles to communicate and organize—but rather a rejection of what are understood to be the mainstream values of modern societies. Slow is obviously intended to oppose the "fastness" of the modern economy; I return to this question of time later, as it hints at the key question of giving the future due importance in today's decisions, although the issue is more of time horizon than being fast or slow. Beyond that, the emphasis is on community, relationships, and the environment, things that unfold and evolve over long periods of time, all of which are felt to be threatened by the relentless push for more growth, more productivity.

This triad—community, relationships, environment—has been identified as the victims of economic growth ever since modern capitalism began in the Industrial Revolution. As André indicates, the Romantics were swift to identify the cultural and social costs of the changes driven by economic imperatives, and to contrast the values of nature and industry. William Blake famously wrote of the dark satanic mills. John Ruskin, better known now for his artistic criticism, wrote a bestseller on "political economy" called *Unto This Last*, which was one of the most impassioned and articulate blasts against the turmoil created by industrialization. The drive to get rich, he argued, ignored the social relationships involved in the movement of money: if your neighbour doesn't want money, it has no value to you. The "mercantile economy" centers on money, whereas genuine "political economy" includes the social context. True riches, Ruskin said, sounding like an early prophet of the Slow Movement, lie in:

> The farmer who cuts his hay at the right time; the shipwright who drives his bolts well home in sound wood; the builder who lays good bricks in well-tempered mortar; the housewife who takes care of the furniture in the parlour and guards against all waste in her kitchen; the singer who rightly disciplines and never overstrains her voice, are all political economists in the true and final sense; adding continually to the riches and well-being of the nation to which they belong.[7]

Here, Ruskin explicitly includes well-being, or happiness, as a target. The Romantic themes have been picked up again recently by Richard Bronk. In his book *The Romantic Economist* he advocates a new emphasis in economics on imagination: "The Romantics stressed the central role of the imagination in creating and envisioning the future, and in forging our own identities and aims out of the incommensurable and conflicting values and discourses we face."[8] This perspective ties in with the argument that measures such as GDP are an inadequate way to assess economic progress; that we can't capture it in monetary terms.

These are only two examples plucked out a vast literature highlighting the adverse cultural and social consequences of economic growth. Each economic crash, following a period of boom and excess, has brought a new surge of criticism. Karl Marx was inspired, if that's the right word, by the financial crises of Victorian Britain such as the railway manias and stock price crashes of the 1840s and the mid-nineteenth-century banking collapses. But the reaction was perhaps most dramatic in the 1930s, when the inevitable result of the Great Crash and the Depression was to encourage many different attempts to reimagine the fundamental purposes and aims of the economy. Some of the reactions, as we know with hindsight, had profound and terrible political and historical consequences.

If fears for culture and the importance of human relation-ships have a long history, the last issue in the Slow triad, the environment, has much greater resonance today than in the past. The explanation obviously lies in climate change, which is the subject of the next chapter. The environment has always been affected by economic growth, but only now does that impact threaten to be both irreversible and catastrophic. With a global population of more than 6 billion, forecast to peak at 9 billion by the mid-twenty-first century, it isn't surprising that environmentalists argue that the planet cannot sustain ever-growing levels of resource use and consumption. As Nicholas Stern, author of the 2005 Stern Review for the UK Government, and the follow-up book *Blueprint for a Safer Planet*, puts it:

> The problem of climate change involves a fundamental failure of markets: those who damage others by emitting greenhouse gases generally do not pay. Climate change is a result of the greatest market failure the world has ever seen. The evidence on the seriousness of the risks from inaction or delayed action is now overwhelming. We risk damages on a scale larger than the two world wars of the last century. The problem and the response must be a collaboration on a global scale.[9]

IS HAPPINESS THE RIGHT GUIDE FOR LIFE?

From the dawn of capitalism to present-day environmentalists, then, there has been a tradition of suspicion about growth. So why is growth still so central as a policy goal? How is it related to the welfare of society?

The reason is not just that economists have a stranglehold on government policies. Economics asks how best to use the available resources in a society in different activities. Most often economists are interested in questions of efficiency, or how to get the most out of a certain amount of resources. Sometimes economists also look at questions of distribution, or how income is shared between members of society. Less often still, economists consider questions about *social welfare* by asking more fundamental questions about what the available resources should be used to produce, and how to reach such decisions collectively in the interests of everyone, as well as questions about the share-out between the different members of society. But although economists don't typically spend much time pondering such questions, economics has never insisted that social welfare depends only on income or wealth. It is a myth that only money matters in economics.

On the contrary, economics recognizes that social welfare will certainly depend on more than money and the things money can buy. For example, it will depend on physical security and the rule of law, on the quality of the environment, and on the civility of everyday life. These aspects of society and many others entirely unrelated to income and wealth contribute to each individual member's welfare and therefore the aggregate. What's more, economics also explicitly recognizes the importance of different preferences and even moral choices. The preferences of each person are equally valid, whether they're material or spiritual, ascetic or consumerist. Whatever the preferences of the society and its members, the central question for economists is then how to allocate resources in order to achieve them as efficiently as possible. "Social welfare" should be maximized, but it can be a multidimensional and capacious concept.

However, this standard economics approach to social welfare as depending on a wide variety of aims and emotions has recently been overshadowed by the emergence of "happiness" as the main or only candidate for assessing social welfare. A number of prominent scholars (including economists) argue that we should only use that lens to assess how societies are organized, and therefore what they should make their top economic and political priorities.[10] The "happiness" approach seeks to sum up the many aspects of welfare considered in conventional economics in a single idea or measure. Governments are then urged to aim to maximize the sum total of happiness.

This approach is a descendant of utilitarian philosophy, first set out in the nineteenth century by thinkers such as Jeremy Bentham and John Stuart Mill. Their recipe for social welfare is usually described in shorthand as the greatest happiness for the greatest number. Some modern happiness theorists such as Richard Layard work explicitly in the utilitarian tradition. It is a distinguished philosophical tradition that was most notably continued in the twentieth century by John Rawls in his landmark *Theory of Justice*. It is also a controversial approach, because in its own way emphasizing happiness (or "utility" or "well-being") as the sole measure of welfare is just as reductionist and inadequate as saying only the pursuit of income matters. Indeed, almost all other approaches to ethical rules for the good life would say that social welfare—the good society—has several dimensions, and sometimes other principles should outweigh happiness.

In fact, the psychological state of happiness has not until quite recent times featured prominently in the centuries-long debate about the meaning of life. Aristotle, who set the framework for all subsequent discussions of ethics, emphasized the living of a virtuous life and the development of character. It was not until the late eighteenth century that individual psychological well-being became more prominent as an issue. America's Founding Fathers of course enshrined the right to life, liberty, and the pursuit of happiness. And as already noted, the nineteenth-century utilitarian philosophers wove happiness effectively into the debate about what makes for a just society. The concept of utility also became a central analytical tool in economics. Individuals are assumed to try to maximize their utility, which will depend on their preferences and be constrained by their income, talents, and effort. Individual welfare does depend on utility. But even among the utilitarians there was a vigorous debate about whether utility could be boiled down to individual happiness.

Indeed, John Stuart Mill, one of the first and certainly the best of the utilitarian philosophers, acknowledged that the pursuit of happiness was an inadequate principle for either personal or social welfare—better Socrates than a happy pig, as famously he put it.[11] I doubt he would have regarded either GDP or self-declared happiness an adequate guide for policy-makers. And many other economists and philosophers have argued that a focus on a single outcome, whether it is called happiness or utility, misses out some important dimensions of social welfare.

What this discussion highlights is that thinking about how to improve social welfare isn't a matter of choosing between increasing economic growth or increasing well-being, in which case only selfish or philistine materialists would choose to focus on money rather than happiness. Economists don't believe that social welfare only depends on money incomes or economic growth. It would be equally restrictive and narrow to believe that social welfare depends only on happiness. So the first premise of those urging governments to focus on happiness is flawed. Growth alone is not enough for a good society—but neither is happiness alone.

Does Growth Increase Happiness?

The second step in the argument of the "happiness" advocates is that happiness is not increased by economic growth. That too is incorrect.

There has been a lively economic debate about claims that there are no links between growth and happiness.[12] Some of the claims in this literature are supported by good evidence; others, contrary to popular opinion, are not proven by the available data. On the contrary, there is good evidence that growth and happiness *are* linked. There is also a growing body of psychological evidence about what "happiness" can sensibly be taken to mean when it comes to drawing up economic and other policies. After all, there are (and surely ought to be) limits to the scope for governments to affect our deepest emotions such as falling in love or experiencing religious joy—or even being happy. Like precision about the links between economic growth and happiness, being specific about what kind of "happiness" we mean also sharpens the focus when it comes to policies.

But first, let's look at that widely believed but empirically doubtful claim that we're no happier for all the growth in GDP there has been in modern times.

Economic growth has had such a huge impact on everyday life that on the face of it it's strange that anyone should doubt its benefits, especially when you think about the changes it has brought about over a period of decades rather than years. Yet despite the amazing increases in prosperity delivered by capitalism, and the benefits economic growth brings for people's health and well-being, there is as we've seen a long and deep-rooted cultural heritage of suspicion about money, or the desire to amass money. This suspicion is shared by most religious traditions. Consequently the ownership of great wealth is almost always believed to bring great responsibilities. We applaud the very rich who, like Bill Gates or Ted Turner, give away large amounts of their wealth through charitable foundations. In some societies the "big man" is expected to help out his extended family or social group and display lavish hospitality. Few are the businessmen in literature or drama, and those there are tend to be, like Trollope's Melmotte or Fitzgerald's Gatsby, either flawed characters or outright villains.[13]

Yet, of course, there always have been some individuals who get rich, and we admire that, or aspire to it, too. Almost everyone can think of something they could buy or do if they had more money. The rich fascinate us, and we pore over them in magazines or on TV or online, part of the cult of celebrity. Sports and pop stars are rated by their earning power. The praises of entrepreneurship and wealth creation are loudly sung, and so widely accepted as desirable that there are popular TV shows about making money in business or getting rich via the stock market. Above all, politicians the world over boast about delivering economic growth when they can, or blame others when they can't, because a strong economy wins votes.

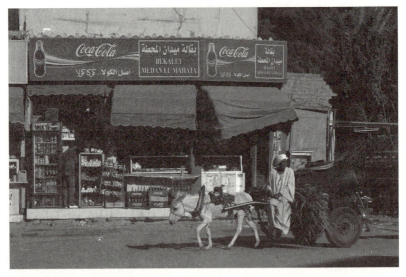

Figure 2. Consumer dreams.

There would certainly be wide agreement that more than 4 billion of the world's 7 billion people are very far from having enough. At least 2 billion do not have enough to eat, do not have adequate housing and water, are unable to educate their children or afford health care. These "bottom of the pyramid" billions can hardly be considered greedy when they aspire to be consumers and buy the global brands that signal joining the modern economic world.[14]

Consumerism on the part of the poor is hard to criticize, although some campaigners, fans of Naomi Wolf's argument in *No Logo*, are at the same time dismayed by the cultural baggage of consumerism.[15] It is impossible to ignore the benefits of economic growth in poor countries, providing what we consider to be necessities for a decent life, better health and increased longevity. Even so, there is great ambivalence—paradoxically on the left—about poor people having the money to spend on the things we already have.

If the cultural, environmental, and moral concerns aroused by economic growth as described above have a concrete focus, rather than a generalized sense of unease, it is the inadequacy of growth as our measure of progress. The attack on growth has two prongs. One looks literally at the measure used as the target for policy and challenges the use of GDP. Other measures are argued to be more appropriate. The second challenges the merits of growth per se as a policy target.

MEASUREMENT ISSUES

The standard metric for economic success is GDP, adjusted for price increases to reflect true purchasing power, and divided by population to give a per capita measure. The concept of GDP dates back to the need during the Great Depression to be able to measure how much the economy was producing, no more than that. It was never intended to measure social welfare. As a measure it has many well-known flaws, most of them recognized by its creators right from the outset. These are the main ones:

- GDP measures paid-for goods and services including things many people regard as "bads," or at least "regrettable necessities," rather than "goods," such as weapons or tobacco or spending on the police.
- It excludes many positive things such as a parent's care for children, cooking at home, and housework, because they are not paid for.
- GDP doesn't take account of the negative consequences of growth, and in particular does not net off the environmental costs such as pollution and greenhouse gas emissions.
- A simple per capita average does not take account of the distribution of incomes and the different weights that might be given to increases in income at the top and bottom of the scale.
- GDP fails to take full account of the improvements in quality and new goods, which are never fully captured in the statistics; this is especially true for big changes in technology.
- GDP does not include many indicators of progress we rightly care about such as health, levels of education, infant mortality, and life expectancy.

The first three of these adjustments would reduce measured GDP, the fourth would do so to the extent that incomes are becoming more unequal, and the fifth would substantially increase measured GDP. The sixth consists of indicators that are not the same kind of measurement at all. Considered important welfare indicators by economists, they feature prominently as measurements of how economies are performing.

One response to this list of inadequacies is to produce an adjusted or alternative measure. A well-known example is the Index of Sustainable Economic Welfare (ISEW), originated by Herman Daly and John Cobb in 1989. The ISEW adjusts for the first three points above and therefore paints a much gloomier picture than the conventional economic statistics.[16] "Gross National Happiness" is another contender.[17] The most recent one of this type is the Happy Planet Index from the New Economics Foundation.[18] All are similar in their emphasis on subtracting environmental impacts from GDP, and in showing next to no "progress" in recent decades. This is wholly because of the way they are constructed.

An alternative, widely used by economists, is the Human Development Index (HDI), which derives a single measure from GDP and other indicators (of health, literacy, access to technologies, and so on) measuring human capabilities to lead a satisfying life; this addresses the sixth point on the list. It combines into a single index a range of underlying indicators of well-being. The HDI includes GDP per capita as one of its components, along with others including inequality, health and longevity, education, and access to resources.

Most of the debate has been about the adjustments under the first three categories listed above, and it's therefore easy to get the impression that GDP greatly overstates "true" welfare. Yet few people appreciate the absolutely enormous understatement of GDP which is due to our failure to measure the impact of new and improved goods and services. Recent examples include the impact of consumer electronics such as computers, cameras, or mobile phones, whose quality and capabilities have increased far beyond the extent captured in the figures, and the impact of new medicines or medical techniques. But there are countless everyday examples too—zippers, shampoo, sliced loaves, smoothies, pantyhose, noniron shirts, breakfast cereals—apparently more trivial but nevertheless making a big contribution to the ease and enjoyment of life.

I am not aware of any attempt to take account of the undermeasurement of GDP by the omission of new and better quality goods apart from the Boskin Commission in the United States. It looked mainly at capturing better the improved quality of electronic goods. Its 1996 report found that the statistics had overstated U.S. price inflation by about 1.1 percent, and correspondingly understated real GDP growth.[19] National statistical offices do by and large now try to incorporate some allowance for improvements in quality of goods such as computers or cameras. However, William Nordhaus has shown that for some technologies—he looks at lighting and computers—the improvements are far, far greater than has been reflected in GDP statistics.[20] No estimates exist for the understatement of GDP by failing to take account of the whole range of new goods and quality improvements; whatever the figure, it would be extremely large.

Although this failure to measure the benefits of innovation is a significant blind spot, ignoring the profound structural changes in the economy, the effort to find better measures than GDP to guide policy has become more vigorous. The high-profile Commission on the Measurement of Economic Performance and Social Progress, founded by French president Nicolas Sarkozy and led by two Nobel-winning economists, Amartya Sen and Joseph Stiglitz, is a recent example. Its opening statement of issues declares:

> There is a huge distance between standard measures of important socio-economic variables like growth, inflation, inequalities etc, and widespread perception. The gap is so large and universal that it cannot be explained by reference to money illusion and/or

to psychological characteristics of human nature. Our statistical apparatus, which may have served us well in a not too distant past, is in need of serious revision.[21]

The commission selected three main directions of study: (1) the limits of GDP as an indicator of progress or economic performance; (2) the quality of life, taking a broader perspective on well-being, including asking people about how they themselves feel; (3) sustainable development and the environment. The commission's central conclusion was that governments should supplement conventional economic statistics with a much wider range of measurements, including environmental indicators and direct measures of well-being.

An initiative by the Organization for Economic Cooperation and Development takes the same approach. At the close of its second World Forum on Statistics, Knowledge, and Policy held in Istanbul in 2007, participants (including the World Bank and the UN Development Program) agreed on the need for national statistical offices, academics, and public and private bodies to work with civil society to identify a "new paradigm" of social progress going beyond GDP. Included in these indicators are health, education, and the environment, as well as employment, productivity, and purchasing power. The third world forum was held in September 2009 in Busan, Korea.[22] At its conclusion the OECD committed to producing a "road map" for the international community to develop an agreed set of indicators of "progress."[23]

The weight of opinion seems to be tipping firmly toward the dashboard approach, introducing a range of supplementary indicators in addition to GDP.[24] Many national statistical offices now produce "satellite accounts," usually looking at environmental measures, and more are also producing other types of measures such as time-use surveys looking at unpaid work at home. By far the most practical and informative approach is to monitor several indicators in addition to GDP, rather than trying to find a single number to replace GDP. One government already does this. The Australian Bureau of Statistics each year publishes a wide array of indicators selected in consultation with the public. The Measuring Australia's Progress (MAP) indicators fall into four categories: individuals, the economy, the environment, and living together. The MAP summary depicts the average annual rate of change of the indictors in these categories over a period of ten years.[25]

THE ANTIGROWTH ALTERNATIVE

Criticizing the indicator being measured is one approach; an alternative is to reject the use of any growth indicator at all, preferring to focus on *happiness*. The inspiration for this approach stems from an influential 1974 paper by economist Richard Easterlin presenting what has come to be known as the Easterlin Paradox.

He noted that levels of happiness were higher in richer than in poorer countries, and higher for rich than for poor people within a single country; but over a period of decades, GDP had risen much more than measured happiness. In fact beyond a certain threshold level of income, higher GDP didn't seem to increase average happiness at all. Other economists followed up Easterlin's paper and confirmed the finding. This body of work has come to create a sort of received wisdom about growth and happiness. These pieces of research find the same apparently conflicting evidence between cross-section samples of data (comparisons between countries or between people in one country at a point in time) and time-series samples (over time in one country). The conclusion typically drawn is that money does increase happiness but only up to a point. As Richard Layard put it in his well-known book *Happiness: Lessons from a New Science*: "Once a country has over $15,000 per head, its level of happiness appears to be independent of its income per head."[26]

There are two explanations given for this paradoxical result. One is that people usually adapt to changes in their circumstances to become pretty much just as happy as they were; this is true of certain positive events such as winning a lot of money and of some negative ones such as becoming badly disabled by an accident. A second and related explanation is that because people quickly get used to better circumstances, they need more and more income just to sustain their happiness—it's called the "hedonic treadmill."[27] Richard Layard writes: "I grew up without central heating. It was fine. Sometimes I had to huddle over a fire or put my feet into a bowl of hot water, but my mood was good. When I was forty, I got central heating. Now I would feel really miserable if I had to fight the cold as I once did. In fact, I have become addicted to central heating."[28] Together, adaptation and the hedonic treadmill seem good explanations of why at any point in time rich people are happier than poor people, yet over time higher incomes don't raise happiness. Some of the happiness authors have concluded that government policy should stop seeking to achieve economic growth, as it doesn't make people any happier. This is sometimes linked to the finding from psychological research that people have a "set point" of happiness, at least partly genetically determined, to which they almost always return.[29]

The Easterlin Paradox, along with the strong policy conclusions some researchers draw from it, has struck a chord. Robert Frank (in *Luxury Fever*) argued that high taxes should be used to discourage consumer spending, which won't buy happiness. Barry Schwartz has written about *The Paradox of Choice*, whereby the great variety of goods and services available to Western consumers only makes us unhappy (despite the fact that consumers do buy a huge variety of products). The Kingdom of Bhutan has become an icon for its policy pursuit of Gross National Happiness, despite the country's miserably poor human development indicators.

However, recently the evidence on growth and happiness has been persuasively reassessed. As described below, recent research strongly suggests that there is no paradox, as growth and happiness are in fact usually positively linked.

To me it always seemed odd to expect happiness to rise fully in line with GDP in the first place—not least because the fall in GDP associated with a recession always causes great unhappiness. Of course, higher incomes should make us happier on average but why would anyone expect GDP and happiness to rise *in proportion* to each other? Higher incomes make us taller on average too, but nobody would expect height to continue rising at the same pace as GDP.[30] This instinct was articulated rigorously by Helen Johns and Paul Ormerod when they pointed out that the happiness measures used in the studies are derived from surveys that ask respondents to rate their happiness (or life satisfaction) on a scale with three or five choices. The way the figures are constructed means they simply cannot increase as much as GDP figures, which are constructed completely differently and do not have an upper limit. No firm conclusions can be drawn from empirical research that does not acknowledge this statistical issue.[31]

Several recent papers redo the empirical testing with due account taken of the very different character of the two variables. These look at the links between happiness measures and the *logarithm* of GDP (the log measure increases at an ever slower rate than the absolute measure).[32] These economists find that in both cross-section and time-series data there is good evidence from a number of different datasets that happiness rises with GDP, and does so at a consistent rate. There are two caveats. First, the questions in surveys change over time, and different countries are included in surveys—so the time-series estimates are less precise than the cross-section ones, although they show the same kind of relationship. Second, there is one country where indeed there is no clear link over time between average GDP per capita and happiness, namely, the United States. In their paper, Betsey Stevenson and Justin Wolfers suggest that this is because the United States, almost uniquely, has become steadily more unequal over the decades for which we have the happiness survey data. The average of (the logarithm of) household incomes has been flat, in contrast to (the logarithm of) average GDP, so it should be no surprise that average happiness has not increased. This is an interesting and plausible hypothesis; I return to questions of inequality in a later chapter.

However, these authors conclude that the United States is an exception; in other rich countries such as Japan and the EU member countries, happiness has continued to rise in line with GDP. Stevenson and Wolfers conclude: "There appears to be a very strong relationship between subjective well-being and income, which holds for both rich and poor countries, falsifying earlier claims of a satiation point above which higher GDP per capita is not associated with higher well-being."[33] Other work is now coming down on the same side of the debate. For example, one paper reports rising happiness in forty-five of fifty-two countries for which times-series data are available (for the years 1981–2007) and links it to rising freedom and economic development.[34] Another confirms that income, alongside social indicators, explains much of the difference in self-reported happiness levels within countries and between countries.[35]

This seems a much more credible result than the original Easterlin Paradox. But the temptation to read too much into this should be resisted. This is partly for reasons of sensible caution about the statistics. All of this work looks at statistical correlations and not at causation. Happier people might be more productive, leading to higher growth and incomes, rather than the causality running the other way. Alternatively, other factors that do cause happiness might be linked in turn to growth—such as better health or greater access to education—making the observed correlation between happiness and growth an indirect one.

Moreover, there is other evidence on the relationship between economic and social measures and happiness that gives useful insights when it comes to policy. Some of this evidence comes from similar statistical studies to those described above, but using other economic and social measures as the potential explanations for happiness levels. Some of these are linked to GDP but may do a more direct job in explaining happiness. This work shows that among the other economic indicators apart from income, having a job is the most important; unemployment makes people very unhappy, although inflation also contributes to dissatisfaction. Other important personal and social indicators are: being married, being in good health, having strong religious or moral values, living in a strong community, and having political freedom.[36] These results place particular emphasis on political institutions and the importance of freedom.

More than a debate among economists is at stake here, because the two different approaches lead to contrasting policy conclusions. Those researchers like Richard Layard and Robert Frank who believe the link between growth and happiness tails off to nothing above a certain income level argue for taxes to make people stop working so hard or spend less on various consumer goods. The government must prod us into being happy because we're simply adapting to each new level of income. The rat race means that like caged guinea pigs scrabbling around their wheel, we keep running to earn and spend more without making any progress in terms of happiness.

However, this kind of policy conclusion has been strongly challenged by other researchers. In his book *The Idea of Justice* Amartya Sen agrees that people's happiness depends on their expectations, which are shaped by their own social situation.[37] But he turns the argument about adaptation and the hedonic treadmill back on the happiness crowd: if we just aim for people to be happy with their lot, where is the social discontent that will create the momentum for a better life? Would women have ever gained the vote if many had not been unhappy? Would there have been a civil rights movement without discontent? Is poverty acceptable because poor people say they are pretty content? Obviously not; most people would agree the world with the discontent and change was better than the contented and static one.[38] Other researchers, looking at the wider array of explanations as to what makes us happy, argue that strong growth is desirable because it keeps employment high, and this is important for happiness. Other things that empirically contribute to measured happiness are traditional social values and political freedoms. It will be obvious that these findings would be more acceptable to people with libertarian rather than interventionist political views.[39]

It also makes sense to look at indicators of unhappiness. Many of the researchers who built on the original Easterlin Paradox have pointed to other measures that suggest that richer societies are not automatically happier. For example, mental illnesses such as clinical depression, illegal drug use, alcohol abuse, and suicide have increased over time in some rich countries.[40] These indicators tie in with the argument that countries are not getting happier as they get richer, so solving the Easterlin Paradox perhaps replaces it with another paradox: Why do some indicators of unhappiness rise at the same time as the average general level of happiness is rising too? Are the same people both happier and more stressed? Or are a minority of people increasingly unhappy while the majority pulls away from them? Or is it just happenstance? The evidence is not consistent—for example, suicide rates show a lot of variation that obviously has no relation to income levels, going up and down over time for unknown, noneconomic reasons. But to the extent that some indicators of unhappiness do increase as incomes rise, this, like the paradox of happiness and growth in the United States, may be an inequality issue. Certainly, the final word on how to interpret all of the evidence has not yet been written.

The Psychology of Happiness

Perhaps an alternative approach can help. Psychologists too have been looking more closely at happiness—the "positive psychology" movement. It would be easy to make fun of some of this work. For example, two techniques of collecting data on happiness are commonly used by psychiatrists. One version asks people to keep a diary during the day about their feelings when doing various activities. Another involves people recording how they feel when prompted to do so by their mobile or PDA at random points during the day. The results so far seem unsurprising and without many obvious policy implications. One of the best known involved 909 women from Texas. They liked sex and socializing best, followed by praying, eating, exercising, and watching TV. They liked least commuting and being with their boss, then housework and childcare. No big surprises here, nor any obvious policy conclusions.

Yet the psychology of happiness offers a useful alternative perspective. Its leading authorities have explored what contributes to a positive baseline frame of mind.[41] The problem, as Mihaly Csikszentmilhalyi has put it, is that we live in a universe that's indifferent to us: "How we feel about ourselves, the joy we get from living, ultimately depends directly on how the mind filters and interprets everyday experience. Whether we are happy depends on inner harmony, not on the controls we are able to exert over the great forces of the universe."[42]

Most people are somewhat happy most of the time, no matter where they live or what their conditions are, although with some cultural variation, and the differences reported in the surveys used in the economic research described earlier should be seen in this light.[43] The explanation lies in the process of adaptation, the hedonic treadmill. It moderates or limits the psychological highs and lows that the vagaries of experience would otherwise impose on us. "Just as it acts as an emotional ceiling that keeps us from experiencing non-stop joy, it also protects us from being dragged into the emotional pits."[44] Adaptation is a marker of human psychological resilience; it is a desirable characteristic. It can be kept at bay to some extent. Haidt writes: "Variety is the spice of life because it is the natural enemy of adaptation."[45] And perhaps this (rather than the keeping up with the Joneses mentality of conspicuous consumption) explains one of the underlying drives toward consumerism: the variety that characterizes modern capitalism does indeed make us happier, until we adapt and seek the next new experience or item.

However, adaptability does limit the scope either for us as individuals or for governments on our behalf to increase happiness levels. This is not to say that each person's level of happiness is immutable. The research on what it is that enables us to experience an inner harmony rather than disharmony is expressed in several different but essentially similar ways. Csikszentmilhalyi describes happiness as deriving from "flow," the focused immersion in an activity that challenges our skills but does not go too far beyond what we're capable of. Activities that create a sense of flow are those in which you lose your sense of time. You are concentrating and absorbed in what you're doing; worries and fears fall away. Anybody who has watched young children play with a pile of bricks or toy cars on the rug will recognize this description. So will anyone who plays a sport or does yoga, or reads a gripping book, or has any other experiences requiring an intense focus that makes other thoughts evaporate.

Flow forms one part of a wider formula:

Happiness = Biological set point + Conditions of your life + Voluntary Activities

We all arrive with a given genetic predisposition to happiness, or a "set point." Neither this nor some of the conditions of life (sex, age, race) can be changed. Other conditions of life may be amenable to change (marital status, location) and some will have a large effect on happiness: the results suggest that noise is one of these, for example, commuting another. Voluntary activities are those where we can make a big difference to our happiness by finding greater "flows" which suggests people should pay careful attention to their work and leisure choices, as well as lifestyle choices such as getting married and finding a home.[46]

Flow is an inner phenomenon. It can be learned or cultivated. According to Jonathan Haidt, mediation and cognitive therapy are the two effective methods, in addition to certain drugs, for improving an individual's happiness.[47] Some of the conditions of life are also perhaps amenable to personal action, such as choosing a home that is not too noisy or too far from work.

Other life conditions might be affected by public policy action so it is worth setting out the external conditions that can affect happiness in a lasting way.[48] They are:

Noise. People never fully adapt to a high level of chronic noise, especially if it is variable or intermittent. This is relevant to noise abatement policies and also policy questions such as new roads and airport expansion.

Commuting. People don't fully adapt to a long commute, especially if driving in heavy traffic. This puts a premium on measures to reduce congestion and to deliver good public transport.

Lack of control. Giving people more control results in large and lasting improvements in their happiness. The lesson here is for the manner of making public policy—I return to this in later chapters.

Shame. Feeling ashamed has a powerful influence on people's happiness, which explains why apparently frivolous changes such as cosmetic surgery have a lasting impact on happiness.

Conflict in relationships. Personal conflicts make people very unhappy and they never adapt to it.

This is quite a long list of nontrivial issues, but far from the public policy agenda usually considered in the economics of happiness literature. However, there is one further issue arising from the psychological research, which speaks more directly to the way society is organized, and that is the role of what could be described as cultural anxiety. Here's how Mihaly Csikszentmilhalyi describes the issue:

> One of the major functions of every culture has been to shield its members from chaos. . . . This is as it should be but there are times when the feeling that one has found safety in the bosom of a friendly cosmos becomes dangerous. An unrealistic trust in the shields, in the cultural myths, can lead to equally extreme disillusion when they fail. This tends to happen whenever a culture has had a run of good luck and for a while seems indeed to have found a way of controlling the forces of nature.[49]

When this rude awakening occurs, he writes, making it plain that progress is not inevitable, people feel anxious and apathetic.

There is a sense of a general malaise, with no single obvious external cause. He believes we are at such a point now in Western societies. Jonathan Haidt expresses it in different terms, with reference to the concept of *anomie* proposed by the sociologist Émile Durkheim:

> Anomie is the condition of society in which there are no clear rules, norms or standards of value. In an anomic society, people can do as they please; but without any clear standards or respected social institutions to enforce these standards, it is harder for people to find things they want to do. Anomie breeds feelings of rootlessness and anxiety and leads to an increase in amoral and anti-social behavior.[50]

He too believes that Western societies are missing something, the richly woven tapestry of shared values and the sense of virtue they had in the past. What's more, he argues that the cultivation of a virtuous character through socially engaged activities such as altruism or voluntary work is one way for people to experience the sense of flow.[51]

These thoughts have taken the research agenda of positive psychology from the recording of data that link individuals' feelings to their activities during the day to much broader hypotheses about the nature of society—about the way work is structured, the impact of cultural diversity, and the importance of a sense of wider meaning in life. As Ed Diener and Robert Biswas-Diener put it: "Humans are unique among animals in many respects; perhaps chief among them is the ability to live virtuously and find purpose in life. As humans, we actually require a sense of meaning to thrive."[52]

The importance of meaning, which underpins our happiness via our sense of "flow," is clear in studies of how people feel about their work. For example, Csikszentmilhalyi, along with Howard Gardner and William Damon, looked at whether certain professions can be classed as "healthy" or "unhealthy"—to be the former, doing *well* professionally and doing *good* need to be in line. The researchers found that this was true for geneticists but not for journalists, for example; the former had a sense of social meaning and purpose in their work. The diary methods for collecting happiness data, described earlier, show that about half the time people in a wide range of jobs do experience a sense of flow at their work, whereas outside work they do so only about a fifth of the time. These results had the social gradients you might expect, with managers and professionals experiencing the good emotions more frequently than manual and low-status workers. Yet in a seeming contradiction people also say much more often when they are at work than outside that they'd rather be doing something else. Csikszentmilhalyi concludes: "When it comes to work, people do not heed the evidence of their senses. They disregard the quality of immediate experience, and base their motivation instead on the strongly rooted cultural stereotype of what work is *supposed* to be like."[53] In other words, for many people, their job does not intrinsically give them a sense of purpose—it is an imposition on them made by someone else, making them prefer activities outside work.

The salience of meaning or purpose emerges in other aspects of life apart from work. Jonathan Haidt argues that happiness depends on "coherence" between our psychological and cultural conditions. Some of his research makes him wonder whether in the efforts of many modern societies to embrace demographic diversity, we've created too much moral diversity and ignored the need to create a common shared identity in society. "Diversity is like cholesterol: there's a good kind and a bad kind, and perhaps we should not be trying to maximize both."[54] We would be happier in general if we had causes to fight for which unite us, he argues. Ed Diener asked his students to compare the happiness they derived from a purely hedonistic activity such as going out to party and a virtuous activity such as volunteering; the former was fun but the happiness was ephemeral, while the latter was not enjoyable at the time but created a lasting feeling of satisfaction.

So the positive psychology movement has brought this debate full circle to the views of many philosophers over the ages—for example to Aristotle's emphasis on the importance of behaving virtuously in everyday life, and thus developing a virtuous character, and to the long tradition in many religions of activities that underpin spiritual meaning. Just as in the standard economics approach, social welfare can't be reduced to a single dimension, whether it is income or happiness. There are many facets to welfare, all of which need to be included in any assessment of policy.

SHOULD GOVERNMENTS TRY TO INCREASE HAPPINESS?

As just discussed, the balance of the evidence is that monetary incomes and material goods *do* increase happiness; and there is *no* strong empirical evidence that rich Western societies have reached a point where people are sated. Happiness seems more directly related to many noneconomic variables, although having a job is key as well. Being married, holding religious beliefs, being in good health, and enjoying political liberties are strongly correlated with being happy—something in that list, perhaps, for those of both liberal and conservative political views.

Significantly, there is good evidence that both freedom and social cohesion make an important contribution to happiness.[55] Much of the "happiness" advocacy concentrates on the empirical evidence regarding levels of income, and consequently on policies to force people out of the rat race. But this emphasis flies in the face of the full breadth of the evidence, and to the extent that it ignores individual freedom is dangerously paternalistic. What equips expert economists and psychologists to manipulate other people's work and spending patterns, and what legitimacy do they have in trying to do so? This concern is increasingly being flagged by some of the economists working in this area.[56]

As we've seen, the psychological research shows that each individual has a genetically gifted baseline level of happiness; that we adapt reasonably quickly to most kinds of changes in circumstances, but not all; that happiness is the product of a process, of engagement in an absorbing and satisfying activity; and that this sense of "flow" needs to be informed by the meaning or purpose we as individuals find in life, rather than anything we have to do because others tell us to. Our individual happiness depends on others. As social animals, our individual sense of purpose will almost always lie in the wider society. It also seems we are happier if our community or society has a purpose too. The pioneers of positive psychology seem to agree that this is lacking now in the rich Western societies. They identify signs of disillusion or "anomie," which is consistent with rising rates of depression and suicide. Although happiness is rising as economies continue to grow, some indicators of distress are on the increase too.

There is a clear conclusion: economic growth contributes to happiness, and GDP growth should remain a policy target. Governments should make a special effort to ensure that growth delivers jobs, to keep unemployment low, and to ensure people are not left unemployed for years—as all too many have been due to the transition from traditional industries to services and higher-tech industries. Many governments pay lip service to ensuring employment is high without taking the measures needed to deliver on their promises. Sometimes particular beliefs about the jobs market get in the way—for example, the view that young people should not have a lower minimum wage than older and more productive people, or that unions should concentrate on delivering higher pay for their members rather than creating new jobs for nonmembers. Sometimes governments do not want to commit the effort and resources needed to find people jobs and prepare them for the work; it can be achieved but it's a long and slow haul that doesn't fit well into political timetables.

The immense effort that has gone in to measures to *replace* GDP is irrelevant, resting as it does on the incorrect conclusion that there is no link over time between an economy getting richer and getting happier. There's no doubt that in a number of ways GDP is a flawed statistic as a measure of welfare. But any replacement would be flawed too, not to mention much harder for many countries to collect and measure; at least with the familiar GDP statistics we know what we're getting.

At the same time, it is equally clear that GDP growth will not in itself give members of society an adequate sense of meaning or purpose. Policymakers need to aim for more than just GDP growth. Thus one conclusion is that we should look at a much wider array of indicators. The "dashboard" approaches I described should be given due prominence when politicians are assessing how they are doing, or when citizens and journalists are holding politicians to task. There has been a big international effort to build this consensus about statistics, including the work of the Sen and Stiglitz commission and the OECD; now governments need to implement it. The following chapters will be more specific about the kinds of indicators that should be included.

But I want to round out this first chapter by discussing, not whether we should care about whether people are happy (yes, of course), nor whether people's happiness should be the overriding aim of policies (no, as argued above). Instead, I want to describe more carefully what it means to improve social welfare, where the standard approach of welfare economics has a lot to offer. Because, as argued earlier, neither happiness alone nor GDP alone is enough to define social welfare.

Economists typically use what is on the face of it a limited definition of welfare. A policy or change improves welfare if it improves the potential welfare of one person without diminishing that of anybody else—this is known in the jargon as a Pareto improvement. But although this seems oddly limited, what it means in practice is that economics defines welfare in terms of increasing people's range of choices. A welfare improvement is something that expands the options of one person while reducing no others. This approach also makes it very clear that while there is no inherent conflict between wealth and happiness, welfare is inextricably tied to free choice. Welfare rests on freedom. Economics in this way is entirely consistent with the psychological evidence about the importance people place on freedom. It also means that social welfare incorporates in a straightforward way the value of a clean environment or a good life, in addition to income or wealth. A government seeking to maximize social welfare should not *only* maximize GDP growth.

Amartya Sen also makes a convincing case that our assessment of social justice should not rest only on the outcome—what is the happiness level—but also on how it comes about. Are the society's institutions and its decision-making processes fair? Do people behave in a reasonable way? And in particular he emphasizes the importance of freedom, not only in the conventional political sense but also in the sense of people having the capability to choose and to lead the life they want.[57] This resonates with the importance in the psychological research of a sense of control for reported happiness.

The second half of this book returns to some of these questions. First, the following chapters look at how we can reconcile more growth with our strong instinct that we have reached a point of "enough."

Because to insist that GDP growth is desirable is not the same as believing that it is the only correct focus for improving society's welfare. The next chapters turn to the ways in which economic growth is presently unsustainable.

One chapter picks up directly from the findings on inequality reported earlier in this chapter. Growth needs to deliver higher income for most citizens: the "average" person is a mythical creature, and if many people are getting no better off while only a few are growing vastly better off, happiness economywide will not improve. People everywhere have a strong sense of fairness, and although different countries will accept different degrees of inequality in income and wealth, in some cases inequality has become excessive.

What's more, although economic growth is helping make us happier, and new technologies are helping boost growth, the social trends and rise in debt resulting from the fundamental structural changes under way in the economy are working in the opposite direction. The complaints about capitalism voiced so stridently during the past few years are at heart about the accompanying cultural and social change, not about what has in fact been stupendously impressive delivery on the economic promise. The financial crisis of 2007–8, and the recession it caused, has grabbed lots of attention. But whether it's tulips or credit default swaps, there's nothing new about financial crises or about their causes, greed and selfishness. The crisis doesn't lay bare a fundamental economic problem so much as a social and political crisis. Just as at previous times when technological progress reordered the economy and society, the political and social sustainability of capitalism comes under strain. These challenges of sustainability come together in today's widespread sense of crisis, of dissatisfaction, of being at a turning point in individual societies and humanity's global society as a whole.

TWO Nature

WHENEVER THE ECONOMY IS IN A RECESSION, a wave of books and feature articles will discover the joys of a simpler, less acquisitive lifestyle. This recession has been no exception. Except that, compared with the downturn of the early 1990s, there is a much greater emphasis now on the green benefits of buying less and making do instead. Downshifting made its first appearance in the early 1990s, but the "Downshifting Manifesto" that appeared in the United States in 2008 had the title, "Slow Down and Green Up." For those out of a job or short of cash, this really is making a virtue out of a necessity.

It can certainly be very helpful to people struggling financially to get advice about cheaper recipes, home-grown foods, and secondhand clothes. Nevertheless, there is an off-putting air of smugness in some of this recession-chic literature. Much of it is written by people who are themselves well off by any standard, and yet they obviously get great satisfaction from circumstances that mean many people are struggling to make ends meet. It's as if homespun is *morally* superior to something bought for money. The moral fervor gets an extra edge these days from the fact that it's helping the environment as well as saving money.

No doubt some people do enjoy making their own things, but many others prefer to buy their clothes or meals ready-made in the shops. It's why consumer spending on items which people—mainly women—used to have to put a lot of time into doing at home grew so much in the first place. Having to do-it-yourself in feeding and clothing a household costs less money but much effort, and leaves people with less choice and lower quality. Even in situations of real poverty, people want to spend some of their money on stuff from the shops. George Orwell made this point in his powerful book about the poverty of the 1930s, *The Road to Wigan Pier*. He was commenting on well-meaning advice to the poor to stretch their money further by cooking wholesome, cheap foods like lentils.

> When you are unemployed, which is to say when you are un-derfed, harassed, bored, and miserable, you don't want to eat dull wholesome food. You want something a little bit "tasty." There is always some cheaply pleasant thing to tempt you. Let's have three pennorth of chips! Run out and buy us a twopenny ice-cream! Put the kettle on and we'll all have a nice cup of tea! That is how your mind works when you are at the P.A.C. level. White bread-and-marg and sugared tea don't nourish you to any extent, but they are nicer (at least most people think so) than brown bread-and-dripping and cold water.[1]

More money makes people happier because it means they can buy more. As the last chapter described, contrary to what many people have come to believe, a proper assessment of the evidence means there's no sign that people have come to the end of want-ing more, even in the richest countries in the world. A reces-sion does not in fact offer an ideal opportunity to topple lots of people off the consumerist treadmill so they can get digging or knitting, and be happier with it; on the contrary, declining GDP and rising unemployment mean a big increase in unhappiness.

This is a conclusion that will be rejected by environmental-ists, many of whom have eagerly embraced the idea that the economy doesn't need to grow to make people happier. If not growing—or even shrinking—the economy could be better managed, the environmental pressure of the world's nearly 7 billion inhabitants on the planet could clearly be reduced, and everyone would be happier.

So the fact that the economy does need to grow to improve society's well-being puts human happiness back on a collision course with environmental sustainability. There is no win-win outcome of being able to abandon economic growth and make voters happier at the same time. With those 7 billion people all wanting their own share of GDP to rise, how can their wishes possibly be satisfied without destroying the climate and denuding the Earth of other resources? Some campaigners believe climate change is already causing more extreme weather phenomena—floods, droughts, hurricanes—and changing the normal seasonal patterns around which the production of food for the growing number of people has been shaped. Many countries have already recently experienced unusual weather patterns, which could be interpreted as frightening omens of the impact of global warming on everyday life, and on the structure and potential of the economy. Not all of these events have affected distant countries—unusually severe or unpredictable weather has been experienced in a number of Western countries. Many environmentalists believe this is related to anthropogenic climate change, although there are strong differences of opinion on this question. If temperatures are likely to rise enough to cause upheavals in the climate in most countries, destroying lives, homes, and livelihoods, should people be made to settle for less *now* in order that there is an economic future, even if it makes them unhappier?

This chapter explores the environmental question, which has become one of the most widely discussed but also increasingly contentious areas of public policy today. Do we need sustainable growth, which will help prevent environmental degradation and avert climate change, rather than plain old-fashioned economic growth? If so, what is it? With so many books and research papers written about environmental sustainability, I will be picking out some key issues for the questions about social welfare.

The issues will prove to be similar when I look at sustainability from some different perspectives in the following chapters—because growth needs to be financially, politically, and socially sustainable as well as environmentally sustainable. But this chapter starts with the environmental questions, which many people would consider to be the most urgent. It is certainly the context in which the policy dilemmas seem most acute and the arguments have become increasingly ill-tempered. On the one hand, for many people the threat of catastrophic climate change is the most serious risk to our way of life, or possibly life itself—and most Western governments are already implementing policies to address and mitigate the threat. On the other hand, the political and social imperative to continue delivering economic growth makes it difficult to achieve large reductions in adverse environmental effects—and the political opposition to environmental policies is vigorous. Not surprisingly, the debate is highly charged because a lot is at stake, and the political divisions are hardening—both between rich and poor countries and in domestic politics between those who would halt growth and those who do not believe the environmental threat is so serious that such drastic action is needed.

What's the best way to navigate through such a sharp difference of opinion? Especially for what I suspect is the silent majority who don't have strong views about climate science, who are vaguely worried that it might be true, but not to the extent of wanting to make large material sacrifices? I argue here that the route out of the dilemma is to lengthen the time frame we consider when making decisions about the consumption—or not—of natural resources. Policy needs a new criterion, that we must leave later generations at least as well off as us in terms of social welfare—with at least as wide a set of choices as we have, in the framework set out in the previous chapter. A key first step in achieving this is in measuring wealth as well as GDP or income, including natural wealth. A longer time horizon doesn't resolve the conflict of views but does bring the two sides closer together in terms of practical next steps. And the switch to a longer-term perspective will prove important in the other contexts covered in the following chapters.

The Climate Change Dilemma

Some, perhaps most, environmentalists would advocate less, not more, economic output in order to preserve the planet for the future. They rarely make a point of saying so in concrete terms in public, however. "Enough" might not have majority support and "Less" is downright unpopular. It would take a brave politician to run on a platform of shrinking the economy outright for the sake of the environment, including spelling out the consequences this would have for jobs and incomes.

Yet opinion polls suggest that in most countries the majority of people (albeit a declining majority in several cases) accept that the changing global climate due in large part to the buildup of emissions of carbon dioxide and other "greenhouse" gases (GHGs) poses a serious threat to future well-being. The central forecast of the Intergovernmental Panel on Climate Change (IPPC) published in 2007 was for a 0.2 degrees centigrade a decade increase in temperature, with the risks of a bigger rise. The UN's latest report on climate change forecasts says the chances are increasing that the increase will lie at the upper end of the IPCC's range of forecasts; and that some events previously expected to occur on a longer-term time horizons are already happening or set to happen far sooner. Recent increases in greenhouse gas concentrations have led scientists to predict a warming of between 1.3 and 4.3 degrees centigrade above preindustrial surface temperatures. This is sufficient for the experts to predict substantial and damaging changes in weather patterns, ecosystems, and water resources. The balance of risks, these experts say, is that the actual temperature change will be even greater.[2]

These forecasts mean it has become obvious to environmentalists that for growth to become remotely sustainable, big changes in the way we run the economy will be required, and in particular reduced consumption. Although governments' stated targets for reductions in greenhouse gas emissions most likely will not be met, there has been a widespread shift toward policies recognizing environmental imperatives. To give just a few examples: in 1989 a landmark international treaty, the Montreal Protocol, successfully agreed to phase out chlorofluorocarbons, important greenhouse gases; the use of unleaded gasoline and/or diesel fuels has become almost universal; the EU announced in 2009 that it is phasing out incandescent light bulbs in member countries; power stations around much of the world have been subject to increasingly tough emissions targets or financial incentives for lower-carbon energy generation, including renewables.

The full list of policies would be a long one. But even among the majority of people who accept that the challenge exists and is urgent, the question of how to respond effectively, and by how much, is still controversial. The reason is that, at least according to environmental experts, much bigger changes in behavior in the future are going to be needed to limit the rise in global temperatures enough to have a hope of averting catastrophic changes in the climate and weather patterns. The steps taken so far are inadequate from this perspective. "We . . . find it hard to imagine making the massive changes that are now necessary to solve the crisis," former vice president Al Gore said in his Nobel Prize acceptance speech. "We must quickly mobilize our civilization with the urgency and resolve that has previously been seen only when nations mobilized for war. . . . The way ahead is difficult. The outer boundary of what we currently believe is feasible is still far short of what we actually must do."[3]

The same conclusion was reached in a large-scale study commissioned by the UK Government and carried out by economist Nicholas Stern. Lord Stern said, just like Vice President Gore in his film *An Inconvenient Truth*, that consumers everywhere, but especially in Western countries, need to make big changes in their lifestyles, and thereby big reductions in the carbon emitted in the course of their economic activity. The Stern Review concluded that the fall in output required is about 1 percent of world GDP immediately and permanently—that is equivalent to a reduction of $104 a year in consumption spending by every person on earth, if it were shared equally. If all of the burden is borne by the rich countries, the required reduction is 1.8 percent of OECD GDP, or $667 per OECD citizen. These figures might sound low, but the power of compounding over the years mean they are in fact enormous consumption sacrifices. One estimate is that a 1 percent a year reduction in consumption is equivalent to about twice what U.S. households would lose in purchasing power from a 10 percentage point increase in inflation, and about twenty times the welfare cost of business cycle fluctuations since 1945. For every American it amounts to a cut in consumption now of about $277 a year, or more than one month's average spending on food.[4] This might seem a small price to pay to save the planet and secure humanity's future, but to demand it is like calling for a Great Depression.

Received wisdom among many "opinion formers," and also the political momentum, lie at present with the Stern and Gore view that we should be making these big sacrifices right now in order to limit the rise in the Earth's temperature and ensure changes in weather patterns are no more catastrophic than we can help at this stage. However, nobody in the rich Western democracies has yet been asked to make any sacrifices they might notice. Indeed, being green is regarded as a consumption choice—energy efficient light bulbs or normal ones? A hybrid car or a diesel? Plastic carrier or canvas bag?—rather than a matter of *cutting* consumption. The leading environmental economist Partha Dasgupta has pointed out that if poor countries will not adjust so the burden demanded by the Stern Review and its supporters falls on the rich West, the amount involved is equivalent to asking voters to pay two or three times as much to reduce carbon emissions as they currently pay to donate aid to developing countries. So the first serious electoral tests of this demand will be interesting. Consumers might have other good reasons for cutting spending, as we'll see in the next chapter, but it isn't at all clear that a majority yet see reducing their environmental impact as a compelling reason for doing so. Especially as any policy to bring it about will bear more heavily on some people than others.

A vast amount has been written about climate change and what needs to be done, and I am not going to try and sum it up here.[5] My focus is not on the science or even on what specific policies would be needed to curb GHG emissions by enough to stabilize the climate, but rather on the implications of the environmental challenge for how to go about setting policies to improve social welfare. How do we know whether big economic changes are needed to achieve environmentally sustainable growth? How can consumers be persuaded to change their way of living by enough to avert the worst potential impacts of climate change? And how can we start to address these questions when there's a diminishing degree of political consensus about, on the one hand, the sharing of the burden of adjustment between rich and poor countries, and on the other hand, about the extent to which there is a climate problem at all?

Global Climate Politics

The consensus—or at least the convention—in international politics at present is that climate change does pose a serious threat to human lives and livelihoods. So far the international policy response on climate change has been shaped by major international conferences under the auspices of the United Nations. The first international agreement was the Kyoto Protocol, signed in 1997, which came into force in December 2005. As a result various governments have announced targets for reductions in carbon emissions in their own countries. For example, the EU has said it will cut its greenhouse gas emissions up to 95 percent by 2050, with a short-term target of 20–30 percent reductions by 2020, provided that a global climate deal was signed in Copenhagen in December 2009 (it wasn't, and as of mid-2010 EU countries were divided about whether they should adopt the tougher target unilaterally). Each nation that has accepted the treaty has started to translate these high-profile commitments into specific actions, such as limits on GHG emissions by power stations, taxes on high carbon fuels, energy efficiency incentives, and so on. However, it took some leading industrial countries many years to sign up to Kyoto. Australia didn't accept the Kyoto obligations until the election of a new left-wing government in 2007. The United States signed but never ratified the treaty, and President Barack Obama seems (as I write in mid-2010) hesitant about what kind of international obligation could pass Congress. America was until 2008 the world's biggest emitter of carbon, and Australia makes a significant contribution, so their hesitations make it clear that from the start the policy process had clear weaknesses.

One key weakness is a fraught debate about the responsibilities of the developed as against the rapidly industrializing developing countries. At issue is how to share the burden of adjustment between rich but slow-growing Western countries with high levels of energy use per capita and poor developing countries with low per capita resource use that is growing rapidly.

China recently overtook the United States in absolute terms as the biggest carbon emitter, and India, Indonesia, and Brazil are also now among the largest contributors of carbon to the atmosphere. But all lag far behind the industrialized economies in their levels of per capita emissions. The Kyoto Treaty embodies a principle described as *common but differentiated responsibility,* which places the burden of emissions reduction on the developed economies. But regardless of what the treaty says, the planetwide level of emissions can only be kept to levels that— so experts hope—will not cause catastrophic climate change if countries like India and China also restrain their energy use. By 2050, eight-ninths of the world's population will live in the developing world, so unless poorer countries accept a share of the burden there is no hope of making significant reductions in global GHG emissions.

As Nicholas Stern puts it: "It is profoundly inequitable that the difficult starting point is largely the result of actions by the developed nations, but the numbers on population and future emissions are such that a credible response cannot come from the rich countries alone."[6] He argues that the imperatives of economic development and responding to climate change can't be separated: if we try to tackle either one without also addressing the other, we will fail on both fronts. Either economic development will be derailed by the impact of the changing climate on agriculture and output in developing countries if climate pres-

Figure 3. Beijing traffic.

sures are ignored, or it will prove impossible to address global warming if the justified claims of poor countries for economic growth cannot be met at the same time.

More ambitious international targets still have been sought more recently. The Kyoto Protocol will expire in 2012. The summit in Copenhagen in December 2009 tried to broker an agreement to replace it—and failed, despite the high-profile efforts of the prominent world leaders who flew there to contribute to the sense of urgency. The reason for the failure was precisely the inability of the developing and developed countries to agree on a fair allocation of the burden of adjustment.[7]

What demands should be placed on how people in each country lead their lives? Should countries reduce emissions in equal absolute or proportionate terms, over the same or different time periods, or to target the same level at a certain date? There could be justification for any of these paths, and the implications would be dramatically different for different countries.

Why should people in China reduce their still low use of energy and transport at all if Americans, with their extremely carbon-intensive and resource-intensive lifestyles, guzzling gasoline, water, and minerals to sustain a high standard of living, are not making much bigger sacrifices? The tension between the aims of economic growth and environmental sustainability are acute enough within each rich nation, and all the more so when taking into account simple justice between nations. It is untenable to argue that Indians or Brazilians should not aspire to air conditioning, cars, and fridges now that the great majority of people in the Western world have attained the comforts of ample consumer goods. What's more, much of the recent growth in emissions by countries like China has been generated by industries producing consumer goods for export to the rich countries, so all the more reason for the rich countries to make the bulk of the necessary adjustment.

The Western countries will therefore not find much support in international negotiations if it seems we're trying to pull up the rope ladder behind us. And so it is. India's government has firmly rejected the attempt of the "international community" to use the Copenhagen negotiations to share the burden of adjustment between the rich West and the emerging economies, though it has recently announced that it would voluntarily reduce its carbon emission by 20–25 percent of 2005 levels by 2020. The environment minister told his parliament that India's transition to a low-carbon economy would be on its own terms and in its own self-interest: "We are not doing the world a favour. Forget Copenhagen. Forget the US. Our future as a society depends on how we respond to the climate change challenge."[8] As I write this, it is entirely unclear what the prospects are for a new international agreement on emissions targets. It might well be a matter of every country or region deciding what individual course of action to take. For people seriously concerned about the impact of human activity on the climate, this is unlikely to add up to enough of an adjustment.

Domestic Climate Change Dissent

The lack of an international consensus on where responsibility for adjustments should fall is a big enough barrier to changing behavior. But another looms even larger. A vocal and growing minority of people in the Western democracies distrust what they've been told by the scientific and political establishment about the risks of catastrophic climate change. For example, a March 2010 Gallup Poll found that the proportion of people in the United States regarding environmental issues as a higher priority than economic growth had declined to 38 percent from 42 percent a year earlier and 49 percent in 2008.[9] The level of concern about climate change is the lowest since polling on the issue began. An Ipsos Mori poll in the United Kingdom found a similar drop in the proportion agreeing that global warming was "definitely" a reality, from 44 percent in 2009 to 31 percent in 2010.[10]

The recession and a cold winter played their part in causing these opinion shifts. But another reason is the growing doubt about the legitimacy and truthfulness of the institutions that have played leading roles in forecasting damage to the world's future climate. The leading expert institution is the IPCC, the UN-sponsored body of scientists monitoring the climate that forecasts likely trends in the decades ahead. Some prominent environmental economists and activists, as well as political campaigners, have raised serious doubts about the methods of the IPCC and the extent of its genuine commitment to peer review and a transparent discussion of the science. For instance, it has been criticized for refusing to publish data, for failing to use appropriate statistical methods despite criticisms, and for failing to engage in standard scientific peer review processes or even publish the debates between the scientists involved in drafting its reports.[11] In January 2010 the IPCC was forced to admit its latest report had been mistaken in its prediction of when the Himalayan glaciers were likely to melt. Subsequently the United Nations asked the InterAcademy Council, which represents national science academies, to review the IPCC's methods, and a number of submissions to its experts listed numerous procedural and methodological weaknesses.[12] One of the leading global centers of climate change research, at the UK's University of East Anglia, was at the heart of an even more damaging scandal when hacked emails seemed to suggest that scientists had actively been rigging results and misleading people they regarded as hostile. Although a review cleared the scientists of the most damaging allegations, even prominent environmental campaigners concluded that climate scientists must engage more honestly and openly with their critics.[13]

Serious institutional failings of this sort play to political parties and industry lobbies opposed to various types of response to climate change. What's more, given the bitter state of emotions in this debate, and the mutual suspicions of climate scientists and climate change skeptics, the area of agreement is shrinking rather than expanding.

So a growing number of people, mainly politically conservative, and including some prominent economists, reject the claim that climate change is so urgent an issue that dramatic lifestyle changes and economic changes are needed now. They argue that a more gradual approach will be sufficient—if they believe that change is needed at all. At least some of the dissenters from conventional environmental wisdom are serious people whose views should be seriously assessed. Relatively few of these particular climate change refusniks rebut the basic scientific data measuring temperature changes in certain locations, or argue that human activity has not contributed to climate change at all. Their focus is instead on the interpretations of the data, the methods used, and the conclusions governments and international agencies have drawn from those basic facts. These weaknesses mean the policies are being shaped inappropriately, they argue. While some of the criticism maps onto conventional left-right politics, there are obviously reasonable questions about the role and motivation of the IPCC and its related groups such as the scientists at the University of East Anglia. The climate change establishment has not had due regard to its own legitimacy and accountability, especially if it wants to change minds and votes in democracies.

The dissenters argue further that the official forecasts are unduly alarmist and that the temperature rises against which governments need to take mitigating action are not likely to be as high as the IPCC predicts. David Henderson, a former chief economist at the OECD, is one of the people who has led the intellectual charge.[14] Henderson argues that the IPCC is institutionally biased toward pessimism and also has insufficient knowledge of the proper methods for assessing the likely economic effects and necessary adjustments (not that economists have a terrific forecasting record of course—but at least we can't fail to be aware of the fallibility of any prediction). There are other voices making the same point. The economist Ross McKitrick, whose work has been used by the IPCC, writes: "I believe the core group that influence the IPCC's reports and conclusions is biased toward the view that greenhouse gases are the cause of major, deleterious global warming, and . . . I think this bias leads them to censor or even misrepresent opposing evidence. . . . Over time, it is possible that the IPCC's analysis and forecasts would be vindicated. But I doubt it."[15] A third highly credible critic is the Yale environmental economist William Nordhaus, who has made a similar point about the inbuilt bias of those who are sounding the alarm about climate change. He writes that the UK government-commissioned Stern Review, which gave such an impetus to global public policy on climate change and fed into the Copenhagen Summit, was written with undue haste and without peer review, in order to satisfy a political agenda: "The Review was published without an appraisal of its methods and assumptions by independent outside experts. Nor can its results be easily reproduced. These may be seen as minor points but they are fundamental for good science. The British government is not infallible in questions of economic and scientific analysis of global warming."[16]

These kinds of allegations about the institutional flaws of the climate change "community" are supported by the behavior and errors that have come to light recently.

Other critics of the consensus also say the forecasting methods used by the IPCC are flawed. It must be true that the margin of uncertainty in these forecasts is very large, not only because the Earth has experienced big swings in climate in the distant past not caused by human economic activity, but also because forecasting a complex dynamic system like the world's weather is hard for the next two days never mind two decades. What's more, there is an uncertain economic forecast superimposed on the uncertain climate forecast: future emissions forecasts, which affect the predictions about temperature change, depend on future economic growth and also future innovation and investment in energy-efficient technologies, which in turn depend on the incentives created by the price of carbon-based and alternative energy sources. But the specifics of the critique matter less than the fact that respected economists with a record of work on the environment are making such strongly worded criticisms of the international institutions assessing the risk and shaping government policies that might impose big costs on their citizens. This points to the conclusion that the IPCC process is flawed. The IPCC represents a massive intellectual and scientific effort, and almost all climate scientists back its conclusions. However, it is not sufficiently transparent, has not engaged effectively with critics, and lacks political legitimacy. Even if everyone involved in the debate agreed about the climate science, no political consensus on what action to take will be possible without a better policy framework ensuring accountability to voters. In the second half of the book I return to what seem like rather minor points about process, which in fact turn out to be profoundly important for sustainability.

In addition to these doubts about the climate change establishment, there is also a divergence in philosophical approach between economists and environmentalists. It is encapsulated by a well-known bet between economist Julian Simon and Paul Ehrlich, author of a popular book, *The Population Bomb*, which warned of environmental catastrophe due to the pressure of population growth. In 1980 Simon challenged Ehrlich to name five commodities of his selection and predicted their price would be lower (relative to the general price level) in a decade. In 1990, Ehrlich had to pay up. Every one of the five commodities he had expected to soar in price because of the pressure of demand was *cheaper* than it had been at the time of the wager. The moral economists draw from this tale is that it is misleading to extrapolate trends far into the future, as Ehrlich and many environmentalists do. If pressures emerge such as growing demand for a particular resource, its price will rise and people will switch their behavior to use something else, or invent a new technology to replace the shortage commodity. Even accepting that markets underprice energy and many other resources, given the externalities involved, economists are inclined to believe that changed patterns of demand and technological innovation will go a long way toward solving any environmental problems. Ensuring that markets set a price for carbon, taking account of the climate externalities, emerges as the most important weapon against climate change. In economics, as long as markets are allowed to operate, metaphorical time bombs never explode. Price changes defuse them.

Economists are therefore strong advocates of establishing a carbon market which, if it set up effectively, will deliver a long-term market price for carbon. William Nordhaus writes: "Carbon prices must be raised to transmit the social costs of GHG emissions to the everyday decisions of billions of firms and people."[17] Existing carbon markets are flawed. The price of carbon they set has turned out to be volatile and too low, mainly because governments have given in to industry protests in setting up the market, making too many exceptions for too large an amount of emissions for the market to work well. But a carbon price will need to be sufficiently high and stable to incentivize investment in low-carbon forms of energy and in energy saving.

Governments can increase the carbon price by themselves if necessary by charging a carbon tax—indeed some have already introduced carbon taxes albeit again in a half-hearted way due to effective lobbying by certain industry groups.[18] Ross McKitrick suggests tying the rate of the carbon tax to global temperature, so that the more serious the problem becomes, the greater the incentive that will be created to reduce energy consumption.[19] Indeed there is a substantial economic literature on the use of taxes and the creation of markets for carbon, all aimed at increasing the price consumers and businesses must pay to use energy and carbon-intensive products, and thus changing their behavior. Price is a powerful incentive, quieter than campaigning rhetoric but more effective.

CLIMATE CHANGE AND SOCIAL WELFARE

So far, this chapter has focused on the obvious political tensions in the climate change debate. I turn now to a subtler question about how the debate should treat our responsibilities to the future. This is at the heart of the sustainability question: what we mean by sustainability is precisely about the legacy we will leave for the future. Looking at the impact of policies over a longer time horizon gets to the heart of how governments could deliver improved social welfare in other dimensions, too, not just environmental issues.

Consider one powerful critique of advocacy of radical economic change in order to reduce GHG emissions significantly. It says the impact of climate change lies in the future, but economic growth between now and then means that people will be much more able to afford compensating action when the time comes. We are poorer than succeeding generations will be, so it is for them, not us, to make the necessary sacrifices in terms of giving up consumption. This seems an appealing argument: it doesn't deny climate change but postpones any need to sacrifice much if any consumption today, and so evades the difficult moral question about how to cut economic output while being fair to the aspirations of poor people in developing countries.

Surely this is too good to be true? Put so simply, it probably is. But the intergenerational issue has been raised by some of the economists who are most expert and thoughtful about the interplay between the demands of the environment and economic growth. William Nordhaus summed it up:

> Global per capita consumption today is around $10,000. According to the [Stern] Review's assumptions, this will grow at 1.3 percent per year, to around $130,000 in two centuries. Using these numbers, how persuasive is the ethical stance that we have a duty to reduce current consumption by a substantial amount to improve the welfare of the rich future generations?[20]

The question is how, as a matter of morality, we should treat people in future generations when we make decisions about consuming environmental resources now. No answer to the question of how to respond to the prospect of climate change can avoid taking a position on the ethics of how those of alive today should treat those yet to be born.

Part of the controversy about the Stern Review is that it did not discuss the ethical framework explicitly but implicitly took what other economists regard as an extreme position. There are two separate ethical judgments involved. One is whether people in future have the same value as people now and should therefore be given the same weight in decisions. To the extent that they should be given less weight, we should *discount* their views—in technical terms this is done using a discount rate. In many circumstances, including assigning values in the financial markets, we assume the appropriate discount rate is a small positive number—say 1 or 2 or 4 percent. Apart from anything else, impatience to have money now rather than later (economists call this "time preference") and uncertainty about the future make this sensible. In the ethical context of the environmental debate, there is wide agreement that the discount rate used should by contrast be zero, or very low. Stern does this and nobody disagrees with the value judgment that people's well-being should carry the same weight regardless of when they were or are to be born.

However, there is a further point, which has been emphasized by William Nordhaus and Partha Dasgupta. The Stern Review also attaches equal weight to people who have a lot and a little money, whereas many people would argue for placing more of the burden of adjustment on the rich than on the poor. Thus even if people in future are much richer than us, it concludes that we should still be making sacrifices so they can be better off still. In other words, there are two sets of weights involved in the choice about consumption sacrifices, the weight attached to an individual's date of birth (equal for all) and the weight attached to their income (poor or rich, at whatever date they are born).

Dasgupta criticises the Stern Review for not exploring the sensitivity of its recommendations to the values of the parameters in its model that embody underlying ethical assumptions. He writes,

> Where the modern economist is rightly hesitant, the authors of the Review are supremely confident. Climate change has been taken very seriously by all economists who have studied the science since the late 1970s. To be critical of the Review isn't to understate the harm humanity is inflicting on itself by degrading the natural environment—not only in regard to the stock of carbon in the atmosphere, but also in regard to so many other environmental matters besides. But the cause isn't served when parameter values are so chosen that they yield desired answers.[21]

Responding to these criticisms, Nicholas Stern is dismissive of these economists' questions about the appropriate ethical judgments to apply to future consumption. For him, the framework of analysis they bring to the question misses the point that the scale of the potential catastrophe means the future is potentially much poorer, not much richer, than the present. The havoc wreaked by changing weather systems is likely to destroy the economy, he suggests. The economists who quibble about parameter values are, to him, the modern-day equivalents of mediaeval scholars debating how many angels could fit onto a pinhead. He agrees that we need to choose a rate at which to convert an extra unit of consumption gained in future to an extra unit of consumption given up now; and also that it will be less than one to one if future generations will be wealthier. But he writes: "What we do now on climate change will transform the circumstances and income of future generations." If we fail to sacrifice some consumption now to mitigate climate change, future generations might in fact be much worse off than we are now. "If these strategies—and it is an unavoidable question in the context of climate change—are a matter of life and death for many, then the issues are different."[22]

Moreover, Stern says the damage that will be caused by climate change is irreversible and large, so it makes no sense to think about the choices as trade-offs, a bit more here for a bit less there, which is what the conventional economics approach does. The "price" of environmental goods in the future will rise so much that there is no sense in discounting them: the cost-benefit analysis will be overwhelmed by the prospect of catastrophic and irreversible environmental change. Economics assumes that there is a relationship between amount consumed and global temperature: a bit more consumption means a slightly larger increase in average temperatures, and conversely. From the environmental perspective, the idea that there could be incremental changes in temperature is wishful fantasy; the only choice is catastrophe or not, with extreme weather threatening the fundamentals of human life and society. Others support his view that conventional economic tools for assessing the costs and benefits of different choices are not applicable in the context of a potentially massive change in the environment.[23]

Unfortunately, this makes the policy choice about what scale of costly changes to impose on citizens' lives more or less a matter of faith. Perhaps Al Gore and Nicholas Stern are right; but unless a majority of their fellow-citizens agree with their assessment of the urgency and scale of the reduction needed in

Figure 4. What threat does climate change pose?

consumption today, it is unlikely that the policy actions they'd see as necessary will be feasible. Passionate campaigners for urgent action against climate change are impatient with talk of political realities. They prefer to put their energies into trying to convince others to share their views. Which is fine. But it's in the nature of faith that others will challenge it. There is a valid debate about the scale of the actions needed now to safeguard the world against damage from climate change, and it is foolish to be dismissive of the sincere argument that the sacrifice we make right now does not need to be as large as the very big estimates some campaigners are advocating. This, surely, is an area of policy where pragmatism is essential, no matter how much it antagonizes the true believers.

How to Take the Future Seriously

In chapter 1 I described the evidence undermining the fashionable argument that higher GDP—that is higher income and spending—doesn't make people any happier. On the contrary, there is good evidence that more income and more consumption do make people happier. The idea that it will be easy to give up policies for economic growth is therefore a false trail.

The environmental issues set out in this chapter have put at center stage the dilemma of persuading voters that some growth must be sacrificed, in a context of increasingly bitter dispute about the scale of the necessary change. The idea of environmental sustainability leads us to think about the future. People my age in the West are likely to live another forty or fifty years. Parents care about the well-being of their children. Many people have religious beliefs or come from a cultural tradition in which the concept of good husbandry is a moral imperative. Whatever our individual rationale, many of us do care about the future and therefore about sustainability. A good society will deliver economic growth with due regard for the next generation. What measures will steer us toward that goal? Using annual increases in GDP has not done the trick and has been too short term as a focus for policy, whether in terms of the natural world or—as described in later chapters—the social world. Indeed the framework for shaping policies during the past half century or so has brought economies to the point of unsustainability in a number of ways.

Decisions to consume now rather than conserve for the future have long-lasting implications. "We" (meaning a majority of people in rich Western societies) have been consuming "too much," according to the evidence from the scale of the increase in the amount of carbon dioxide in the atmosphere, and the likely increase in the Earth's surface temperature. Economic growth is certainly possible—and in fact necessary, not least to create the means of paying current debts and to create the incentive and scope to invest in greener technologies. But a larger share of the additional economic output created each year must be saved and invested. The next chapters will show that this is needed for multiple reasons, not just for the sake of limiting the damage to the climate and environment. But by how much?

The question of a practical definition of sustainability is far from new. The debate about environmental sustainability took its present shape following the publication of the Brundtlandt Report, *Our Common Future*, in 1987. This UN-commissioned work, led by former Norwegian prime minister Gro Harlem Brundtlandt, defined the term:

> Sustainable development is development that meets the needs of the present without compromising the ability of future generations to meet their own needs. It contains within it two key concepts:
>
> - the concept of "needs," in particular the essential needs of the world's poor, to which overriding priority should be given; and
> - the idea of limitations imposed by the state of technology and social organization on the environment's ability to meet present and future needs.

It continued:

> Development involves a progressive transformation of economy and society. A development path that is sustainable in a physical sense could theoretically be pursued even in a rigid social and political setting. But physical sustainability cannot be secured unless development policies pay attention to such considerations as changes in access to resources and in the distribution of costs and benefits. Even the narrow notion of physical sustainability implies a concern for social equity between generations, a concern that must logically be extended to equity within each generation.[24]

This steps beyond the bounds of the debate about climate science and into the areas covered later in this book.

Subsequently, the concept of sustainability has been extended. Partha Dasgupta has argued that the Brundtlandt definition does not go far enough. He says of this definition of sustainability: "It doesn't, for example, demand that development be *optimal* or *just*. But how is a generation to judge whether it is leaving behind an adequate productive base for its successor?"[25] So he introduces the dimension of social welfare and the practical question of how sustainability is to be judged.

The economist Robert Solow has also argued for a more capacious definition of sustainability, leaving for the next generation "whatever it takes to achieve a standard of living at least as good as our own and to look after the next generation similarly."[26] The focus on living standards is more generous than the mere fulfillment of needs, and the formulation passes on the responsibility for sustainability in all successive generations as well, as it is recursive. Economist Paul Collier adopts a similar ethical test for today's use of natural assets, the test of stewardship, which he contrasts with both utilitarianism and "romantic environmentalism." Future generations should be able to benefit not only from the preservation of resources but also the ability to use them productively. He notes, too, that this ethical concept has great resonance in a number of religions and seems to accord widely with our moral intuition.[27] Amartya Sen also thinks the emphasis on equal access to the resources available for economic activity by successive generations is incomplete. Sen emphasizes that the environment should be understood to include humans and our activities—it is not just a "state of nature" separate from us—and we should aim to enrich the environment in this wider sense.

He also argues that it is too meager an ambition to conceive of future generations only in terms of their needs; we should include their potential to act, participate, have different values and make different choices, so that they are not just passive elements of our choices. In other words, even a concern for future living standards is inadequate in his view—we need to ensure also that future generations have the same capabilities so they are actively able to safeguard what they care about. The example he gives is the concern many people now have for the preservation of species close to extinction.

There is an economic cost to extractions. A UN project, The Economics of Ecosystems and Biodiversity (TEEB) is estimating the monetary value of aspects of nature such as keeping water and air clean, protecting coasts from storms, and maintaining wildlife species. It estimates the annual cost of forest losses at $2–$5 billion, for example.[28] But in addition to concern for the economy and our own living standards, Sen articulates an expression of the value we place on the existence of different creatures—and this is a value that would not have been widely shared in previous generations. He writes: "If the importance of human life lies not merely in our living standard and need-fulfillment, but also in the freedom that we enjoy, then the idea of sustainable development has to be correspondingly refor-mulated."[29] We need to sustain our freedom too, including the freedom to meet our needs but going beyond it—we should aim to ensure that future generations have at least the same capabilities.

All of these definitions tally with the formulation of social welfare in economics in terms of the range of choices open to people. But there is still a question about how any formulation of sustainability, necessarily abstract, can be put into practice. How much less consumption does it imply now? One practical proposal is that the amount we save rather than spend now should leave the next generation with at least the same amount of *capital* as we inherited ourselves, specifically natural capital in the environmental context.

Natural capital is the stock of natural resources of all kinds, the world's environmental wealth. The natural capital of con-cern for sustainable economic growth is not just the climate. Many of the world's various ecosystems, large and small scale, are under threat, whether areas of rainforest that provide a liv-ing to poor rural communities, coral reefs, or major fish stocks in the oceans. When an ecosystem collapses, so do the societies relying on it; indeed the human society should be thought of as part of the ecosystem. Humans and our activity are part of the environment, not separate from the natural world.[30]

This rule about leaving behind no lower a level of capital than we inherited directs us toward an inherently longer-term framework than focusing on how much is generated each year, or the flow of income and resources a measured by GDP. In just the same way, a key measure of the success of an oil company is its reserves, not just how much oil it pumped this year; or the success of a university investment fund is the value of the endowment as well as the income contribution for the year. A stock of wealth is a measure of future potential, exactly what is needed to implement any of the definitions of sustainability set out here.

What does it mean to leave at least as much capital as we inherited? How can natural capital be measured? There are no easy ways to calculate natural wealth because markets undervalue many natural assets—there are many externalities that make property rights over natural resources hard to enforce and the "tragedy of the commons" ensues. This means that resources owned in common—such as fish in the ocean or clean air—are overused and therefore depleted. No individual owner takes responsibility for their stewardship, in the absence of any successful collective agreement to limit their depletion. The price we pay (essentially free) is lower than the price that would reflect the true cost of our use of them. This has distorted the development of advanced economies to make them far too hungry in their use of such resources. As Dasgupta says: "Distortions in the pricing of primary factors of production filter down to influence research and development. The latter in turn influences the character of technological change. Because nature's services are underpriced in the market, innovators have little reason to economize on their use. We shouldn't be surprised when new technologies are rapacious in the use of natural capital."[31]

So the absence of "true" prices for environmental goods poses a dual problem: they are overconsumed, and we are unable to easily measure their value.

GDP is a good indicator of production, which is what it was designed for, and even, as we've seen, a reasonable indicator of happiness, but as a guide to the effectiveness of economic policy and how much growth is enough, it is inadequate. Its key flaw from this perspective is that it doesn't incorporate the true value or the depreciation of natural (and other) assets. In other words, it makes no allowance for what will ensure the potential for future growth, as opposed to recording past growth. The inclusion of "satellite accounts" for nonmarket issues, such as the environment or indeed household satellite accounts measuring unpaid work in the home, are recent innovations in national accounts statistics. They should remain an important priority for statistical offices. But to avoid being forced by what we do now measure into an excessively short-term focus, we urgently need better statistics on natural and other forms of capital.

Although an economy's "comprehensive wealth," as it has been termed, is hardly an easy indicator to build, neither is GDP. The statistics of the national accounts are extremely complicated, with all kinds of ad hoc assumptions and patches. A growing number of economists who study environmental and welfare economics are coalescing around a measure of comprehensive wealth. Economic growth means that GDP must increase; sustainable growth requires also that investment in comprehensive wealth is positive.[32]

Some early estimates of comprehensive wealth do exist. They add investment in human capital (measured by education spending) to conventional measures of capital and deduct disinvestment in natural capital—for example, reductions in the stock of oil and minerals, increases in the concentration of carbon in the atmosphere. The adjustments made in these early estimates fall short of the ideal—improvements in human capital due to improved health are left out, as are losses of fish stocks—but it is certainly the avenue to pursue. Kirk Hamilton and Michael Clemens (1999) and the World Bank (2006) estimated comprehensive investment in the period 1970–2000 in over 120 countries. Their analysis is inevitably preliminary. Still, it is a start.

Kenneth Arrow and his coauthors (2007) also used estimates of comprehensive wealth and concluded that economic development had gone backward in a large number of developing countries in the years 1970–2000. China was one exception; other countries, including India and Pakistan, had seen total comprehensive wealth rise, but not in per capita terms because of their high rates of population growth. In developing countries, the aim is not to demand less consumption by people who are very poor, but to seek better policies and economic institutions so that their use of resources is more productive. Dasgupta writes: "In poor countries the production and distribution of goods and services are highly inefficient, implying that consumption and comprehensive investment there do not compete for a fixed quantity of funds. Better institutions would enable people in the poor world to both consume more and invest more."[33]

The statistics we need do not yet exist. But then neither did GDP before the need arose in the Great Depression of the 1930s to have a reliable measure of what was happening to the economy's level of production. The need precedes the development of the appropriate measures. Cross-country measures of comprehensive wealth are needed now. The Sen-Stiglitz commission discussed the concept of "extended wealth," a concept they defined as the relevant economic counterpart of the notion of sustainability. This would include not only natural resources but also those other ingredients necessary to provide future generations an opportunity set that is at least as large as what is currently available to living generations.[34]

Adopting comprehensive investment as an additional guideline for policy, and one to trump GDP if something that raises GDP would reduce comprehensive wealth, is clearly essential. It isn't the same as the answer to the question of how much consumption needs to fall now to avert catastrophic climate change. I suspect the answer to this is, as much as is politically feasible, and Nicholas Stern's 1 percent of global GDP (1.8 percent of the developed world's GDP) is an upper limit on the feasible. However, switching the policy focus to a measure taking account of the future, from one that only looks backward, would be a huge stride toward sustainability, both environmental and social. Evidence about long-term impacts from new statistics might make for a more constructive political debate.

Also essential is reform of the scientific and governmental institutions responsible for gathering the evidence on which scientific research is based. Not only the IPCC but also other UN environmental agencies, and national bodies and universities, have suffered a damaging loss of credibility recently thanks entirely to the way they've been run and their lack of transparency. It's always hard to rebuild a damaged reputation, so there is a lot of work to be done by the climate change establishment in order to regain trust and create the political conditions for a different approach to spending and consuming. One of the lessons of this chapter, one of the reasons for dwelling on the bitter politics of the climate change debate, is that institutions matter enormously for the kinds of policies that can be introduced. The evidence and arguments relevant to policy decisions are completely entwined with the processes for reaching decisions, not just in the case of the environmental questions but also of all the social issues addressed in this book. The processes—the institutions or people making the decisions and the rules according to which they operate and engage with the wider public—affect how everybody else evaluates the issues. A wise and kindly dictator could not decide how much GHG emissions and therefore energy use need to be cut, on behalf of everyone else, because even if he got the calculation exactly right he would not have persuaded people to alter their behavior.

CONCLUSIONS

Sustainability is about how we weigh up the present against the future. How do we ensure that we have a sufficiently long-term focus in our everyday decisions? It takes us back to the measurement question of chapter 1 and what *more* and *enough* ought to mean.

It has been a damaging error to steer the assessment of welfare, and public policy, by looking at measures of how much is produced per year—that is, measures of income. Instead, we need measures looking also at changes in value, that is, measures of wealth, both natural and financial (the subject of the next chapter). This apparently small change of focus—after all, don't income and wealth go hand in hand?—is in fact vital because it changes the time horizon over which we assess our decisions and policies. A sustainable economy will require us to set policies with reference to a much longer time frame than at present.

We do want *more* in order to be happier—but how much more is feasible without destroying the natural and social environment, and how much more is fair to the people who will come after us? The answers to these questions point us toward sustainability.

However, the dimensions of unsustainability go much wider than the environmental issues, important as these are. The following chapters go on to look at other features of our economic arrangements that also pay too little regard to the long term.

The next is the unsustainable burden of debt, especially government debt. Debt should not be mistaken for a merely financial indicator. It is an indicator of social obligations and excess debt is a sign of the depletion of social resources. Later chapters will explore two other aspects of unsustainability, the collapse of trust in fundamental economic and political institutions, and the increase in inequality, much more extreme in some countries than others but increasing almost everywhere.

All of these reflect the failure of political and social institutions to keep pace with the ways the economy and technology have developed in the past generation. The natural world is the most urgent and potentially catastrophic manifestation of the inadequacy of the institutions we have for coordinating the lives and decisions of 7 billion people. But these crises of sustainability are related. They are all—including the environmental challenges—the symptoms of a failure of the institutions that shape our economies and societies, the forms through which we reach collective decisions. The term *institutions* encompasses both markets on the one hand and political and governmental structures on the other. The second half of this book will look at the economic and political institutions, and the processes for taking policy decisions, needed for the world of Enough.

THREE Posterity

SERIOUS ENVIRONMENTAL CHALLENGES are only one aspect of the widespread sense that the economic and social framework of our world is in crisis. The other dramatic and immediate crisis of recent times has been the financial crisis, the near disintegration of the global banking system, which started slowly in 2007 and reached a crescendo with the collapse of the investment bank Lehman Brothers in September 2008 and its impact on financial transactions around the world. The literal failure of the financial system, and the deep and long recession it triggered, offered a dramatic demonstration of the unsustainability of the way the global economy had been operating. Although there has been a vigorous public debate subsequently, for example, about the need for tougher financial regulations or the break up of some big banks, the immediate opportunity for fundamental reform provided by the crisis has slipped past.

Yet reform is needed. The huge burden of public debt created in the course of the financial breakdown remains, and remains unsustainable. The figures are simply staggering—the increase in government debt due to the financial crisis adds to existing large but hidden debts. The debt burden due to the financial crisis comes on top of existing government debt burdens, sometimes acknowledged, more often off the books either as a deliberate sleight of hand or because they are implicit in the promise of future pension and welfare payments. As well as repaying the debts incurred in sorting out the banking crisis, taxpayers will have to shoulder the debts created by a system of pensions and social welfare, which are going to cost more than will be readily available to pay them in future. This is partly due to the structure of the pension and benefits systems and partly because in many countries birthrates have fallen so much that the population of working adults is going to decline. I'll argue here that the full debts are unlikely to be honored. It would be politically unsupportable to do so. What's more, in some countries the scale of the government debt is so large that it could depress the economy's potential to grow enough ever to meet the burden of repayment.

For more than a generation Western governments have been borrowing on a large scale from their own citizens but increasingly also from foreigners in much poorer countries. The cost of these promises will be piled onto taxpayers as yet unborn or too young to vote, and to these now are added the costs of the debts created by the banking crisis. In the next decade or so, as those taxpayers start working and earning and voting, it will become clear that these large transfers from all taxpayers to specific social groups (those with enough income to have lent part of their savings to the government), or to citizens of other countries whose governments have bought these debts, are unsustainable.

I will look in this chapter at this financial unsustainability, at government debt in particular. Our environmental legacy is not the only serious question about fairness between generations facing governments now. This debt is another potential burden people living now will bequeath to their children. Like the environmental burden, the debt burden will mean reductions in the amount that can be spent on consumption. However, the debt burden is less obviously catastrophic and urgent, more hidden— and what's more, likely to be in part repudiated in various ways, discussed below. Michael Burry, the investor who predicted the 2008 financial meltdown (and profited from it by "shorting" the market) said in a comment on the U.S. federal government deficit: "Strictly looking at the monthly Treasury statement of receipts and outlays, ... as an 'investor,' you see a company you might want to short."[1]

It's also a distributional, or to put it another way, a political, issue. OECD governments have borrowed vast sums from both their own citizens and from foreigners. Citizens who have accumulated savings, typically the better-off members of society, and the governments of countries with a large pool of savings, China prominent among them, have lent the money to pay for current government services. All future taxpayers will have to make the repayments. Both the domestic politics and the geopolitics are likely to be fraught, so large is the accumulation of debt.

The links between the world of high finance and the wider organization of society are not obvious. But from time to time, the intuition that there are in fact deep links comes to the fore. This usually happens in times of crisis. Even then, it is not apparent to everyone that something important is taking place. In a speech in New York's Federal Hall on 14 September 2009, the anniversary of the Lehman Brothers bankruptcy, President Barack Obama said: "Unfortunately, there are some in the financial industry who are misreading this moment. Instead of learning the lessons of Lehman and the crisis from which we're still recovering, they're choosing to ignore those lessons. I'm convinced they do so not just at their own peril, but at our nation's."[2] His speech was greeted with a distinct lack of enthusiasm by the financiers in the audience and got mainly critical reviews the business press. The banking world is extraordinarily blind to the implications of the crisis.

People who work in the world of finance seem not to understand that those of us outside their world will not accommodate their wish to return to business as usual. Across the Atlantic Ocean at the same time as President Obama's speech, seventy-two London-based financial traders were taking their former employer, the investment bank Dresdner Kleinwort, to court over the bank's failure to pay them €34 million in bonuses for 2008. In September 2008, Dresdner Kleinwort had been rescued in a €6 billion takeover by Commerzbank, 25 percent owned by German taxpayers. Other such lawsuits were reportedly in the pipeline. Meanwhile, the bankers have also fought a largely successful battle to prevent governments—major shareholders now—from limiting their ability to receive large bonuses. Their success reflects an extraordinary and unforgivable lapse of political nerve among elected officials to confront bankers' greed. What, the rest of us ask, are these multimillion-dollar bonuses supposed to be rewarding?

Conversations with people working in the financial markets in the twelve months after Lehman Brothers "fell over" (to use the term for bankruptcy financial folk prefer) made it plain that Planet Banking is in a different universe to Earth. Bankers complain about being demonized, about the recession not being their fault, about the need to ensure regulation of the financial markets doesn't hinder their ability to compete and make profits in future. They argue that bonuses are essential to attract the best talent and stay competitive, despite the evidence that bonuses incentivized excessive risk-taking rather than productive effort. Others are unable to comprehend the cheek of the banking fraternity (and it is mainly male) in making such arguments when their industry has received a multitrillion dollar, euro, and pound bailout from taxpayers around the world.

Why did the banks need rescuing on such a large scale? In mid-September 2008, the bankruptcy of Lehman Brothers set off a chain reaction affecting the whole global financial industry. Lehmans had massive, complicated, and extensive transactions outstanding with lots of other banks and insurers, and they in turn with others, and nobody knew which of these would be honored as a result of its collapse. Banks overnight stopped trusting each other and ceased pretty much all lending and borrowing within the financial system.[3] A downward spiral began, as the uncertainty about the value of some assets reduced the value of others linked to them. It seemed possible that the collapse would extend to the everyday movement of money and the settlement of checks and direct debits around the domestic banking system.

This would have been catastrophic. Economies are built on the security of money, and money in a modern economy mostly takes the ephemeral and intangible form of electronic transfers. The zeroes and ones zipping between banks' computer systems, the marks they make against the accounts of businesses and individuals, make possible all the transactions of everyday life—buying the groceries, paying the electricity bill, making payments to suppliers, receiving a salary. If the electronic payments systems were not functioning, workers wouldn't get paid, supermarkets wouldn't be able to restock with goods, shoppers wouldn't be able to buy, cars couldn't refill with gasoline. All the economic transactions of modern life are mediated through money, and without a functioning banking system the whole sophisticated structure of the economy would crumble leaving us scrabbling to survive.

An exaggeration? Not at all. Look at the social corrosion caused by hyperinflation, the extreme debasement of the value of money by rising prices. Whether in Weimar Germany of the 1930s, many Latin American countries in the 1980s, or Zimbabwe in recent years, a nonfunctional monetary system has caused misery and political turmoil. The next chapter will return to the wider issue of trust and economic sustainability. In this chapter I concentrate on the long-term fallout of the government debts created by the banking crisis on top of a preexisting but slow and largely silent debt crisis due to welfare systems. Government funded by future tax revenues that can't be collected has been steadily undermining the fundamental consent required for a society to function. In almost all developed economies, recent generations have promised themselves a comfortable income if they become unemployed or fall ill, and also when they retire. They have built health systems that spend a large proportion of tax revenues, and will spend more in years to come.

Demographic change is intensifying this financial unsustainability. Longevity has increased a lot in most countries in the world, albeit with important exceptions. People have been having fewer than the number of children needed to keep the population constant. Indeed, there are many countries now where the population is declining and getting older. The demographic structure of the developed world and some developing countries including China has altered radically in the past generation.

These two seemingly unrelated debt burdens, one created by the immorality of bankers, the other by the frailty of politicians, both reflect societies (or rather governments) that have mortgaged their future. Future taxpayers will have to work harder and consume less if the accumulated public debts are going to be repaid. Today's debts will cast a long shadow into the future. Social tensions are bound to rise as younger citizens realize they will not enjoy the same welfare benefits or pensions as their parents and will also pay higher taxes to repay the debts incurred on past benefits. The risks are very different from the kind of catastrophic physical threats posed by climate change, but they are in their own way equally damaging. Sustainable economies have to leave more than a mountain of IOUs for posterity.

This chapter will start with the immediate crisis, the legacy of the financial crisis for government debt. Then I'll describe the existing and often hidden debt, mainly due to implicit welfare and pension promises made by governments. What matters about the scale is whether or not the repayments can be made relatively easily, so the following sections will turn to the arithmetic of public debt—when does it become so large that it depresses economic growth to the extent that the debt can't actually be repaid?—and then to the question of who has done the lending. I'll argue that for both reasons many governments will effectively default on their debts, in one of several ways.

The Debt Legacy of the Financial Crisis

The numbers are so large that they are hard to make sense of, but it's worth starting out with an idea of the headline figures. IMF estimates as of mid-2009 suggested that the total cost of the financial crisis has been $11.9 trillion (that's $11,900,000,000,000).

This includes guaranteeing debts and giving banks new capital as well as the upfront cost of the banking rescues. The total might change. Some of this government bailout money might not be needed but even if only half is spent it will amount to an average cost of about one thousand dollars for every person, children included, in the world. The amount per taxpayer in the rich economies is much higher. Some countries are worse off. The United Kingdom's situation is worst of all with an upfront cost of about one-fifth of the economy's whole annual output and a total potential cost of more than 80 percent of GDP, but the United States isn't far behind.[4]

It's a lot of money—and that's only the start of the cost. In country after country, other banks that were in danger of failing because of their spiraling losses in the bond and derivatives markets were bailed out by governments. A worldwide recession followed, prompting central banks to slash interest rates and provide massive cash injections to the banks, and governments to step in with stimulus packages—enormous sums of taxpayers' money in the United States and elsewhere. Most governments put in place measures to avoid a severe recession, by spending more money on public services and cutting taxes. The efforts have succeeded in the sense that the recession has been less severe than had initially been feared, although also prolonged. But the resulting budget deficits are the largest since the Second World War, at 10 percent of GDP on average for the big economies, and 13.5 percent of GDP for the United States. The cost of bank bailouts has come on top of "structural" deficits that were already much larger than was warranted by the state of the economy before the crisis. The U.S. budget deficit trebled between 2008 and 2009. The burden on taxpayers who must finance the interest and eventual repayment will be long-lasting. In most of the leading economies, the ratio of government debt to GDP will have risen by 2014 to the region of 100 percent of GDP, compared with 60–70 percent before the crisis. Again, the picture differs from country to country. Japan, which started with a high government debt ratio because of its 1990s economic crisis, will end up with a figure of about 240 percent likely by 2014.[5]

Many people will already have glazed over under this onslaught of percentages; the point is that the numbers are truly large. They are larger than government debts ever before incurred outside periods of wartime, when fundamental national interests are at stake and people are therefore ready to support the financial sacrifices their governments ask of them in order to service large debts.

What's more, these large figures need to be added to another debt burden.

THE PENSION AND WELFARE BURDEN

That is the burden of future government payments to the recipients of state pensions and other welfare payments, including medical care paid for by the government. Of course, governments of the future will receive tax revenues from their citizens. The question is how much the revenues will need to go up to deliver governments' promises to make pension, medical, and other benefit payments. Even before the financial crisis, some governments had "structural" deficits, a long-term shortfall between revenues and payments, and more had large implied future deficits. This implicit debt is rarely considered and isn't part of the official statistics. How has it come about?

The share of government in the economy has increased in all developed countries over the decades, although it varies widely between different countries. At the low end of the spectrum are the United States and Singapore, at the high end the Scandinavian nations and some continental European countries. All of these are prosperous places. The difference in the size of government reflects political and cultural choices made in those societies. However, there is no exception to the general long-term trend of government spending accounting for a rising share of national output. The few partial exceptions reflect either a one-off windfall (such as the United States being able to temporarily cut defense budgets in the early 1990s after the end of the Cold War) or massive and divisive political determination (such as the Thatcher and Reagan years, when the United States and United Kingdom briefly halted the upward climb). Indeed, one of the markers of a country making the transition from developing to developed status is an expansion of government, because the creation of a welfare state is an important means by which citizens can be insured against an uncertain future when they move from village to town or take new jobs.

The catch is that governments have struggled and failed to raise taxes in line with spending. It is much easier to borrow, and indeed there is no reason they shouldn't borrow. Until his resolve collapsed under the desire to spend, British Labor prime minister Gordon Brown had a so-called "Golden Rule," that the government could borrow to spend on capital projects such as infrastructure spending, as these would generate a long-term return to the public. Borrowing is also an essential tool for limiting the impact of recessions. Sadly, all such sensible rules—budget rules, or deficit limits as in the Eurozone region—reach a point at which they come unstuck. Governments over and over again have proven unable to commit themselves genuinely to financial discipline. Budget deficits are the norm in the leading economies. Before the financial crisis struck, the average for the rich OECD economies was already about 1.5 percent of GDP (in 2007, a boom year when tax revenues were buoyant). So in almost every rich economy governments have already borrowed some money to finance welfare, health, and pension systems, and will have to borrow a great deal more in the future to continue with these systems.

Estimates of the debt burden implied by commitments to health and pension spending, such as Medicare and Social Security, are harder to come by. One thorough assessment of the U.S. government's indebtedness, now a few years out of date, estimated this part of the debt at the equivalent of 8 percent of all future GDP, a gap so big it would need a permanent doubling of payroll taxes to close it.[6] One estimate, from the OECD, is that the average member country's government will need to borrow 5 percent of GDP more than they do now within a decade, if there's no change in the pension and elderly care system.

These long-term deficits and the rising mountain of government debt will become ever harder to finance. Governments can borrow either from those of their own citizens with savings to invest or from foreigners with savings. The former may have distributional implications, as all taxpayers will owe the interest to those who do the lending; but usually the benefits of the borrowing mean that doesn't matter. The latter type of borrowing is potentially more fraught. The large pools of savings available to lend to the American and British governments lie for the most part in developing economies, especially China. It seems inherently problematic to use money from relatively poor Chinese savers to support the relatively generous pensions paid to elderly Americans, or bailouts to investment bankers. At some point, too, this flow of savings will be directed to better uses paying higher returns, such as investment in Chinese enterprises; it could dry up quickly. There is a geopolitical dimension too, with the flow of funds so large that it makes diplomatic relations between the two countries harder—witness the row over the level of the dollar-renminbi exchange rate—and fuels U.S. insecurity about whether China is overtaking it as the world's major power.

Does it matter? Yes, because these rich countries have reached a stage of crisis that will unfold more slowly than the financial crisis but is if anything more severe. The amount of spending implied by existing patterns of entitlement such as how much pension the state will pay and at what retirement age, what medical payments the government will cover, what benefits are received by the long-term sick, and so on is on the point of rising sharply. Pensions and health care (as older people need more treatment for longer) are the main culprits. Western societies (and some others) are aging rapidly. The ratio of old people to young ones is rising, and ultimately populations will start to shrink. A long-heralded demographic time bomb is exploding and taking government finances up with it.

THE DEMOGRAPHIC IMPLOSION

The human population started growing rapidly about two hundred and fifty years ago, when the dawn of the capitalist economy permitted an escape from the "Malthusian" trap of food production limiting the increase of the population. For the first time since then, there are many countries whose birthrates are well below the replacement level, and whose populations are aging and will soon start shrinking.

This might seem surprising as so much attention has been paid to the headline global numbers, which are climbing in a slightly scary way: the world's population is above 6.5 billion in 2009 and is expected to peak around 9 billion, and we rightly worry about the environmental impacts globally. Much of this expected growth will occur in poor countries. Yet in fact, population growth has already declined in many developing countries too. The key seems to be the education of women, along with their participation in the work force, as much as the well-known "demographic transition" of a high enough level of income that it is no longer necessary to have many children as an investment for one's old age.[7] And there is not one of the rich countries with a birthrate above replacement level. Those such as the United States and United Kingdom whose populations are growing are attracting enough immigrants to offset declining "native" birthrates. In some cases, including Germany, Italy, Japan, and a number of eastern European countries, the demographic change under way is startling. Italy's population, for example, is expected to shrink by a quarter between now and 2040, while the average age is likely to rise from 44 to 54. Among poorer countries, China faces the same unknown waters of demographic transition due to its strict one-child policy

Figure 5. Just one child.

under authoritarian communism: two parent couples producing one child each makes for a rapidly shrinking population, and a disproportionately male one as so many baby girls have been aborted or killed in early infancy to ensure the sole permitted child is a son.[8]

Certainly in these countries people who are working will have to devote an increasing amount of their income to supporting older people who have stopped working, and—if nothing changes—a lot of this support will take place through the tax system. This has nothing to do with the financial structures of pension systems and whether they are "funded" or not (that is, whether or not there is already a pot of investments earmarked for paying them in future). Much of the policy debate has focused on this question of whether or not schemes are "funded" by investments, but this is a bit of a red herring. Whatever the formal financial arrangements, at any moment the amount available to consume has to be split between people who are working and those who are not. Nobody can eat future meat and vegetables, no matter how much money they have. This will alarm anyone who thinks they have a healthy amount in their pension fund, and it should. Financial assets held in a pension fund are claims on returns to economic activity in the future, and those returns will not be high enough unless there are enough people engaged in sufficiently productive economic activity at that time. All that can change is the geographic scope of the resources being claimed by pensioners—a point I return to below.

For several decades now, since the creation of the welfare state as we know it in so many Western countries after the Second World War, people have worked for about forty or forty-five years, and been retired for another ten or, more likely now, twenty or twenty-five years. Partly this is due to unanticipated increases in life expectancy, which stands now at seventy-eight in the United States and eighty in Europe, compared with only sixty-six in 1945. But these generations should also think of themselves as reaping a reward for their efforts in the Second World War and the "golden age" of growth in the following thirty years. For retirement ages will certainly increase from now on. The average OECD ratio of the number of dependants (children and pensioners) per worker will climb from sixty-five per hundred workers in 2005 to eighty-eight per hundred projected for 2050.[9] This implies that the number of pensioners will have to fall—retirement ages will have to rise.

Later retirement will not completely remove the burden on the future, however. Despite improving health in middle and old age, people do slow down as they age, and need more medical treatment. And in countries with sharply declining populations—such as Germany, Italy, Japan, or Russia within about two decades, or China just a little later—the figures seem to remove the prospect of retirement altogether. Will we have to return to the prewelfare state era of old people working until they fall irretrievably ill or die? Is the possibility of a pension becoming extinct?

For several decades, many governments have ignored the demographic pressures by letting the level of their debts rise. They have mortgaged their future citizens' tax payments in order to spend on citizens of the present. A good tactic for winning elections is a bad strategy for sustainability of the state. The Italian government is already in debt by 106 percent of the country's entire annual GDP (as of 2008), and annual interest payments out of tax revenues are 5.1 percent of GDP. Its population is shrinking now. The financial markets, through whom money is borrowed (taking the savings of Chinese peasants as well as Europeans, and lending the money to the Italian government so it can provide pensions and health care for its elderly), have taken note: the interest rate on Italian government debt is significantly above the U.S. government's rate for borrowing money. At some point, the game will be up. This point could be quite close. By 2050, a third of the Italian people will be over sixty-five. Italy and Japan are extreme cases in their demographic change, but this is a widespread problem.

The debt implied by future social and pension obligations is, for the most part, not acknowledged by governments, because the consequence, that pensions, health care, and social security need substantial reform, is politically toxic. There are exceptions. David Willetts, a minister in the UK coalition government from 2010, has acknowledged in his book *The Pinch*: "Our fears about our society and the strains in our economy reflect a breakdown in the balance between the generations." He predicts a decade of painful adjustment, without creating political hostages to fortune by suggesting specific measures.[10] How big an adjustment will be needed? The OECD estimates that if there were no change in work or retirement patterns, the ratio of older inactive persons per worker could rise to almost one older inactive person for every worker by the year 2050 in Europe. It further estimates that on the basis of unchanged participation patterns and productivity growth, the growth of GDP per capita in the OECD area would decline to around 1.7 percent per year over the next three decades, about 30 percent less than its rate between 1979 and 2000.[11] This would also likely be lower than the real interest rate on government debt, raising the prospect of an ever rising debt spiral.

Indeed, some people believe this large debt burden created in part by demographic change, as well as ever-more generous systems of state payments, is in turn contributing to an even greater decline in population in a slow but equally vicious spiral. Faced with the accumulation of debt created by current and past governments, what do future generations of taxpayers think? Axel Weber, president of Germany's Bundesbank, said, only half-joking: "They are doing the only thing they can. They're avoiding being born."[12] The economic incentives (on parents) are certainly not the only influence on birthrates—and, of course, these can change in the space of nine months or so—but to the extent that economic pressures reinforce cultural and social influences, they are certainly not encouraging more babies to be born.

Does this matter? Some environmentalists would argue that it is desirable: the population needs to shrink in order to bring the burden humans are placing on the planet's ecosystems and climate down to a manageable level. But even if you accept the need for a smaller human population—and not all would agree—all the people who are alive today need to be fed, sheltered, clothed, and kept in all the other goods and services they want—health care, cinema trips, furniture, books, schooling, phone calls, cameras—using the efforts of the people who are working today. If the ratio of nonworkers to workers rises, either the workers have to get much more productive or the nonworkers have to do without.

What is certain is that governments can't keep on ignoring the demographic change by borrowing more, especially not on top of their acknowledged debt due to expensive bank rescues and the recession. The funds have to be borrowed from somewhere. Debts are owed to specific lenders. Both debt burdens—to pay for pensions and social spending, and to pay off the banks—are owed to a mix of lenders at home and abroad. Many of those at home are pension and investment funds, so the government is borrowing from its own voters. A growing proportion of the debt is being funded, however, by developing countries with high savings rates, especially China. As of March 2007, China held $421 billion of U.S. Treasury securities. By October of that year, its holdings were $388 billion, a reduction of $33 billion. Its net purchases since then have been small.[13]

Now, as noted earlier, small enough debts don't matter because the interest on them can easily be paid from future taxes. Is the double debt burden on the rich economies now, the post-crisis financial debt and the unfolding crisis of social debt, too big? After all, the banks had to be bailed out in order to prevent an unprecedented economic collapse, and every rich country—even the small-government nations like the United States—believes a social welfare and pension system to keep citizens out of extreme poverty is a minimum requirement of a prosperous and civilized society. The question really is whether debt has grown to the point of unsustainability. I believe many countries are close.

How Much Does Government Debt Matter?

In the months after the scale of the financial crisis became apparent, and the need for a fiscal stimulus by the government to prevent a deep recession was accepted, one of the (many) disagreements among economic commentators was about how much the government needed to stimulate the economy, and for how long. The most entertaining row involved Harvard economic historian Niall Ferguson and Princeton economist Paul Krugman. Ferguson, a conservative, warned (at a 30 April symposium at the Metropolitan Museum of Art in New York) that if the U.S. government carried on borrowing at the current pace, "the financial credibility of the United States would be called into question." He drew on his detailed studies of finance in an earlier era of terrible instability, the 1930s. Paul Krugman, the leading liberal columnist in the United States, soon responded on his blog, saying this was the "back to the dark ages of economics." Krugman is a supporter of the case for deficit financing first espoused by the eminent 1930s economist John Maynard Keynes. The clash between these two titan egos continued in newspaper columns and blogs until August, trading accusations of ignorance on the one hand and racism on the other. Finally, Krugman accused Ferguson of being a poseur, while Ferguson accused Krugman of playground immaturity.

This issue has stimulated a partisan row between the political left and right, not just in the United States. Yet there is a genuine intellectual debate behind the row, with many respected economists on each side. Paul Krugman is the most ardent advocate of deficit spending as large and long-lasting as needed to ensure the economy does not get stuck in a deep recession that will cause many people to lose their jobs and incomes. He has the authority of the IMF on his side, although its tone is far more measured. A comment by some of the IMF's top economists said fiscal stimulus is necessary and what's more: "It is essential for governments to indicate from the start that the extent of the fiscal expansion will be contingent on the state of the economy. Sizable upfront stimulus is needed, but policymakers must commit to doing more if needed. This should be announced at the start, so later increases do not look like acts of desperation."[14]

The world of economics has split into two camps on this question. When different eminent economists can disagree so sharply, it's clear this is an area of judgment rather than hard science. What does economic analysis actually tell us? The greater the government demand to borrow, the higher the interest rate needed to be paid to increase the supply of savings available to meet it. So governments will need over time to pay higher interest rates in order to continue borrowing more and more. At a certain point, rising government borrowing becomes impossible for an economy to sustain. The point is reached when the interest rate (after adjusting for inflation) exceeds the economy's long-term potential growth rate. Either large-scale borrowing that pushes the interest rate higher than that point or depressed economic growth can act as the trigger. The long-term growth rate will depend on many factors, including innovation and productivity, the average age and skills of the workforce and thus birthrates and immigration, on the use of natural resources, and also on the impact of the government on the economy through tax levels and borrowing. According to John Lipsky of the IMF: "We have estimated that maintaining public debt at its post-crisis levels could reduce potential growth in advanced economies by as much as ½ percentage point annually compared with pre-crisis performance."[15] These debt spirals, when the interest still due grows faster than the amount by which the outstanding debt is repaid, are a real possibility, not a theoretical one—Japan has been on or over the edge of one since the 1990s.

Many economists had started to say by the middle of 2009 that governments were going too far, and were building up unsustainable levels of public debt. One was a Japanese economist, Keiichiro Kobayashi, drawing on the experience of Japan's "lost decade" of the 1990s. He argued that the lesson of that financial crisis, in which many of Japan's banks went bust under the weight of bad or "toxic" debts, was that government borrowing adding more debt onto an existing debt problem makes matters worse. He wrote:

> If Krugman—who won the Nobel Prize in economics last year and enjoys a high profile—continues emphasising the importance of fiscal expansion while downplaying the need to tackle the bad asset problem, he will be giving the U.S. public an excuse for avoiding the painful job of dumping the toxic assets. His theory will mislead U.S. citizens into believing that big government spending can save the day, thereby making it impossible to build the solid political consensus needed for grappling with the challenge of eliminating bad assets.[16]

The United Kingdom is another extreme case, with the government's budget deficit unavoidably reaching 12 percent of GDP in these years immediately after the financial crisis. Interest payments by the government in 2009–10 are likely to be £30 billion a year, or equivalent to just over 2 percent of the economy's output for the year. Assuming a strong recovery in the economy in 2010–11 onward, and assuming that government spending on services at best is flat after adjusting for inflation for at least eight years, the annual budget deficit is unlikely to return to balance until at least 2017–18. Not until after that would the level of debt on which interest must be paid start to fall. There is no period of so many years in the past in which government spending did not rise. Since 1970 there has been the odd year of decline—one of them was in 1977–78 when the International Monetary Fund had to step in and help the UK government sort out its finances. All these occasional years when government spending declined slightly in real terms felt like a painful squeeze so it's hard to imagine what an eight-year freeze would be like. This likely pain suggests it will in reality take much longer to stop the debt-GDP ratio rising. And, of course, this is just the immediate deficit—the retrenchment measures needed to cover future pension, health, and welfare obligations will be far bigger.

To spell it out, the crisis of government we face now is more serious by orders of magnitude than that of the late 1970s, a tumultuous era of strikes, cuts in public services, and political upheaval.

The UK's position will be worse than most but it is not alone. The U.S. situation is similar, and all the rich country governments have mortgaged future tax revenues to a degree that will compromise their ability to provide in future the services and benefits (including pensions) they pay for now. Even if Professor Krugman is right that fiscal stimulus has been and remains essential for now, the existing debt burden means future taxpayers (declining in number, remember) will be paying a higher share of their incomes to their governments for a lower entitlement to services and benefits from their governments. Governments can't possibly honor the much greater burden of future pension and social entitlements implied by today's systems, if they were to carry forward into the future. What does this mean? How will the dual debt crisis unfold?

What Will Governments Do?

The debt time bomb is metaphorical—and metaphorical devices never explode because unsustainable trends are not sustained. (This is a version of Herbert Stein's Law, which he expressed as: "If something cannot go on forever, it will stop.") The accumulation of debt, a massive obligation we have imposed on people in the future, will therefore lead to certain more or less inevitable changes. There are a limited number of ways this can work out, and the less unpalatable routes will require an explicit acknowledgement that present choices are required by future obligations.

What are the possibilities? The debts incurred by rich Western countries represent a transfer of resources from the future to the past, and also from future citizens of other countries, to the extent that foreigners are buying the government bonds being issued to raise the money. So there is an international as well as intergenerational aspect to this transfer. We are maintaining today's levels of consumption not only at the expense of tomorrow's consumers at home but also consumers abroad, now and in the future. We—adults alive today and benefiting from state-funded cradle-to-grave social systems—have created huge obligations to these different groups of people, living as we have beyond our means.

Any resolution of the unsustainable debt burden, whether this happens in unintentional or planned ways, will involve a mix of:

- reduced consumption and increased saving in the indebted rich economies, either through higher taxes or higher private saving to pay for services governments will not be able to afford to offer in future;

- more work and less leisure, in order to support aging populations and reduce the ratio of dependents to earners, which can come about in several ways, set out below;
- more effort, or higher productivity, so that the growth of the economy can help make the debt burden easier to service;
- investment of Western savings in faster-growing emerging economies, again to help pay off the interest and debts;
- improving the demographic profile, creating more taxpayers, through increased immigration of working age people, or a higher birthrate;
- default on debts, either overtly—unlikely given the obvious costs in terms of higher interest rates that would have to be paid for subsequent borrowing and the upheaval in trade and financial markets—or covertly by allowing inflation to eat away at the real value of existing debt.[17]

Each of these options has a different degree of political and social palatability, and can come about in different ways. The route through will be the result of political choices, most of which politicians do not care to talk about. So it's worth exploring the different possible routes back to sustainability.

Reduced Consumption, Increased Saving

Just as in the case of environmental sustainability, if we are overconsuming resources there will have to be a reduction in that consumption and an increase in saving. As the financial debts that have piled up have been incurred by governments, much of this adjustment will have to come about through reduced government expenditure and increased taxes: a government deficit is "negative saving" by the state. Some groups of individuals in some countries, especially the United States and United Kingdom, are burdened by debt too but household debt even in these two countries is small beer compared to government debt.

As discussed above, the scale of the adjustment in the role of the state implied by the required debt reduction is staggering. The dual financial and social debt crisis will mark a significant turning point, likely to be just as significant as the long expansion of the state during and after World War II. However, there will be a huge political battle. Part of the adjustment will or should involve a switch from debt-funded government pension provision to private pension saving and lower levels of private spending—the figures cited earlier in this chapter make plain this need. People today have been spending up until their retirement at a level possible only by borrowing from the living standards of people not yet born or grown.

But, of course, the level of pension payments is a political shibboleth and moves to reduce pensions will be extremely contentious. Reasonably enough, the cohort of voters who have paid taxes for other people's pensions and welfare receipts but will perhaps not receive the same entitlements themselves will be aggrieved. In aging societies, politicians will have to be brave indeed to pledge to reduce the pensions bill. The baby boom generation, born between 1945 and 1960 and beginning to retire now, is likely to be extremely vocal about such policies— they used to be known as the Grateful Dead generation, but one analyst has said they will become the "ungrateful undead," demanding more by way of pensions and health care through their long retirements.[18] It is not obvious that governments in Western democracies will have the political will to reduce social and pension spending, even in a slow transition. If this proves to be the case, other, less orderly, adjustments will take place.

More Work, Less Leisure

One relatively easy way for governments to reduce the public sector bill is raising the pension age. Whether to save the public finances or to ensure an adequate private pension, people of working age now can expect to work longer than their parents did. In recent times a retirement period of a quarter of a century hasn't been unusual; in the 1960s a decade was the norm. That's probably what we need to return to, which with current life expectancies implies a retirement age of at least 70, up from 60 or 65 now. Early founders of the pension system never imagined that its financing would have to stretch to keeping people on the golf course for the whole final quarter of their lives. (Indeed, the United Kingdom's postwar state pension system was set up with a retirement age older than life expectancy at birth at that time.)

Furthermore, in many countries more people of working age will have to work and pay taxes. The participation rate—the proportion of people of working age who actually work—varies widely between countries. In the flexible labor market "Anglo Saxon" economies, it is typically high, with around four-fifths of those who can work doing so. In some others, such as Italy or France, it is lower, around two-thirds—reduced by high rates of long-term or youth or ethnic minority unemployment, high levels of long-term disability, and less likelihood that mothers of young children will work. Participation in the job market depends on cultural norms, on what is socially acceptable, as well as financial necessity and incentives created by the tax and benefit system. Even so, the rate of participation can increase within the space of a decade or so, and that is needed now.

Productivity Improvements

One "easy" answer to the need to provide more resources for posterity is for people working now to do so more productively—produce more for the same effort, rather than having to consume less. Politically, this is certainly the easiest option. In reality, faster productivity growth is difficult to achieve. The impact of the new generation of information and communication technologies did boost productivity growth in the leading economies during the late 1990s and early 2000s—the estimated trend growth in the U.S. economy went up by a full percentage point to around 4 percent a year.[19] However, if it took a technological revolution to achieve that increase, it would be foolish—although politically tempting—to assume the same again will be possible in the decades ahead. We can hope that higher productivity is part of the mix of solutions, but we shouldn't count on it. Nor would it be enough. In a boom year in the high-productivity growth 1990s or 2000s, a typical Western government could reduce its government debt-GDP ratio by perhaps 2 percentage points just through economic growth. However, under current economic conditions, it would take decades, relying on faster productivity growth alone, to reduce debt ratios to sustainable levels.

Another way to get more output for the same effort is to invest savings overseas in economies that are growing faster, such as China and India. People saving more for their own retirement will be able to earn a higher rate of return if they invest the money in places where productivity is growing faster than at home. But this might prove more politically contentious than it seems now, at the tail end of a long period of increasing globalization of capital flows. There will be a temptation for governments to restrict the freedom of investors to put their money to work overseas if things look tough at home, and in particular if investing in national government debt is seen as a patriotic duty.

Migration

More migration can be expected from countries with growing populations to those with shrinking populations. The recession has more or less put a halt to a big surge in emigration from Africa to North America and Europe, but it is likely to resume. The movement of young people from countries where there are too many to those where there are too few will not only rebalance the pressures between countries, it will also increase global productivity. The reason is that migrants from poor to rich countries become more productive overnight, as soon as they have access to the capital and the social institutions of their host countries, enabling them to make better use of their personal talents and experience.[20]

International migration has been an emotive topic, generating political controversy. Paradoxically, perhaps the greatest tensions have arisen in countries whose demographic need for larger numbers of younger people is the greatest—Italy is one example, where there is great hostility to the influx of young workers from the southern shores of the Mediterranean. A number of Western governments have felt obliged to try to slow the inflows of immigrants, especially those from much poorer countries.

Although there are without doubt costs involved in large-scale immigration—in terms of pressure on housing and transport in some areas, for example, and in terms of cultural adjustment—I have no doubt that the flows should and moreover will continue. It doesn't take much awareness of the desperate attempts of some would-be migrants to reach Europe and the United States—the leaking boats and airless trucks, the frightened scurry across the border or panicky wait in line at the airport—to realize the strength of the demographic and environmental pressure behind the massive movement of people. The number of international migrants in the world increased from 155 million in 1990 to 191 million in 2005. Developed countries absorbed most of the increase in the number of these migrants during this period, or 33 million out of 36 million, and there is now an increasing concentration of international migrants in the developed world, specifically North America and Europe. The proportion of migrants living in North America increased from 18 percent in 1990 to 23 percent in 2005 and the share of Europe rose from 32 percent to 34 percent during that period.[21] We are still in the midst of one of the great eras of migration that occur from time to time in human history. One of its by-products will be a small improvement in the demographic structure of the population in the rich economies, a slowdown in the rate at which their populations are aging.

An alternative is an increase in the birthrate of the native born in aging societies. Baby booms do occur, and the reasons for demographic waves of this kind are not well understood. However, they do seem to be linked to the prospects potential parents see in the world around them—there was a postwar baby boom but a Depression era baby bust. So it seems unlikely that a period of major economic adjustment of the kind we are in for would encourage a higher birthrate.

Figure 6. The desperation of migrants.

Default

The final option is that governments will not honor the debt they have accumulated. This is unlikely to be explicit. A formal default makes it impossible to borrow again for a long period in the future, casts a shadow over private sector borrowers by raising the interest rates they have to pay, makes it harder to engage in international trade, and causes recession and economic turmoil. However, quiet default by allowing inflation to rise so the real value of the debt is eroded is extremely likely. It was the way governments tackled an earlier build up of debt in the 1970s.

This might sound like an easy way out, but high inflation is socially corrosive. It harms people on low incomes, which never keep up with price rises, and small savers, whose interest rates turn negative in real, inflation-adjusted terms. The well-off and big investors find ways to protect themselves. Extreme cases illustrate dramatically the social impact—the hyperinflations of the 1930s, or of Zimbabwe now, for example. Inflation of 20 percent or 25 percent is certainly not comparable, but shouldn't be dismissed as minor either. We experienced that in the United Kingdom in the late 1970s, and I remember going short of certain foods in my ordinary, not poor, family—coffee and sugar for example becoming unaffordable treats.

Besides, inflation doesn't address the real transfer of resources from smaller future generations to larger old generations, which current systems of pensions and health care imply. Disguised default is not an attractive option, although it will probably seem the least problematic politically.

What should governments in fact do?

Nothing is not an option. The unsustainable won't be sustained; but governments and voters can either decide to respond to the pressures or just to let events unravel. And a mix of the various possibilities is likely. Higher growth would be terrific but is hard to achieve. Additional migration on a large scale is probably unlikely given that it has already reached such high levels compared with the recent past, although it will continue. According to Carmen Reinhardt and Kenneth Rogoff, default is a surprisingly common policy response to financial crisis, in a mix of the forms described above, and often described as "restructuring." In their thorough study of the history of financial crises, they conclude that not only do crises commonly cause very large increases in public debt, but also that subsequent default on this wide definition is nearly universal.[22] It seems only realistic in the light of their findings to expect many governments to take this route.

Economists would rather urge long-term reforms of entitlement spending on pensions, health care, and welfare as well as higher taxes and other spending cuts. For example, the IMF's John Lipsky said in a speech: "Just keeping debt ratios at a postcrisis level will require new policy action. Unwinding the discretionary anti-crisis stimulus measures would contribute only 1½ percent of GDP to the [necessary 8 percent] fiscal adjustment. As a result, the bulk of the required progress will have to reflect reforms of pension and health entitlements, containment of other primary spending, and increased tax revenues."[23]

Many countries will end up having to restructure the way they pay pensions and provide medical and social care to the elderly, although reform is likely to be incremental and slow, given the political challenge of achieving such reforms with an aging electorate.

Ultimately, too, people in the OECD countries will need to increase their work level and increase their domestic savings. Retirement ages will climb. The long-term trend toward shorter workweeks and longer holidays will come to an end or go into reverse.[24] And, just like the response required for greater environmental sustainability, debt sustainability will also call for lower consumption and higher savings. This can take many shapes, but one important factor will be the realization of those not yet retired that we'll need to work longer and more productively, and to save more of our own incomes to finance our later retirement years.

WHAT DO WE OWE TO POSTERITY?

The postwar generations lived through the Cold War and the fear of nuclear annihilation; but they took other elements of their security for granted. This has applied in particular to economic security. This rested on an assumption of the plentiful availability of natural resources, including carbon-based energy, with no impacts so large or irreversible in their scale that normal market mechanisms can't handle them. And also on the fundamentals of social security, everywhere founded on old age pensions, dating back to the earliest introduction of social welfare by German chancellor Otto von Bismarck in the 1880s but greatly extended after 1945.

Now it has become clear that we have borrowed massively from the natural and human resources of the future—to an extent that means an end for the first time in more than two centuries to the easy assumption that people in future generations will be better off than we are. Not only have we left nothing for posterity, we've made it likely that standards of living will be lower in the future when people have to service our massive financial debts and live with unknown environmental changes.

Debt is not just a financial indicator. It reflects the depletion of social as well as financial resources. Borrowing creates political and social as well as financial obligations. The crisis has greatly increased the degree of indebtedness of most of the governments of the leading economies; but there is a dual debt burden, and the more onerous part is the hidden part created by government promises to pay pensions and health care and other benefits to their aging and declining populations. The promises can't be kept. The only question is how they will be broken, given the enormous political strains involved in fundamentally changing what people will get from their governments. The role of the government has been to raise the living standards of their current aging populations by borrowing the money rather than paying for it from current tax revenues. Demographic change makes that impossible to continue.

So far this book has identified two dimensions of unsustainability—the depletion of environmental resources, and the vast borrowing from posterity implied by current and prospective levels of debt. Both imply that current and recent generations in the rich economies have been living beyond their means and will need to correct that by saving more and consuming less. A lack of due attention to the future, the failure to exercise proper husbandry, is the other side of the coin to excessive consumption. The Economics of Enough require that the future should get more attention now. The following chapters will explore two further ways in which the way we live now has damaged prospects for the future, namely, the collapse of trust and the increase in inequality in at least some societies.

FOUR Fairness

Do people have an innate sense of fairness? Or are we intrinsically selfish and bound to come into conflict with each other? In the past philosophers have disagreed. Thomas Hobbes was famously pessimistic, holding that our self-interest was bound to lead to a "war of all against all" in the absence of a strong state to enforce peace. Jean-Jacques Rousseau disagreed with this dark vision, set out a few decades earlier by Hobbes in *Leviathan*. Rousseau agreed that humans have a drive to self-preservation but also held (in *Discourse on the Origin and Basis of Inequality among Men*) that a sense of compassion, an aversion to causing pain, is in our nature.[1]

The philosophical debate continues, but there is now an accumulation of scientific evidence bearing on human nature. In this chapter I'll describe some of it. On the whole, it indicates (among other things) that a strong and rooted sense of fair play is innate, and important for the way we organize society and the economy. A society that offends its members' sense of fairness is, in important ways, unsustainable.

One of the main questions I will examine in this chapter is economic inequality and the extent to which the inequality we observe now is compatible with that fundamental sense of fairness. I will also look at the evidence on the sustainability, both political and economic, of current levels of inequality. Perceived unfairness can create a political backlash, which can take various forms. It can also potentially undermine the strength of the economy, both the aggregate growth rate and the prosperity of citizens. There is indeed evidence that in some countries inequality has increased to an unsustainable degree and is corroding society and indeed the economy; these countries include the United States and United Kingdom. The disgust widely felt in these countries about bankers' bonuses, self-awarded out of tax dollars or pounds, has brought this into sharp focus.

Already some readers might be bristling at these last words. Inequality is a fraught topic. It arouses strong ideological beliefs—it is an issue distinguishing political parties. In the international context, it arouses the passions of antiglobalization campaigners. And because the question is one that does arouse philosophical and political passions, the heat of argument inflames what ought to be objective questions of measurement and evidence. So I will try to set out the building blocks of my argument in this chapter carefully.

This is how the line of argument will go.

The first section will look at the evidence on the existence of a sense of fairness as part of human nature, and on the evolutionary origins of a fairness instinct. This includes a diversion into how this understanding of human nature ties in with the standard assumption made in economics that people act in a self-interested way. I argue that economics is not only consistent with an appreciation that we have a fairness instinct but is actually fundamentally making the same assumption as the evolutionary sciences. "Self-interested" should not be interpreted to mean "selfish"—certainly not "selfish and rationally calculating at all times," as a typical (and sometimes deserved) caricature of economics would have it.

The following sections will look at the statistics available on the degree of inequality in incomes—first, at inequality at the global level between nations; second, at the degree of inequality within different nations, and what has happened over time. There is a much smaller amount of evidence on the distribution of wealth, but it indicates that wealth inequality is greater still.

Then I will turn to the explanations economists offer for the pattern of inequality, and how well the evidence supports them. The main point of this section is that no single universal cause can explain differences in how income distribution has changed in different nations, so marked are the divergences. Even if there is one important economic cause (and it does seem to be technology that plays the main role), the wide variety of political and economic institutions means that the underlying forces play out in country-specific ways. Inequality is fundamentally a political and moral choice, although the politics involved is as much a matter of the acceptable long-term norms of the society as of short-term election issues such as top tax rates and welfare spending.

The final two sections will go on to consider the consequences of "too much" inequality. One considers the evidence—incomplete as it is—on the relationship between inequality and growth. The other looks at evidence on the impact of inequality on well-being and the long-term strength of society. One of the most important issues is how inequality affects social capital. This is, as will be discussed in the next chapter, fundamental to any economy and more so now than ever before as technology increases the complexity and interconnectedness of the global economy. In some countries—the United States and United Kingdom foremost among them—income and opportunities have become so unequal as to corrode the social fabric. The trend toward greater inequality is, if not yet unsustainable, well on its way to being so.

THE FAIRNESS INSTINCT

The evidence for the existence of a fairness instinct in humans comes from psychological experiments, evolutionary psychology, and primatology.

Some of the experimental results have become well known, thanks to the fashion for behavioral economics. One example is the "ultimatum game." One of two players is given some cash to divide between the two of them. The second player can take or leave the offer, but if he rejects it, neither of them gets any money. Typically, offers that are too low are rejected, with the threshold being about a quarter or a third, even though the second player punishes themselves as well as the insufficiently generous first player. Much has been made of the fact that this contradicts the assumption in economics of rational self-interest—taken to its logical conclusion, this would suggest the second player should accept even a cent as better than nothing. This experiment and others indicate that a sense of fairness, and unfairness, trumps this strong version of the rational self-interest assumption.[2]

Too much weight is placed on this experimental psychological evidence, however. Behavioral economics has become so fashionable partly because the experimental results are fascinating but also partly because so many of its new aficionados are delighted that it seems to overturn a key assumption in economics.

Their delight is misplaced. For one thing, other experimental evidence indicates that humans behave selfishly in other contexts. In some experiments, economists have shown that markets operate exactly as conventional economic models based on rational self-interest would predict.[3] For another thing, subtle changes in the design of experiments can change the outcomes dramatically, as economist John List has documented.[4] List cautions against drawing hard and fast conclusions about human nature from the results available to us now: "A first lesson that I take from this body of research is that what we do not know dwarfs what we know."[5]

Having admired this modesty in an economist, however, there is a good amount of experimental evidence from a wide range of contexts that people do have an innate sense of fairness. For example, psychologists have accumulated a body of research about the way our moral judgments are rooted in intuitions, some of which vary widely between cultures or at different times—think about how attitudes to smoking have changed in recent decades—but a handful which seem a constant part of how humans are constituted. Jonathan Haidt has identified five of these universal moral themes: avoidance of doing harm, due respect for authority, striving for cleanliness or purity, loyalty to group or community—and a sense of fairness.[6]

The last two of these have been specifically identified by evolutionary scientists as aspects of *reciprocal altruism*. This theory about the willingness to help others in the valid expectation of being helped by them in turn originated in 1971 with an article by biologist Robert Trivers entitled "The Evolution of Reciprocal Altruism,"[7] and was further elaborated in 1976 by Richard Dawkins in his classic, *The Selfish Gene*.[8] As Steven Pinker explains it, reciprocal altruism is not a calculating, selfish thought process but the outcome of a set of human emotions: "Sympathy prompts a person to offer the first favor, particularly to someone in need for whom it would go the furthest. Anger protects a person against cheaters who accept a favor without reciprocating, by impelling him to punish the ingrate or sever the relationship. Gratitude impels a beneficiary to reward those who helped him in the past. Guilt prompts a cheater in danger of being found out to repair the relationship by redressing the misdeed and advertising that he will behave better in the future."[9] Reciprocal altruism is the evolutionary basis for our sense of fairness. The sense of community, likewise, is a moral emotion of evolutionary origin, rather than a rational choice, although there may be many good objective reasons (or rationalizations) for our having it.

Fairness is consistent with the "selfish" gene: very often acting in a seemingly nonselfish way delivers better outcomes for an individual, because so much of human life is characterized by the scope for mutual benefit (or by non–zero sum games, as a game theorist would express it). A woolly mammoth is more easily brought down by a group than by a lone hunter, while individuals in a modern economy are richer when working cooperatively and engaging in trade.

The role of fairness, or reciprocal altruism, in economics was given a big boost by Robert Axelrod's 1984 book, *The Evolution of Cooperation*. Axelrod translated the concept into the formalities of game theory and showed that in a tournament setting different strategies against each other, those involving being "fair" performed best, and best of all was the self-explanatory "tit for tat." Axelrod showed that the key to this result was the probability that the players would meet each other again—the more frequent the interactions, the greater the likelihood of co-operation emerging as the best *self-interested* strategy.

Further support comes from the study of our close evolutionary relatives. Primatologist Frans de Waal has studied extensively the behavior of capuchin monkeys and other primates. De Waal makes the point that reasoned decisions have a basis in our emotional nature: "People can reason and deliberate as much as they want, but, as neuroscientists have found, if there are no emotions attached to the various options in front of them, they will never reach a decision or conviction."[10] In a large number of studies, he and coauthors have documented the evidence of fairness and cooperation in other primates. De Waal concludes from this work: "A solitary person would have no need for morality, nor would a person who lives with others without moral dependency. Under such circumstances each individual would just go its own way. There would be no pressure to evolve social constraints or moral tendencies."[11]

However, as we are social and do depend on each other, we have evolved to be moral. Moral views vary greatly for different people—in any conflict each party thinks it has right on its side, and in some conflicts the contenders have entirely different worldviews about right and wrong—but there are also a few moral universals. Prominent among these is a sense of fairness. Moral sentiments such as fairness and reciprocity are common to all primates; some add to these fundamental instincts the social pressures that favor a cooperative group life through punishment and reward. Humans apply judgment and reasoning on top of these two levels of morality, in particular the notion that objectivity or impartiality is an important part of morality. All in all, evolutionary science points firmly to the basis of a sense of fairness in the fundamentals of human nature.[12]

ECONOMICS AND FAIR PLAY

The importance of these basic evolutionary instincts has long been recognized in economics, although only recently in these scientific terms. Adam Smith's *Wealth of Nations* built on

Figure 7. Social animals.

his earlier work, *A Theory of Moral Sentiments*. His near-contemporary David Hume had coined the term *moral sentiments* in his 1739 *Treatise on Human Nature*.[13] He argued that people who carried out virtuous acts were often not motivated by specifically moral considerations but rather were acting "naturally" or instinctively. Notoriously, however, economics moved steadily away from this rich concept of self-interest in a social creature being manifested in strong moral instincts, including fairness and altruism, and toward the idea that people's behavior is to be explained by a narrower individual selfishness. Although the former perspective never vanished entirely from the subject, by about 1980 conventional economics did take a reductionist view of human nature—rationally calculating, individualistic, selfish—often not out of any strong conviction but rather as a matter of convenience. The mathematics of modeling the behavior of many individuals and working out the collective result was much easier if people could be assumed to make their decisions independently of each other and according to the rules of logic and algebra.

However, the assumption of narrow individualism in economics has been in retreat for the past twenty years or so (there is much more on this in my book *The Soulful Science* [2008]). Not only in behavioral economics but also in the study of growth, economic institutions, social capital, innovation, and other economic topics, not to mention in the widespread use of game theory as a tool, there is a richer version of how people behave and what motivates them. In fact, the parallels and crossovers between economics and evolutionary science are becoming ever more apparent. The two subjects have always influenced each other in both content and methods of analysis. "Selfishness" is an important assumption in economics, but in the same nonliteral sense it applies in the process of evolution. People make "selfish" choices in the sense that they are acting, often according to rules of thumb or instincts rather than an explicit rational calculation, in ways that tend to serve their self-interest on an evolutionary timescale. Self-interest encompasses altruism, reciprocity, and fairness.

It is fair to say that the reductionist notion that selfishness, that is, individual self-interest alone, is the right way to understand the economy and set policies has taken a huge knock with the financial crisis. However, it is a mistake to think economics always assumes everyone acts as a selfish individual. There was certainly a strong strain of that in the subject reaching a high tide in the 1980s, with right-wing governments in some countries—especially Prime Minister Thatcher's Britain and President Reagan's United States—implementing that extreme version of economics in policies that have continued in some shape up to the present time.

But much of economics is about trying to understand the collective outcome of many individual decisions. Sometimes, this will be the sum of those individual decisions, taken for selfish reasons and without paying attention to others: there are many circumstances in which the caricature free-market economics predicts what happens very well indeed. Often, though, people's decisions will depend on what others decide. All of game theory involves looking at the interaction between individuals, whether they are cooperating with each other or not.

The key assumption is not individual selfishness but rather that people will act in self-interested ways, where self-interest can include considerations of the wider good or straightforward altruism.

GLOBAL INEQUALITY

If people universally have a sense of fairness, how is it that there is such glaring economic inequality? The evidence on this is startling.

One of the most neuralgic issues in the debate about globalization in recent years has been whether or not it has been unfair. The "pro" camp argues that the decades since 1980 have brought about the biggest reduction in inequality the world has ever experienced. The "anti" camp argues that globalization has helped a few prosper but left behind the majority, leading to the greatest degree of inequality in history.

Both hold some truth, depending on how you look at inequality. In particular, there is a distinction between inequality within countries and inequality between countries. Starting with the latter, and looking at average income per capita nation by nation, countries such as the United States and United Kingdom have pulled much further ahead of the poorest countries such as Zimbabwe and Niger. At the same time, there has been a huge rise in average income per capita in China and India such that they have narrowed the gap with the richest countries. This latter development means global inequality has decreased substantially, but inequality within nations has not.[14]

In general developing countries divide into sheep and goats—a group including India and China that have been gaining ground on the rich countries in average per capita incomes and a group concentrated in sub-Saharan Africa where this process (which economists term *convergence*) has not been taking place. With their huge populations, the income advances in the two

Asian giants carry real weight in the global income distribution. But national averages, which look only at inequality *between* countries are not fully adequate measures given that there is great inequality *within* many countries—and especially in the rapidly growing countries of Brazil, Russia, India, and China (called the BRICs), which have made such a big difference in the middle parts of the global income distribution.[15] Branko Milanovic reports that about two-thirds of global inequality currently is due to differences in income levels *between* countries, a big shift from the nineteenth-century pattern, when only 15 percent of measured inequality was due to national differences, and 85 percent due to income inequality *within* countries.[16]

Another way of assessing inequality suggested by this pattern is to look at what has happened to individual incomes across the world.[17] The incomes of the Forbes Rich List have soared massively ahead of those of people living in the poorest African countries whose economies have been shrinking. Equally, given the big increases in income for some people (but not others) in middle-income countries, it makes no sense only to look at the extremes of rich and poor.

Ideally, we'd look at the individual incomes of every person, regardless of their country, and see what happened along the whole spectrum of global income distribution. Milanovic, in his careful study of global income distribution, has pointed out that this is not just a philosophical nicety; it has implications for policy if social justice is to be relevant. He calculated that, given the pattern of income distribution in France and Brazil respectively, there is a 10 percent chance that an aid dollar given by French taxpayers to the Brazilian government is a transfer from a poorer person to a richer one.[18]

The data are not available to make this assessment comprehensively, and we are stuck with some imperfect measures. The calculations are made more difficult because of uncertainty about the measures of prices and exchange rates to use for converting income in different countries into comparable figures. The most recent data, using the best estimates available from the International Price Comparison research program, are for 2005.[19] A thorough survey of the range of evidence and data difficulties concludes that there is insufficient evidence to draw any firm conclusions about the direction of change in global inequality in recent decades.[20] However, using the recent figures, and taking account of both inequality between countries and inequality within countries, Milanovic draws some broad conclusions. Inequality has increased steadily between the early nineteenth century and the early twenty-first century. The increase was fastest in the nineteenth century and the very end of the twentieth century—global income distribution was stable for much of the twentieth century.

He also calculates an "inequality extraction ratio," which compares actual inequality to the maximum it could be if the actual average income level came about through averaging the incomes of a tiny rich elite and the rest of the population living at subsistence level. Within modern developed economies, the ratio has typically declined over time, implying that inequality in these countries has either declined or at least not increased as much as it could have as the economy grew. At the global level, however, there has been little change over time in the "extraction ratio."

What this combined with the shift from "within" to "between" inequality implies, Milanovic suggests, is the success of a rich global elite. Certainly this helps reconcile the contrasting perspectives on inequality set out above. There has been both great improvement in incomes for very many people around the world, combined with vast improvement for a small group of the globally privileged. I return to the implications of this later.

UNEQUAL COUNTRIES

The picture becomes more complex looking at the distribution of income within certain countries in the recent past.

There is a distinction to be drawn between the rich and poor countries. Poor countries have long been more unequal than rich ones, largely because only a few people have high incomes in poor countries, so they contrast sharply with most of their fellow citizens. The extremes of wealth and poverty to be observed in the developing world are almost a cliché and have in some cases become even more pronounced because the rich have been getting richer. In those poorer countries that have grown very rapidly since the 1980s, very many more people have seen their incomes grow. These countries, notably China and India, now have a middle class—but also a large rich elite and a group of people living in still-undeveloped rural areas who remain on very low incomes. Even if the net effect in the various formal measures of inequality is small, the shock of absolute poverty—the absence of sanitation and safe water, hunger, childhood disease, and death—is all the greater in societies where many people are now doing well. Ensuring that their growth miracles benefit the poorest members of society has become a political priority in China and India, even though already these two countries have achieved the greatest reduction in poverty ever recorded thanks to their recent growth records.

In the rich OECD nations, the issues are different. All have less unequal income distributions than nonmembers of the rich club. Having said that, there are some important differences between them, both in terms of the current degree of inequality and their recent trends.

The northern European countries and Japan have the most equal distributions of income, and have seen the least increase in inequality over time. Just four though—Denmark, France, Germany, and Switzerland—have experienced a decline in inequality since 1990.[21]

The United States is at the other extreme. It has the most unequal distribution and has seen the biggest increase in inequality in recent times. The United States, closely shadowed by the United Kingdom and Korea, is so unequal that it bears comparison with developing countries.

Other European countries are in between these two in the extent of the inequality in incomes and in the recent trend.

There are several ways to measure inequality numerically. The most thorough is using a measure such as the Gini coefficient, an index running from zero (fully equal) to one (all the income goes to the top people), which is calculated in a way that takes account of the middle sections of the income distribution. It is therefore a good measure of the kinds of change in income taking place in India and China where, as discussed above, there has been a big increase in incomes in the middle. The Gini coefficient has two drawbacks: the calculations have not been done for all countries and all time periods of interest; and it is not intuitively easy to understand. So I will discuss here a much simpler measure, the ratio of incomes of the top and bottom tenth in the income distribution. In the rich countries, most of the action has been at the two extremes, so this will not misrepresent the trends in inequality.[22]

The OECD nations differ from each other a great deal in the extent of income inequality using this measure. Japan and the Scandinavian countries stand out as the most equal. The best-off tenth of households have earnings from work just two or three times those of the worst off. For most other European countries this ratio is in the range of three to four—Austria, Belgium, and Germany are just below the bottom of this, and the United Kingdom, along with Australia, Spain, and Portugal at the top. The United States, Korea, and Singapore stand out clearly as demonstrating the greatest inequality, with the highest earners making five times more than the lowest earners. Adding income from other sources, notably investment income, makes the pattern all the starker—the unequal countries are far more unequal when all sources of income are taken into account. The inequality of wealth, difficult to measure and to compare between countries, is even more extreme.[23]

It is worth dwelling on what has happened in America, not only because many people wrongly imagine that it is representative of a general, international trend, but also because it highlights some of the important issues I want to discuss in this chapter. There has been a dramatic increase in inequality in the

United States since around 1990, taking the contrast between rich and poor to an extreme not seen since the Jazz Age of the 1920s. The return of the kind of ostentatious wealth described by F. Scott Fitzgerald has been a uniquely American experience, albeit extended by globalization to a small international elite in both legitimate and illegitimate businesses. But it has had a much wider moral and political impact, shaping the debate now under way about fairness.

The comparison of the nineties and noughties with the 1920s is not an exaggeration made just for effect, but literally true. Economists Thomas Piketty and Emanuel Saez have gathered data on the share of total income going to the top 10 percent of earners in the United States back to 1913. They found that starting in the mid-1980s this share climbed from just over 30 percent, where it had been through most of the postwar era, to almost 45 percent by 2002, the same as it had been through the 1920s. The picture is even more dramatic looking at the data for the top 1 percent of the income distribution: we are talking about a phenomenon of the superrich, not the ordinarily rich.[24] It is striking that the increase occurred in two big jumps, coinciding with two Republican Administrations (Reagan and George W. Bush), which made a virtue of their policies to encourage enterprise by the well-off and thereby stimulate growth. As I describe below, other forces have contributed to rising inequality but so exceptional is the pattern in the United States that it is certain that politics and distinctive cultural attitudes to wealth in America will have played a part as well.

Paul Krugman, the prominent liberal voice of the United States throughout the administrations of George W. Bush, has emphasized the relevance of social attitudes and political decisions in shaping the pattern of inequality. At a broad level, the differences between countries with similar average levels of GDP per head and similar economic structures means that actual measured inequality must result from differences in the ways their labor markets and tax and welfare systems operate. These economic institutions clearly embed social and political

Figure 8. America has once before seen today's extreme inequality.

attitudes. And it has been frequently noted and confirmed that the United States does have a different culture of money making and an admiration for financial success. For example, Alberto Alesina and Edward Glaeser set out convincing evidence on different attitudes to inequality in the United States and Europe.[25]

Krugman's point was that the recent increase in inequality went well beyond the traditional spirit of can-do and aspiration in America. He argues that partisan political choices have contributed substantially to the massive enrichment of the rich, including tax reductions on capital gains and legacies.[26] In addition—and I think this is more interesting in terms of the long-term trends—he has argued that social norms, the unspoken agreement in society about what is acceptable, have shifted toward acceptance of excessive reward for the few and a tolerance of the extremes of poverty and wealth. He noted that in his youth, corporate executives were not that different from their workforces, and people expected everyone to lead a similar lifestyle. By the 1990s that expectation had completely changed, and the very rich and their lifestyles had become celebrated. As Krugman put it in a long 2002 magazine article:

> The New Deal had a more profound impact on American society than even its most ardent admirers have suggested: it imposed norms of relative equality in pay that persisted for more than 30 years, creating the broadly middle-class society we came to take for granted. But those norms began to unravel in the 1970's and have done so at an accelerating pace. . . . Much more than economists and free-market advocates like to imagine, wages—particularly at the top—are determined by social norms. What happened during the 1930's and 1940's was that new norms of equality were established, largely through the political process. What happened in the 1980's and 1990's was that those norms unraveled, replaced by an ethos of "anything goes." And a result was an explosion of income at the top of the scale.[27]

At the other end of the political spectrum, former Federal Reserve chairman Alan Greenspan has actually made a similar point, both about the social acceptability of greed and about the institutional failures that permitted it. Commenting in the wake of the collapse of Enron, he said: "An infectious greed seemed to grip much of our business community. Our historical guardians of financial information were overwhelmed. Too many corporate executives sought ways to "harvest" some of those stock market gains." He blamed pay structures such as stock option schemes: "The incentives they created overcame the good judgment of too many corporate managers. It is not that humans have become any more greedy than in generations past. It is that the avenues to express greed had grown so enormously."[28]

That the scandal of excessive corporate pay has played a part in the broad trends in inequality is confirmed by the Piketty and Saez figures. They looked at the composition of the income of the very well off. Whereas through the 1970s, the very rich made most of their income either from their investments or from running businesses, from the 1980s there was a large increase in the share derived from salaries. Although the contribution of business income also increased, supporting the idea that there was an increase in enterprise, by 2002 salaries formed the largest proportion of the incomes of the superrich.

Excessive executive pay has played a part in all the countries that saw increasing inequality. Chief executives of big companies are paid very well in many countries—typically more than 100 times the average pay in their corporation, and 183 times more in the United States. A big gap opens up at the next layer too, with the average senior executive in the United States receiving 112 times more than the average employee in the company, compared with 50–70 times more in the other countries investigated.[29]

The fact that these trends in inequality have been most pronounced in the United States—made worse there by the fact that in real terms the incomes of low earners have actually been declining—does not make them irrelevant to other countries. There have been significant increases in inequality elsewhere, particularly in the other "Anglo-Saxon" economies like Australia and the United Kingdom. The extent of the increase in inequality there has been the same as in the United States, and the timing has been the same too, although the picture is much less extreme.[30] Some other countries—Sweden, for example—have also experienced large rises in income inequality since the 1990s.

In all cases these social and political forces have been interacting with underlying structural changes in the economy, which have created greater inequality of earnings potential in the first place. It is to the structural trends toward inequality that I turn now, because understanding the causes of growing unfairness in some of our societies, as well as why and how some have avoided the extreme outcomes seen in the United States, are important to thinking about how best to respond.

Structural Causes of Inequality

Changes in the earnings of different people start from fundamental changes in the supply of and demand for certain kinds of labor. These underlying structural shifts are further shaped by the economic institutions, social norms, and political decisions of every society. The United States is more unequal, and has experienced a greater increase in inequality, than any other rich economy. But there are only a few countries that have *not* seen income inequality rise in the past two to three decades. The structural causes are therefore common to all the advanced economies, and they stem from the way technology has changed the skills needed at work, and the way it has shifted activity from rich to poorer countries in a globalizing economy.

Not since the late nineteenth century have we experienced the kind of upsurge in the inequality of incomes (before taking account of the impact of government policy via taxes and welfare benefits) seen in recent times. That was, of course, an era of tremendous capitalist and technological advance, and also tremendous moral and political outcry about the impact on the less well off. From novelists such as Charles Dickens, Mrs. Gaskell, or Victor Hugo to political thinkers such as Karl Marx or campaigners like Charles Booth or Jane Addams, there was a passionate response to the unfairness of an economic system that benefited only the few at the top of the social scale.

Now, as then, there are two main possible explanations for the development of greater inequality compared with the previous economic epoch. One is globalization, in effect bringing a large new source of cheap labor into the domestic economy; either through cheap imports or the offshoring of production, domestic workers have to compete with workers elsewhere who work for much lower wages (although they are also less productive). This could explain downward pressure on blue-collar wages or the low pay in basic services such as call centers.

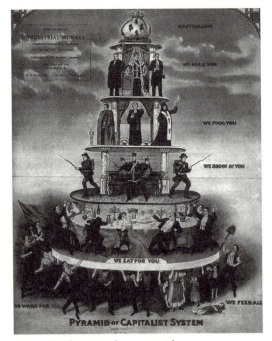

Figure 9. The capitalist pyramid.

The other potential explanation is the adoption of new technologies requiring skills that were initially in short supply. Companies that use computers and other new technologies need people with greater cognitive abilities—computers can do the easy, repetitive work, so the humans need to do the more challenging and creative work. This is great news in the sense that a lot of dull jobs have gone and work for many has become more interesting, but it has substantially reduced the demand for workers with only basic qualifications, and swaths of formerly well-paid shop floor jobs have vanished.

It is difficult to distinguish these two potential causes from each other empirically. Globalization increases the supply of unskilled labor relative to skilled labor by importing it embedded in goods produced in cheaper countries, or by enabling offshoring, or by the immigration of people who will compete for jobs. New technologies increase the demand for certain kinds of skilled labor relative to unskilled labor, for example (as discussed in the next chapter), increasing the need for college-education professionals to work in finance and diminishing the demand for bank tellers. In either case, the earnings of the skilled will increase relative to those of the unskilled. What's more, the two phenomena—technical change and globalization—are closely related, as the extent of the growth in trade and cross-border investment we've experienced would not have been possible without the adoption of ICTs throughout the developed economies.

There has been a good deal of empirical research to try to distinguish the two effects, however. Alan Blinder showed that offshorable jobs in the United States had suffered an estimated 13 percent wage penalty as of 2004.[31] Another study found a 1 percentage point increase in the low-wage import share is associated with a 2.8 percent decline in blue-collar wages.[32] On balance, however, the technical change explanation emerges as the most important driver of increasing income inequality.[33] This is not the popular perception. When a factory or call center closes in the United States and reopens in China or India, or when cheap clothing imports put domestic manufacturers out of business because they can't compete, or when immigrant workers seem to bid down wages for low-skill jobs in the neighborhood, it seems pretty obvious that globalization is the culprit for the fact that low-income families have been faring poorly in recent decades. There is indeed evidence that globalization has played a part in the inequality trends described here. But even though no one is smashing computer terminals the way the Luddites in nineteenth-century England smashed the newfangled textile machinery that was destroying cottage industry, the evidence suggests that a larger part has been played by technological change.

It is not just that the earnings potential of people with degrees going into the professions has increased as new technologies spread in these sectors of the economy. The evidence also lies in the way the very highest levels of earnings have soared by comparison with those of everyone else. This is described in economics as the "superstar" effect, and it has appeared in many types of occupation.[34] Consider a fairly rare talent such as being a world-class opera singer. Opera-goers want to be sure that when they pay for their ticket they are getting the best singers. The clearest signal of the best singer is the one that most people want to go and see. So these performers will be much more popular than the next rank than any objective difference in their talents might justify. Demand to see the top rank feeds on itself. Modern technologies also amplify the potential reach of talented people—the best performers are in demand not only for live performance but for CDs and downloads too.

Both technology and globalization increase hugely the potential demand for talent. These "winner take all" markets have spread superstar pay to many other sectors of the economy, outside sport and the performing arts where they were originally observed.[35] Moreover, this trend means that the increase in inequality due to skills and technology has what is known as a "fractal" character, which means that it is occurring within categories as well as in the overall income distribution: top lawyers' pay has risen relative to those on low incomes; but the top top lawyers have pulled further ahead of the average top lawyer too.[36]

So to sum up, structural changes in the economy driven by new technologies are the fundamental driver of greater inequality, in much the same way that the wave of innovation of early capitalism in the nineteenth century led to great inequality until the workforce as a whole developed the new skills that were needed. Technology has interacted with globalization to exacerbate the trend toward greater inequality, contributing to income inequality within countries through the move of low and medium skill jobs overseas, and creating a rich global elite. The failure of some of the poorest countries to participate at all in these economic trends has made greater inequality a global phenomenon. These structural changes have been universal.[37]

The extent of the increase in inequality varies between countries depending on the scope of structural economic change they have experienced. In some countries there have also been specific changes in social norms and political conditions that have amplified the increase in inequality, as discussed above. The United States stands out in this respect, but the phenomenon of excessive corporate pay has become widespread. In a world of globalized media and international markets for executive jobs, the creeping social acceptability of huge pay packets for some executives and professions has crossed borders.

Does it matter?

CONSEQUENCES OF INEQUALITY FOR GROWTH

There is some controversy about whether income inequality inhibits economic performance. Poor countries are more unequal than rich ones but it is not clear whether the inequality is a cause or a consequence of their failure to grow. Among the rich countries, there is no obvious relationship between level of income inequality and growth rates.

The United States, the most unequal, has experienced the fastest productivity growth in recent decades. There are some reasons to think that in theory greater inequality will *boost* growth—first because rich people save more than poor people, and thus build a pool of savings that can finance investment and growth; second because inequality is often addressed with progressive income taxes, which have an adverse effect on work effort and so might reduce growth.

Equally, there are theoretical reasons for thinking inequality will *reduce* growth, in particular through reducing the ability and incentive of poor people to invest in education and skills for themselves and their children. Another possible channel is that inequality causes social and political instability, which in turn harms economic prospects. Several studies seem to support this empirically. Well-known research by Alberto Alesina and

Dani Rodrik, and by Torsten Persson and Guido Tabellini, argued that distributional conflict was associated with higher tax rates and lower growth.[38]

Given these conflicting theories, and the inconclusive empirical research,[39] the evidence is on balance suggestive of inequality harming growth in the long term, but it is hard to stake a lot on these results. Equally, the negative result implied by this is clear: there is no firm evidence that inequality is tolerable or even necessary because it improves the economy's performance. So if inequality might not harm but probably doesn't help the economy, the obvious question is what we should think about it in itself, rather than as an influence on economic growth. Does it affect social welfare? Does it affect society and the economy in long-term ways that would not harm short-term growth?

One direct consequence of inequality identified by some economists is that it directly drove poorer households to borrow more. Part of the debt burden, including the subprime mortgage borrowing that helped catalyze the financial crisis, is due to people whose incomes hadn't risen much trying to keep their living standards tracking those of their neighbors. During the boom years, nobody could have avoided ads and magazine articles displaying enticing consumer goodies. Luckily, the ads for personal loans and credit cards were equally apparent. According to Raghuram Rajan: "Easy credit has been used as a palliative throughout history by governments that are unable to address the deeper anxieties of the middle class directly."[40] This does not imply a conscious plan on the part of governments to burden the poor with unsustainable debt, but simply taking the line of least resistance by allowing financial services providers to market such products ensured that was the result. What's more, it helped the boom continue and was even rationalized by some commentators as contributing to greater *equality* by allowing low earners to acquire assets—always assuming they could continue to meet the repayments. As if that's not bad enough, inequality has other longer-term consequences too.

Consequences of Inequality for Well-being

In the absence of any evidence on the impact on growth per se, what about evidence of the impact of inequality on more direct measures of well-being?

Some researchers are passionate advocates of a causal link between increased inequality and worse outcomes in a wide range of social indicators, from health and life expectancy to teenage pregnancy and crime. In their recent book *The Spirit Level*, Richard Wilkinson and Kate Pickett make exactly this argument and what's more suggest that in an unequal society even the people at the top of the pile in terms of income have a reduced level of welfare compared to their counterparts in more equal places.

Much of their evidence consists of presenting simple correlations between measures of inequality in different countries and measures of some social bad such a depression rates or prevalence of heart disease. In a few cases they also present time trends in inequality and compare it with time trends in another variable, such as crime rates. They write:

> It is a remarkable paradox that, at the pinnacle of human material and technical achievement, we find ourselves anxiety ridden, prone to depression, worried about how others see us, unsure of our friendships, driven to consume and with little or no community life. Lacking the relaxed social contact and emotional satisfaction we all need, we seek comfort in over-eating, obsessive shopping and spending, or become prey to excessive alcohol, psychoactive medicines and illegal drugs. . . . The truth is that both the broken society and the broken economy resulted from the growth of inequality.[41]

This picture of a broken society echoes many other authors writing about either the consumer debt–fueled boom or its fallout in the financial and economic crisis.[42] It echoes a common theme of many critiques of capitalism.

Sometimes, after reading one of these popular jeremiads against consumerism, I do wonder whether these authors actually know any normal people who like to garden, play soccer at the weekend, join book clubs, or watch TV or movies. The statistics are pretty clear that a rising share of consumer spending, and a rising share of our leisure time, goes to activities like these rather than on material goods. The price of many goods has been declining even as their quality and capabilities have increased. This is one aspect of the "weightlessness" of the economy, that we are spending more on services of various kinds.[43] It is a small minority, albeit much burdened by credit card debts, spending too much on designer goods. Most people are not anxiety-ridden shopaholics, or drug addicts.

Wilkinson and Pickett's book is not in the same category, being a more scholarly study. But it overclaims on the basis of the evidence presented. Some of the correlations they describe show great variation in the relationship with inequality, or patterns strongly suggesting that other factors apart from inequality are playing a causal role. Social and cultural norms are the likely explanation. The causal mechanism is unclear as well, particularly for their claim that even the best-off in unequal societies suffer from the inequality. If the low status that comes with poverty in an unequal society explains why people on low incomes are more likely to be obese, say, why are people on high incomes in that society more obese than high-income people in a more equal society? What is it about American inequality that makes rich Americans fatter, on average, than rich Danes? Other social factors must surely be involved (as economists have indeed shown).[44]

Having said that, in some of the areas these and other authors explore, the extremes of status resulting from income inequality clearly do have an adverse impact on many people. The evidence is strong that stress-related illnesses such as heart disease and depression are more prevalent in situations where people on low incomes have a correspondingly low status and lack of control over their lives. Wilkinson and Pickett present this evidence in chapters 6 and 7 of their book, including a description of the classic "Whitehall Studies," long-term studies of the health of male civil servants in the United Kingdom. Although all the people in these studies were in white-collar jobs, those in the lower ranks were found to have significantly worse health outcomes, overturning the earlier presumption that it was top businessmen who were most likely to suffer heart attacks because of the stress and responsibility of their positions. On the contrary, it is the lowliest who suffer the most damaging stress, and it is lack of control rather than excess of responsibility that causes it. Perhaps the most damning piece of evidence in this vein is research from 1990 showing that black men in Harlem were less likely than men in Bangladesh to reach the age of sixty-five.[45]

So there's little evidence to support the view that inequality harms the rich elite, but it certainly harms the less privileged. As the economist John Kay put it, inequality means that

> rich Americans may suffer more stress and greater risk of crime and be surrounded by a crumbling public infrastructure. But affluent people in the US believe that their higher material standard of living and the greater opportunities available to their children make them better off and it is very difficult to present a convincing argument that they are wrong. So we shall just have to continue believing that bankers' bonuses and preposterous remuneration packages for chief executives are bad for society, not that they are bad for the bankers and chief executives.[46]

THE SOCIAL CORROSIVENESS OF INEQUALITY

The second area in which there is evidence for the damage caused by great inequality is trust. As I will point out in chapter 5, "trust," an abstract concept like social capital, is hard to define and measure. The figures used derive from the World Values Survey, or similar national surveys, which ask respondents whether they agree that "most people can be trusted." Wilson and Pickett present cross-country correlations (and also for U.S.

states) showing a negative correlation between levels of trust and the degree of inequality, although with quite wide variation around the line of best fit between these two variables.

The reported level of trust in the United States and elsewhere has declined substantially over time.[47] Much of the attention on this point has focused on the United States, where Robert Putnam struck a chord with the publication of his book *Bowling Alone*. It presented evidence such as declining participation in social organizations, bowling leagues among these, and other markers of shared activities. But with the exception of Scandinavia and Japan, there appears to be a common pattern of a decline in trust in developed countries during the 1980s and 1990s, as well as reductions in political participation and organizational activity. The earlier part of the twentieth century saw social capital rise steadily in the United States, peaking around 1960. The data show that other developed nations lag behind the U.S. trend by approximately two decades.[48]

The General Social Survey in the United States has tracked changes in trust (among its standard core of demographic and attitudinal questions) over several decades. In answer to the question "can people be trusted?" in 1972, 46.3 percent answered positively; by 2006 only 39 percent did so. In Pew surveys trust was found to be lowest among the youngest Americans, increasing up to middle age, then leveling off.[49] Generations born up to the 1940s exhibited high levels of trust, but each generation born after that was less trusting than the one before.[50] Trends in Australia are similar to the United States, with a general decline in most forms of social capital and particularly in rates of interpersonal trust from the 1980s to the 1990s.[51]

The same is true of many other industrial countries. In the United Kingdom, Peter Hall found that there was no equivalent erosion of social participation in Britain, but there was a decline in social trust. In 1959, 56 percent of adults agreed that most people could be trusted, but by 1981 this had fallen to 44 percent. British Social Attitudes data indicates that this was followed by a two-decade period of stability.[52] There are a few exceptions, however. Across nations, Swedes rank highest on measures of trust and organizational activity. Sweden differs from many other industrial democracies in that it does not appear to have suffered the same sort of collapse in civic engagement; involvement in sporting clubs and charities, as well as rates of informal socializing, were higher in the 1990s than in the 1980s.[53] Civic engagement in Japan has been essentially stable since World War II, and the past two decades have seen a slight rise in social trust and trust in political institutions.[54]

I return to the question of trust in the next chapter. There are good reasons to believe that a negative vicious spiral of declining trust and increasing inequality has operated over the years. In *Bowling Alone*, Putman argued that people's engagement with their community, the level of social capital, has diminished as American society has become decreasingly egalitarian. "What is at stake is not merely warm, cuddly feelings or frissons of community pride. We shall review hard evidence that our schools and neighbourhoods don't work so well when community bonds slacken, that our economy, our democracy and even our health and happiness depend on adequate stocks of social capital," he wrote.[55] The two probably feed off each other: we are more likely to engage in community organizations with people we feel comfortable with because they are pretty much like us, including in their social and economic status as well as their interests or beliefs; and the less contact we have with a wide range of other people in our communities, the more likely it is that the business or job opportunities open to us will be quite narrow in their range. Job offers and deals typically come through informal contacts, so your social circle makes a big difference to your individual prospects.[56] Some evidence of decreased social mobility in the United States and United Kingdom ties in with this.[57]

The increasing distance between the incomes of the rich and poor has unquestionably contributed to reduced trust and social capital in the countries where inequality has become extreme. The very well off lead lives so separate that in some cases they literally lock themselves in behind high walls and security gates. They certainly avoid sending their children to the same schools as those serving less-well-off families. Social contact between rich and poor has become minimal. The inequality has an increasingly rigid geographical pattern as well. Cities have intangible barriers between the areas where the rich and poor live and move. In whole regions of the country incomes stay low, health remains poor, and education levels below average for generations.[58]

Although the pattern characterizes most of the developed world, the United States displays the extreme. It is worth emphasizing for American readers that although many European cities have poor neighbourhoods that could certainly be described as ghettos, nowhere in the rest of the developed world is there the kind of poverty and deprivation we glimpse when we travel to the United States. The shocking realization in my case came on a Metroliner train ride from Washington, DC, to New York, seeing communities next to the tracks that rivaled the visible poverty I had previously only seen in developing countries. Even to someone coming from the relatively unequal United Kingdom, the chasms in American society are shocking.

One consequence of this growing social chasm is that there is also a divergence in the kind of behavior that is socially acceptable as well. This too marks a return to the early twentieth century. It used to be a staple of British comedy to make fun of the fact that poor people used different words for meals or items of furniture, or ate at different times—that they had different norms of behavior. Class distinctions in behavior have returned—many well-off people on both sides of the Atlantic make fun of the dress and speech of poor people. There has been a return to a social division between the language based on received grammar and pronunciation of polite society and street language for everyday.

The last chapter described the evidence that people have an innate fairness instinct and take decisions on the basis of "moral sentiments." The next chapter makes the case that social capital, or trust, plays a vital role in the long-term sustainability of any society. Too great a degree of inequality not only adversely affects the well-being of society's losers, it also corrodes the social scaffolding on which a prosperous economy must be built. This is a long-term result, not an overnight disaster. It is a question of sustainability exactly because it brings into question our ability to bequeath a healthy society to later generations.

This point is made clearly, I think, in microcosm in many businesses. It is clearest in banking, with astounding bonuses paid to individuals for short-term results measured without any attribution made for the efforts of colleagues. Any business's profitability depends on the efforts of many people, even though some individuals will be better or work harder than others. Indeed, there's recent evidence from the financial world that the supposed stars are paid more than their due: it finds that when top-rated analysts move to a new job, their performance deteriorates sharply. Their performance, it turns out, depends on their firm and not their unique individual talents. People who work for better *teams* deliver a better performance. Author Boris Groysberg concludes: "Outstanding performance owes a good deal to the quality and culture of the firm."[59] Of course the most talented or those with the most onerous responsibilities need to be paid more than most of their colleagues. But to pay them tens or even hundreds of times more is to destroy any sense of responsibility for results among those at the bottom of the pile. Let the people with multimillion salaries worry about how things turn out, the underlings will think.

The habit of excessive salaries and bonuses has been a contagion. It spread from investment banks throughout the corporate sector in the United States and (in paler imitation, the United Kingdom, Australia, even formerly egalitarian Sweden). It spread to the public sector too, partly as a genuine response forced by competition for able people in the job market but partly just because of the example set by banks and other companies that were being feted by politicians and the media. It has been corrosive. Bankers have even started to act as though, despite their enormous bailouts from taxpayers, they can get straight back to the high salary and high bonus culture. They seem to have an extraordinary psychological blind spot about the moral outrage their excessive incomes have caused. But their Gilded Age is over. Whether it will be a calm or a turbulent end is yet to be seen.

FIVE Trust

ON WEDNESDAY 10 SEPTEMBER 2008, Lehman Brothers was worth about $5 billion on the New York Stock Exchange. Its shares had lost three quarters of their value during the year, so that valuation was already much lower than the $60 billion it had been worth in early 2007. By the end of the week, it was worth just $100 million or so to its shareholders and owed more than $600 billion. A weekend rescue attempt by the authorities failed, and the bank, founded in 1850, went bust.

Its demise sent shares in other banks tumbling as well. More bankruptcies were feared. The big American investment banks were all (except for Goldman Sachs) taken over by commercial banks or changed their status to ensure the Federal Reserve would save them from failing. The banking crisis wiped out investment banking, and in the few weeks that followed caused declines in share prices that amounted to about $10 trillion globally.

It isn't only banks that are vulnerable to sudden corporate death, destroying value almost literally overnight. There were other startling examples before the financial crisis. Enron was worth $70 billion at the peak of its share price ($90/share), in August 2000. Just over a year later it was bankrupt and worthless. Enron's auditor had been Arthur Anderson. Its value in turn was destroyed by the scandal; the huge accountancy firm, founded in 1913, vanished. WorldCom was another giant company whose value evaporated in scandal. At the peak of its might in 1999, it had a market valuation of $150 billion and reported annual revenues of $39 billion. By 2002 it was almost worthless and the assets it held were sold to other companies.

These are the biggest corporate and financial collapses of recent times but there have been others. They have included long-established and respected names and have occurred in Europe and elsewhere—Parmalat in Italy, Northern Rock and Royal Bank of Scotland in the United Kingdom, Satyam in India. Enron was a relatively new creation but many other companies that vanished in recent times were formed in the nineteenth century or even earlier.

These recent examples were destroyed by the dynamite of innovative financial transactions, which were powerfully destructive, especially when used with criminal intent to defraud. In other recent bankruptcies, deliberate fraud may have been absent but the destructive effect of complex derivatives was similar. Their CEOs and boards had not understood that for all the complexity of the off-balance sheet and offshore vehicles and securitized assets and sophisticated derivatives, finance is really very simple. It transfers the benefit of economic activity from one person at one time to somebody else at a different time and in a different place. If the chain of transactions is not built on solid foundations of trust, it will disintegrate. The failed companies had no idea whose fortunes were now linked with theirs.

This is why large and seemingly substantial corporations and banks could implode. Banks in particular have no value where there is no trust. This is why, historically, banks have always made such a show of their impressive buildings and marble and wood panelling. The grandeur is meant to signal to depositors that they are not fly-by-nights who will run away with their money rather than lending it out cautiously and repaying it with interest on demand. It's also why the 2007–8 financial crisis puts the issues of trust so fully at center stage.

Usually, banks are trustworthy. In most countries banking is heavily regulated and closely supervised. Even in places where it helps to be the president's nephew to run a bank, for the most part banks will repay depositors' trust—otherwise, there will not be any deposits. Sometimes, of course, people are cheated. One example is an elaborate fraud in Uganda involving the creation of a sham bank with an office and printed stationery, which ran an advertising campaign to attract $100,000 in deposits. The crooks then vanished.[1] But this kind of scam is surprisingly rare.

For the most part, finance is a high trust business. In its early stages in late mediaeval and early modern times, the trust was personal, between members of the same social or religious group who knew each other personally. The Fuggers and the Rothschilds built banking empires on the foundations of family bonds. Informal finance such as the current hawala system also relies on close-knit groups, many of whom will know each other personally or have strong social and religious ties. The City of London and Wall Street used to be like this too, a close-knit "club," which unfairly excluded all but a narrow social echelon and aided insider trading; but on the other hand, personal knowledge and the weapon of social sanctions against miscreants acted to keep them more or less trustworthy places to invest money. This is still symbolized on UK banknotes by the printed statement: "I promise to pay the bearer on demand the sum of ten pounds." It was only in times of boom and bust that the conventional network of trust broke down.

Trust is fundamental to any successful economy, at any stage in its development. The simplest transaction can be thought of as a process as fraught as the handover of Russian and American spies at Checkpoint Charlie in Berlin at the height of the Cold War. There was so little trust between the superpowers that when secret agents were exchanged, their walk between the two entrances to the checkpoint had to be precisely timed so they would pass in the middle and there could be no danger of one side reneging on the deal. This was human barter. Other than the simplest face-to-face barter deal in the economy, when items can be simultaneously exchanged, every economic transaction requires one party to trust the other. And as so few transactions involve simultaneous exchange, that trust is embodied in money or financial instruments, which count and store the value, and allow it to be exchanged.

Figure 10. Without trust, all economic transactions are like Checkpoint Charlie.

It is extraordinary, when you stop to think about it, how extensive and also how delicate the web of trust represented by money has become in the modern global economy. All but a few countries are engaged in international trade and vast amounts of financial transactions cross national borders. Much of it now takes the form of electronic records on computer systems, not even paper money or bonds or shares, which are themselves abstractions. The economy is a pattern of zeroes and ones.

Paul Seabright describes this web in the introduction to his wonderful book *The Company of Strangers*:

Most human beings now obtain a large share of the provision for their daily lives from others to whom they are not related by blood or marriage. Even in poor rural societies people depend significantly on non-relatives for food, clothing, medicine, protection and shelter. In cities, most of these non-relatives crucial to our survival are complete strangers. Nature knows no other examples of such complex mutual dependence among strangers.[2]

As he points out, it is almost miraculous that the global economy works as well as it does, so that billions of people can rely without anxiety on the efforts and the honor of complete strangers scattered over the world. Few of us feel the need to grow our own food supplies or dig wells in the garden or keep sheep and spin the wool to make our own clothes. The process of the division of labor and increasing specialization of tasks that first got into gear in the Industrial Revolution—capitalism, in essence—has continued until it now includes almost the whole world. The late-twentieth- and early twenty-first-century era of globalization means that I am fed and clothed by Kenyan farmers or Cambodian factory workers, who are paid through a financial system that stretches from my bank account to their wages in Kenyan shillings or Cambodian riels. In the symbolic global shirt—a simple product—bought in the United States, the design may be Italian, the fabric could be woven in Bangladesh, the buttons made in India, the cutting and sewing done in Mauritius, the finishing and logistics in China.[3]

Finance is a special case, in being dependent *only* on trust. One thing the financial crisis has made plain is that the activities of financial markets had come to obscure the relationships between people implied by financial contracts. As Amartya Sen put it: "The moral and legal responsibilities associated with transactions have in recent years become much harder to trace, thanks to the rapid development of secondary markets involving derivatives and other financial instruments."[4] This loss of traceability and trust is a serious matter. Apart from their buildings and computers, banks have no physical assets. Their stock market value is entirely an indicator of their *intangible* assets—which are, more or less, a measure of the extent to which they are trusted. Until the later part of the twentieth century, other companies had a market valuation that mostly reflected the value of physical assets, such as factories and machines, but a growing share of the value of all companies in recent decades has consisted of intangible items, including the important asset described as "goodwill." This is a sign of the transition of the leading Western economies away from the processing of materials, basic manufacturing, to higher value intangible, or "weightless," activities.[5] A growing proportion of every dollar spent by consumers is paying for clever ideas, design, or service quality or brand cachet, something intangible, rather than the materials from which products are made. Goodwill is real, even if it is intangible. A successful brand such as Coca Cola or Louis Vuitton is valuable because of what customers believe about the products. But the companies that have tumbled have shown that much intangible value can evaporate overnight. Literally so—from billions of dollars to next to nothing due to one announcement. Weightless value is fragile. Modern economies, in becoming increasingly weightless, are more than ever dependent on trust.

The structural shift in leading economies toward intangible activities, and the related globalization of the economy whereby manufacturing has been parceled out around the world in increasingly specialized niches, has made trust more fundamental than ever. That trust is embodied and expressed in global finance. This is why the fraud, greed, and incompetence revealed in the banking system by the financial crisis has struck such a serious blow to the economy. If we seem to have come through it with a relatively minor recession—certainly compared with the Great Depression—that is because governments have laid their credibility on the line to substitute for the collapse of trust in the banking system. The massive expansion of government debt described earlier means that governments at present and for years into the future will be standing as guarantors for the financing of economic transactions, as described above.

This chapter explores some key issues arising from this fundamental importance of trust.

First I set out further the links between trust and economic success, drawing on the economic literature on "social capital." The instinct for fairness and reciprocity in human nature mentioned in the last chapter takes its shape in social arrangements, the unwritten rules of culture and social norms, and the formal institutions through which we embody mutual trust and organize our living together in large and complicated societies. I will argue that social capital is, like natural wealth, one of the forms of capital needing to be constantly replenished for future generations.

The technological and social changes that have given us a globalized and weightless economy are placing immense new pressures on social ties, and I describe what some of these pressures are. The structural changes in the economy resulting from new technologies have increased the importance of trust. A high value economy is a high trust one. At the same time, though, the structural changes taking place in the global economy make building trust difficult and indeed create some social fragility. The simultaneous strengths and social tensions are apparent for example in the megacities that are hubs of the global economy.

Trust is built by and expressed in the institutions that govern the economy and society. As I go on to describe, many of the institutions we have at present, in all their variety right up to the international organizations responsible for the global economy, are not up to bearing the new pressures. This book isn't the place for a thorough exploration of the role and inadequacies of economic governance, a huge subject. Here I simply want to make the link between an emerging shortfall in trust and weaknesses of governance. In the case of trust in our societies, we are currently in an unsustainable situation—just as with our exploitation of natural capital and the unfairness of the distribution of income today and the demands we're making on living standards in future.

This will lead us into the second half of this book, looking at policies that might start to address the challenges set out in the first half.

Why Trust Matters for the Economy

Although it is intuitively obvious, I think, that trust underpins economic growth, it is not so obvious why, or how much it matters compared to anything else, such as education or ideas or roads and bridges. Measuring the importance of trust would require a clear definition, too, and like any abstract concept it proves quite hard to define with enough precision for empirical research. So social scientists have tried to analyze trust using the concept of social capital. This term is usually used as a straightforward substitute. As name suggests, by analogy with physical capital or financial capital, social capital is a stock of wealth. It is something that can be accumulated over time, invested in, but a form of wealth linked to society rather than just an individual.

An important book in stimulating the recent interest in the idea of social capital was a classic study of towns in Italy by Robert Putnam, the eminent Harvard sociologist. He noted from his field research that something intangible but vitally important distinguished towns in the north of the country from the south, making the former prosperous and dynamic places, and the latter persistently poor and suspicious.[6] The "something" in those northern Italian towns comprised civic mindedness, an openness and willingness to help people outside the immediate family group, a sense of being part of a community whose success would bring collective and individual benefits. This "something" Putnam labeled social capital. His definition is: "Features of social life—networks, norms and trust—that enable participants to act together more effectively to pursue shared objectives."[7]

A more recent definition is that social capital consists of the set of relationships between the individual members of a society. Some of the connections between us are impersonal and take place through a monetary transaction; others are "nonmarket" relationships, that is nonfinancial and personal ties of various degrees of importance and strength. The stronger these nonmarket mutual relationships are between different people in a particular society, the greater the social capital.[8]

Social capital defined in this way brings benefits to the people who make up the society in question, but not necessarily to those outside it. So depending on the context, it can be good or bad for the economy as a whole. In the Italy of the 1970s, when Putnam looked at the effects, people in the northern towns identified with the whole of the civic community. In the south, social capital was confined within extended families or other small groups, so the town as a whole suffered from the fact that mutual assistance was confined within small subsets of its population at the expense of the rest. In other contexts, urban gangs or terror cells have strong social capital internal to their membership, which translates into weak social capital for the wider social entities in which they live, whether their estate or their nation.

Strong social capital will improve the way economic markets operate. One example is the way specialized industrial clusters develop in a particular place, where access to market and the availability of employees to hire are part of the explanation, but so are social factors such as the way people in different firms might exchange know-how about their areas of expertise, or move from one job to another via word of mouth. Sometimes, social capital can stop markets from working properly, however. For example, people might decide they will only do business deals with members of their golf club, or their ethnic group, even if that isn't objectively the best deal.

But although social capital doesn't always take a "good" form in terms of its benefits for the wider economy, it seems clear that without trust, without enough of the "good" social capital, the economy will not perform well. Where there is too much distrust, many market transactions cannot take place. Does the evidence back up this intuition?

One hurdle to finding empirical evidence is that there are no obvious data measuring the abstract concept of social capital—after all, there isn't even a single agreed definition. Economists have taken a practical approach. The empirical research has focused on whether an available measure of social capital is positively associated with economic growth—either at the level of the national economy or in other situations. For example, are companies with greater internal "social capital" more profitable than those with lower levels? Social capital in these studies is often measured using the responses to survey questions—for example, one standard question is: "Generally speaking, would you say that most people can be trusted, or that you can't be too careful in dealing with people?"

There are many empirical studies exploring the economic impact of social capital, triggered by Putnam's 1993 book. One early study concluded firmly: "Trust and civic cooperation are associated with stronger economic performance."[9] The vast body of later work, looking at different countries, regions, organizations and businesses, and at historical as well as contemporary evidence, has confirmed this.[10] There is also evidence that high social capital contributes to a more effective and honest political system, as people in such places are less cynical and more willing to take action to punish political miscreants.[11]

In short, the consistent finding, for all the vagueness of the definition and difficulty of constructing a definitive empirical measure of an abstract concept, is that higher social capital, or greater trust, is linked to higher growth. Causality is much harder to pin down—perhaps a more successful economy makes it easier for people to have less concern for themselves or their immediate family and more for the wider community? Untangling causality is difficult given the imprecision of the definition and data for trust or social capital, and given all the other potential contributors to economic success that must be controlled for in the statistical work. For example, there is no clear evidence about whether trust, institutions, unspoken social norms or aspects of culture are more important for the economy—and indeed they must all be related to each other, and all will be affected themselves by the nature of the economy. But even if it proves impossible to untangle the arrows of causality, the evidence of a strong link between social capital and growth has important implications.

The Growing Importance of Trust

The idea of a form of "capital" that requires investment if it is to grow, and which is at the same time a form of wealth owned by society as a whole, achieves two things. It focuses attention on a long-term horizon, and it also links individual fortunes to those of the wider group. To many people this will feel like an intuitively appealing goal, not least as a useful corrective to the individualism guiding economic policymaking for the past two or three decades. Why, after all, has trust, or social capital, or institutions—whichever term is preferred—come to be so prominent in economics and other social sciences during the past decade or two?

Many readers might think it's a matter of economics returning to the real world after a long diversion into an overly abstract and unrealistic realm. After all, it is surely only common sense that institutions and society affect how the economy performs. However, as I've argued elsewhere, economics has been caricatured and was never as unrealistic as critics claimed.[12] The growing interest in the concept of social capital derives from a new salience of the role of social institutions and trust in trying to understand economic performance. The step change in the complexity of the economy resulting from new technologies has made economic performance significantly more dependent on the presence of social capital. Economies have always depended on trust, but a successful modern economy in which the division of labor has become very highly specialized and every individual depends on a large and complex network of other people in many countries is profoundly more dependent on high levels of trust.

New information technologies, from printing to the railways, the telegraph to the Internet, have (like new energy-related technologies and other examples of what the literature terms "general purpose" technologies) always resulted in profound social and economic changes. This comes about in many ways. The results are unpredictable and can take decades to achieve in full, but they are ultimately transformational. This was true of steam power, railways, and electrification. It is just as true now. The impact of satellite television in developing countries from the mid-1990s on the aspirations of hundreds of millions of viewers in village cafes differs in nature and form from the impact of massive computer power on the Western biotech industry. However, in both cases massively cheaper information processing and communication are changing the scope and nature of the ways people interact with others.

The reduction in the cost of processing and exchanging information has been utterly extraordinary. It has been driven by Moore's Law—the doubling in computer power roughly every eighteen months.[13] The decline in the cost of the technology has been the fastest and biggest in history. William Nordhaus has estimated that computing power has grown at a compound annual rate of more than 30 percent for a century, amounting to a real term decline in cost or increase in power of the order of one to five trillion times.[14] The economic and social revolution currently under way due to the microprocessor and its successor technologies will prove to have an extraordinary impact on humanity.

Despite this, for a time in the late 1990s many economists were somewhat skeptical about the likely impact of ICTs. It took some years for any economic effects to show up in aggregate productivity figures. It was not widely appreciated that investment in technology has to be accompanied by much greater investment in organizational change—new ways of running the business, new working patterns, new types of relationship with suppliers. Economic historians offered the first insights into the need for accompanying investments. For example, Paul David drew an analogy with electrification, which required new types of factory building and investment in electric networks, before the economic impact was large and widespread.[15] Nicholas Crafts pointed out that although the estimates of the impact of modern ICTs on economic growth might appear small, they were much larger than the historical figures for the impact of steam, and few people would argue that had not been a pro-

foundly important technology.[16] However, steam, like electricity
or the railways, had taken decades to have its full impact. Businesses didn't invest in steam power until the older technologies
ceased to be profitable, and often it was new businesses that
adopted new technologies.

Like any new "general purpose technology," or in other words
a technology with a wide range of applications, ICTs are reshaping the economy. Elsewhere, I've described this phenomenon
as "weightlessness."[17] This is because advanced economies are
shifting significantly toward the creation of value that is intangible, either in the form of services, or in the form of the innovations, design, creativity, or customization embedded in physical
goods. The UK and U.S. economies literally did not increase in
physical mass in the 1990s and 2000s, although GDP in each
case grew significantly during those twenty years.[18] However,
the structural shift in the advanced economies is taking place
over decades, as businesses and households and governments
slowly adapt. Part of that process of adjustment involves the
development of ever-increasing levels of trust inside these different economic institutions and between individuals. As I'll go on
to explain, trust is more necessary than ever in an increasingly
weightless economy.

Why are the new technologies making more central than ever
the role of trust or social capital in the economy? To understand the reasons, let's look at three different types of economic
change being driven by ICTs. They are the reorganization of
businesses, the process of globalization, and the changing importance of key cities in the global economy.

TECHNOLOGY AND PRODUCTIVITY IN THE FIRM

Let's start with the impact of ICTs inside an individual business. Firms only enjoy the productivity benefits of investments
in the technologies once they have reorganized and changed the
way employees work. Recent research at the level of individual
firms suggests that investment in ICTs needs to be accompanied

by significant changes in structure.[19] The use of the technology improves productivity only when companies at the same time invest effort in changing people's jobs, the flow of work, and the structure of the company. More jobs in the leading economies require people to use their initiative, to be adaptable, and able to think. People need more qualifications and are not as likely as in the past to get through their working life without changing what they do. This is the familiar process of deindustrialization. There are still plenty of "unskilled" jobs; after all, cleaners and laborers are still needed. But a growing proportion of jobs require more than basic skills—the middling sorts of job that were suited to people who did not go into tertiary education, and were based on the kind of skills acquired through repetition, have been shrinking in number. So, for instance, the use of ICTs and automation of banks' back offices have cut the number of bank tellers needed. Fewer managers have secretaries; those that still do will have a highly qualified PA rather than a typist to take dictation.[20] And so on.

This pattern should not be surprising. Cheap information is unlikely to be useful to a business if members of staff are not allowed to use it to improve service or output. Nor will it increase productivity unless they have the capacity to use it well, which is likely now to require a bit of thought and initiative. So employees are likely to need a higher level of education than in the past; their employers will need to trust them to take decisions for themselves, and also to be doing their best for the business. It's very hard, after all, to monitor how well an individual is doing in each separate and unsupervised business decision or engagement with a customer. The relationship between senior managers and frontline staff has to depend much more than in old-fashioned corporate hierarchies on mutual trust. Conventional hierarchical corporations were built in an era of expensive information and communication. Just like a hub and spoke transport system, the most efficient model was passing information to the central hub, where decisions would be taken. When information is cheap, the efficient structure is a decentralized one where many people take decisions (as long as they are doing it according to consistent criteria).

Many private sector organizations have responded to the economic imperatives of introducing ICTs. For example, most large corporations have "delayered," and outsourced many activities to other organizations. The kinds of conglomerates so greatly admired and successful in the 1960s and 1970s broke themselves up into component parts because the advantages of centralizing such varied activities dwindled away. However, many others have not changed as much; the ICT-related "productivity miracle" has by-passed large numbers of companies. I wouldn't want to overstate the adaptability and effectiveness of business. We've certainly not reached a nirvana of empowered and fulfilling employment. There are many companies that are as hierarchical as ever and place no reliance on a highly skilled and motivated workforce. Still, the transition to a business structure appropriate to the weightless economy is under way in the private sector, especially in competitive industries open to international trade. The profit motive has acted as a strong imperative for change.

This is much less true of public sector organizations—a point to which I'll return below. They tend to be organized still on a hierarchical model, with employees not allowed to take advantage of the flexibility and new capabilities created by new technologies. Initiative isn't so highly valued, and there is often also a presumption of uniformity in public services, rather than the customization people have come to expect in their private transactions. However, this will have to change given the huge pressure on public finances, described earlier. Improvements in public sector efficiency on the scale needed will depend on a productivity boost from the technologies, and that in turn will depend on changing the structure of the organizations and the requirements on employees. An effective public sector will also consist of high trust organizations.

GLOBALIZATION

One of the most striking changes in business structures is the move toward networks of companies working together—in effect, complicated supply chains which coordinate closely with each other. These extend across several countries even for quite small companies. Big multinationals in particular have extremely complicated structures dispersed around the globe, and a sophisticated product such as a car or mobile phone consists of many components manufactured all over the world before being assembled and shipped to their final destination.

For globalization is part of the process of the reorganization of the economy triggered by the drive to use ICTs effectively. The globalization that occurred in the late nineteenth and early twentieth centuries was an exchange of capital for raw materials, usually on favorable terms for the imperial sources of capital. That of the late twentieth and early twenty-first century has been different in character. Although the majority of cross-border trade and investment so far consists of rich countries increasing their economic links with each other, developing countries, especially the BRICs, account for a rapidly growing share of world production and trade. The OECD countries' share of world GDP declined from 65 percent in 1975 to 55 percent by 2005. During roughly the same period, its share of world exports declined from 73 percent to 67 percent.[21]

The geographic scope of production has greatly increased, therefore, both in terms of the growth of trade and investment and its geographic distance. Very few manufactured products, and a declining proportion of services as well, are made in one country any longer. Even quite simple products, such as the symbolic shirt or processed foods, will use components sourced from different places. Larger and more complicated items—a laptop, a truck—will have been "made in" many places. Indeed, more than a third of measured trade in goods consists of components, not finished products. A high degree of specialization has developed during the past quarter century. For example, rather than being a center for auto manufacture, like the Detroit of the past, Hungary has become a specialist producer of auto engines, making one in every twenty-five engines in the world, while Poland specializes in transmissions, and so on.

It is not just manufacturing that has globalized. Professional services are global too. Bankers, lawyers, consultants, and the like are likely to be widely traveled with projects or colleagues or postings overseas. Many more routine services, such as call centers and medical imaging offices, have also begun to ship tasks to developing countries with cheaper labor, although this outsourcing is much smaller in scale than the impression given by the media. In both cases, manufacturing and services, globalization and the adoption of new technologies have gone hand in hand. Part of the technology-driven restructuring of the economy, not only bringing about new goods and services but turning value increasingly intangible and increasing specialization, involves changing the geography of economic activity. Supply chains are longer—they involve a larger number of more specialized links—and they cross national borders.

The development of these global networks of business rests on trust, and to a far greater extent than business restructuring in any particular country. They are a delicate and finely spun web of activity covering continents. There are likely to be relatively few social contacts between partners in a global business network, perhaps little familiarity with the country, its cultural norms, its legal framework. In the case of the emerging economies such as China, the history of trading relationships is relatively short, as their engagement with global trade and investment dates back no further than the 1980s. Yet although the social roots of trust are shallow as they're so new, with the just-in-time production chains and complicated supply chains and logistics we have now, the dependence on trust is high indeed.

Yet the arrangements and institutions for managing the far greater trade and investment across borders have lagged far behind the reality. After the onset of the financial crash in fall 2008, world trade declined sharply and has taken some time to recover. It would be a huge challenge, and highly damaging to living standards around the world, if the globalization of production described above were to be unpicked so that we returned to a world where a label saying "Made in Country X" made some sense. But it could happen, just as the globalization of the late nineteenth and early twentieth centuries unraveled.

Even if it doesn't, and I think it unlikely, the question of the governance of the global economy will remain. It is not just nihilistic anarchists on the streets of major cities protesting international meetings of the G8 or G20 who challenge the credibility and legitimacy of institutions such as the IMF and WTO. Many politicians and governments do so as well, including some of the leaders of large emerging economies, which are underrepresented in international discussions. Much of the criticism of the existing international institutions is ill-informed and even potentially counterproductive. However, it is impossible to mount a full-blooded vigorous defense of them when they have adapted so little to an enormously changed world economy.

Their inadequacy was painfully revealed by the lack of international cooperation during the financial crisis. An inherently global problem, given the global reach and interlinkages of the financial system, has been dealt with entirely at a national level. None of the international institutions has played a role in the handling of the crisis or banking reform in its aftermath. It has been handled by national governments with ad hoc international discussions as needed. Another painful gap is the absence of effective international management of the policy response to climate change, described in chapter 1. The mechanism has been overarching targets set at high-profile international conferences—Kyoto in 1997, Copenhagen in late 2009. Both were largely failures. There is no consensus between developed and developing nations about the targets and how to share the burden of adjustment. Policies are on the whole set at a national level, albeit with the exception of the EU.

In fact, the European Union is the only example of an effective international framework for setting policies and governing its members' economies, and it's fair to say both that it too has proven flawed in the light of the financial crisis and that its citizens hold its institutions in low esteem. This esteem varies from country to country—smaller and newer members are bigger fans of the EU. But turnout for EU parliamentary elections is low, while the EU Commission is effective but is not all that well known and not admired. In some member countries, notably the United Kingdom, the "Brussels bureaucrats" are populist bogeymen conspiring to undermine the national way of life. The Commission and European Parliament certainly lack popular legitimacy.

Even so, the EU has created a practical and effective framework for the organization of almost all economic matters, including international trade, defense, the law and police cooperation, and many social matters such as employment law as well. There are twenty-seven nation-states operating in a harmony that is only moderately quarrelsome; fifteen have given up their national currencies for the euro. Citizens of the member states move freely around the whole of the EU, for work and pleasure. Above all, the prospect of a third terrible pan-European war is remote indeed, after the carnage of the first half of the twentieth century. Yet it is fair to say that even this most successful example of international governance in the world suffers from severe institutional weaknesses. National politics is held in low regard throughout Europe; EU politics in lower regard still.

Looking beyond the EU, the picture is even less inspiring. There is a large research literature on issues of international governance, whether at the level of the EU or any other regional grouping, or at the level of the main multilateral organizations, such as the UN, IMF, World Bank, and WTO.[22] On the whole there is a consensus that the governance of the world economy through these institutions is flawed. There have been some moves to increase the representation of rapidly growing economies, and thus the G20 has become more important than the G7, and the voice of countries such as China and India has been increased in the World Bank. Yet on the whole a handful of the largest and richest countries still dominate the various organizations. All of these organizations are politicized and unwieldy, and most find it hard to adjust quickly to circumstances. They tend to lack transparency about the way they operate and their decisions, although this is (very) slowly improving; recently the World Bank made freely available all the data on which it bases decisions.[23] Some—many UN agencies for example—charge very large sums of money for access to their data. None publishes minutes or accounts of their decision-making processes, but prefer instead to issue bland press releases.

However, there is no settled view among scholars as to what improved institutions for a globalized world would look like. The constitutional historian Philip Bobbitt set out in a major book several scenarios about possible alternative frameworks, including a return to a more nationalistic approach, a retreat from our present limited multilateralism, and what he terms the "market state," in which more of the functions of international governance are left to private sector negotiations.[24] At the time of publication, before the financial crisis, he thought the market state the most likely. It is less obvious now that market-driven globalization is as inexorable as it then seemed. In any case, even then, he saw several possible scenarios.

To do justice to those involved in the international organizations, there is a lot of discussion of reform. The rise of the BRICs, and the need to give them a role in the various fora such as the IMF and "G" discussions, is one reason. There have been international commissions to discuss change, such as the Warwick Commission on International Financial Reform.[25] The financial crisis has also provided some impetus to this debate. But, thank goodness, there has not been anything like the crisis of the Depression and the Second World War, which created the conditions for international political agreement to a brand new institutional framework. There is no natural shape for new institutions of global governance to take and insufficient sense of crisis for this to occur. However, they will need to change further to reflect the globalized nature of the changing structure of the economy, a thread I'll pick up again later when returning to questions of governance.

CITIES

Globalization is only one way in which the ICT-driven, weightless economy has become more dependent on trust. A second aspect of the structural changes is the increased importance of face-to-face contact, which seems a paradox given that the technologies have made electronic contact at a distance easier and cheaper than ever. Face-to-face contact occurs in cities: cities have always been hot spots of the economy, but their relative importance has increased.

Many observers of the new technologies in the 1990s assumed that because it was now so easy and cheap to communicate at a distance, longer-distance work contacts would supplant face-to-face interaction. The phenomenon was labeled "the death of distance."[26] Some pundits predicted that there would be a shift toward working at home, and that companies would become more dispersed if they were not tied to specific places by the cost of communicating. Globalization has certainly spread production all over the world, which seems to confirm the theory.

Yet paradoxically, the reverse has happened too. Economic activity has always been unevenly spread, concentrated in towns and cities. Sometimes that was simply due to the presence of a resource such as coal or a geographical feature such as a good harbor. But there are also good intrinsic reasons for locating in a city. Firms can find suitable workers more easily. Workers with a particular skill can find a variety of jobs. When a specialization develops, people also can meet and exchange ideas or industry gossip. Simple historical accident can trigger the kind of virtuous circle that makes an industry thrive in a particular place. And size matters too. A big city is an attractive market and therefore a magnet for many industries.[27] The arrival of ICTs appears to have reinforced the tendency to concentrate in towns and cities, and especially in certain large global cities such as New York, San Francisco, London, Tokyo—and also Shanghai, Mumbai, Mexico City, and Sao Paolo. In 2008 a significant milestone was reached: for the first time more than half the world's population was living in a town or city.

A particularly clear example of what drives this urban clustering phenomenon is seen in Silicon Valley. Of all industries, software is most able to locate anywhere; in fact, it has clustered in a few specific places.[28] The explanation seems to be that face-to-face contact is more important the more sophisticated, complicated, and subtle is the industry in question. The sectors of the economy with the highest "value added," or productivity (that is, with the highest ratio of output sold to input used), are the most geographically concentrated. As well as software, the creative industries such as advertising, biotech, and financial services are good examples.

People who work in companies of this kind need the intellectual and creative stimulus they get from discussions with other skilled professionals. They need to share information and ideas it might be hard to spell out in writing—economists use the phrase "tacit knowledge" for this. In traditional manufacturing, say auto assembly in the 1970s, it was relatively straightforward to set out a lot of what workers needed to know in a manual or teach it in a brief training course. Experience accumulated over many years would certainly make them better at their job, more productive. But by comparison, it would be almost impossible to train a new programmer the same way—she or he will have a college degree at least and will also need the continual stimulus of discussion and brainstorming with colleagues.

The fact is that the most productive parts of the economy now are, counterintuitively perhaps, dependent on face-to-face contact. The fact that computers have taken over much of the mundane activity that used to constitute work mean that humans are now much more likely to have to do the things that computers can't—have ideas, be creative, provide service. New

Figure 11. Urban Babel.

ideas or creative impulses tend to come from other people. Universities have always known this, bringing scholars together in one place, and students to the same place to learn in person. Very many more of us now need the stimulus of other people to do our jobs productively.

So we are congregating more than ever in what are often called "global cities," very large and still growing urban agglomerations with concentrations of high-value industries making heavy use of ICTs. And there is a snowball effect. Concentrations of highly skilled and well-paid professionals lure other industries to the same place and particularly service industries. All those high-value-added creative people need schools, hospitals, restaurants, cleaners, and shops. So the same global cities have also attracted large numbers of migrants—often immigrants from much poorer countries—to fill all of those jobs. These urban agglomerations have grown substantially since 1980 and have a diversity of population that is remarkable compared to a generation ago. They combine in the same exciting, dynamic, diverse geographical area both the extremes of the modern economy, the highly paid, creative professionals and the poorly paid workers in drudge service industries. They have museums and expensive shops alongside slum housing and discount stores, often just across the street. They have the best and the worst, and they are the dynamos of the whole economy.[29]

The global cities are the frontier of the economy. They are both exciting and alarming places, magnets for all that's good and bad in modern societies. Most have pockets of seemingly intractable poverty and crime, while some seem to be irredeemably scarred by social disorder and crime. They are the hubs of global multinational enterprises, centers of the drugs and people trafficking trades. Yet other parts of many huge global cities are astonishingly peaceful and civilized given the number and variety of people living and working in them, and the strains of urban life in a megacity. The level of trust prevailing is a marker of the city's economic success. A face-to-face city at the leading edge of the economy can only function if there is a high level of trust or social capital.

Take my home city, London. Its population has increased from 6.8 million in 1981 to 7.6 million today. Twenty five years ago, 18 percent of the population were immigrants to the United Kingdom, mainly (three-quarters) from former colonies. Now 31 percent are foreign born and they originate from more than forty-seven countries. In 1981 14 percent of Londoners were not of "white British" origin (either because they are immigrants or are the children of nonwhite immigrants); the figure is now 42 percent.[30] It is a large city geographically, but these millions still live at quite a high density per square mile. Their languages and cultural expectations vary hugely. Over that same quarter century, crime rates have fallen, and particularly crimes of violence. The cultural scene is the most vibrant it has been for decades. There is a wonderful diversity of shops and restaurants. It is a surprisingly friendly place. If you fall in the street, of course plenty of people will walk past uncaring; but there will always be somebody who stops to help. So London, for all its remaining poverty and crime, is, I think, a high-trust city. It could not be any other way if it is to succeed. Millions of people from every country on earth could not live together in a large and densely populated city with a thriving economy if it were not a high-trust society.

The mechanisms for the creation of this high level of trust are unclear, and indeed change over time in the same city. A comparison of New York City in 1980 and 2010 would well illustrate the scope for quite dramatic change in a short time in levels of trust and social harmony. Perhaps a lot of it is simply familiarity through diversity—if you attend school with refugee children from Somalia and the children of immigrant workers from Poland and those of Japanese businessmen on a two-year posting, it takes some effort *not* to develop open-mindedness and tolerance.

And, of course, the trust factor is not universal. All global cities have their dark side and some are dysfunctional. There are ghettos of poverty, unemployment, and drugs. The global mafia operates through the global cities, just as legitimate multinational businesses do. But in contrast to those who are nostalgic for a supposedly gentler and kinder past, I would strongly argue that the "average" trust level *can* be higher now than it was twenty years ago and indeed *is* higher in certain cities such as New York and London.[31] These megacities are the successful hubs of the global economy. The higher value activities in which they now specialize are higher trust activities, albeit with clear fragility such as the collapses we've seen in the financial sector in both cases. Others which are low-trust places, such as Mumbai or Sao Paolo, still have to cement their role in the global economy; it's not yet clear whether or how well they'll succeed.

Yet at the same time that new technologies have made high trust essential for economic productivity, they have stretched and strained that trust in new ways. They have brought about a dramatic restructuring of industry and work. They've created the diversity of the modern city and workplace, bringing many people into contact daily with a much wider variety of others than ever used to be the case. And there are much larger geographical distances in production too, due the fact that economies have become more open to trade and investment, and that companies are more likely to be part of a global supply chain.

THE CHALLENGE OF BUILDING TRUST

There are, then, a number of ways in which the technology-driven structural changes in the economy have been simultaneously increasing the importance of trust or social capital and making it more fragile. At the heart of this tension is the way so many people of so many different backgrounds, expectations, and habits are now in contact with each other. The everyday miracle of complex economic organization described by Paul Seabright is becoming increasingly challenging.

Diversity is an important strength in the ideas-based economy. People who are alike, think alike. There is some evidence that more diverse groups are better at solving problems. The underlying intuition is that problems that look difficult from one perspective can appear straightforward from another, or at least can be approached in a fresh way, so a variety of perspectives increases the chances of finding a solution. Perhaps more surprisingly, under certain conditions, a random selection of problem solvers will outperform a group of the best individual problem solvers. Improved results are more likely when there is underlying agreement on aims and values.[32]

However, diversity is also problematic. Like globalization, like increasing urbanization, like the reshaping of companies and other organizations as a result of the new technologies, growing diversity also imposes new strains on the bonds of trust, the social capital, in our societies.

For example, many people find it uncomfortable to deal with others who are different in one way or another. It has been a massive and incomplete struggle for Western societies to acknowledge that women should have broadly equal parity with men in many aspects of life, or that sexual preferences should not matter for the way people are treated at work or socially. Ethnic diversity is a fraught issue in all countries I know of, and all the more so when it involves sometimes quite dramatic cultural differences too. All the leading economies now consist of many groups of people from a range of backgrounds, cultures, and countries of origin, with a huge array of beliefs and ideas about what is socially acceptable. In the early 1980s, most places were still fairly homogeneous in terms of the cultural and racial origins of their population. During the past quarter century virtually every town and city—in all the OECD countries and in many developing ones too—has become kaleidoscopic in its cultural diversity.

Yet the rich economies have an institutional structure built on a rather specific set of social foundations dependent on standard patterns of behavior and cultural homogeneity. This included as part of the social glue the welfare state whereby richer households would support poorer ones through the use of tax revenues to provide welfare benefits. The highest degree of redistribution is found in Scandinavian countries. Until very recently, these were the most racially homogeneous. The least redistribution is found in the United States, where almost all of the richest taxpayers have been white and a majority of welfare benefits are paid to blacks. Harvard economists Alberto Alesina and Ed Glaeser have looked at the pattern in a number of European countries as well as the United States and have concluded that a redistributive welfare state is indeed more likely the less ethnic diversity there is in the population.[33] To put it bluntly, we're more willing to support people who are similar to us.[34]

This is a rather uncomfortable finding for some people of a liberal or leftward-leaning inclination. We prefer, for example, to suppose that decent people want to support the poor by paying tax and are color blind. But equally it is hardly controversial to say there are ways in which racism or cultural intolerance characterizes many or most societies. What's more, the big increase in international migration from about the mid-1990s has brought about quite widespread anti-immigrant sentiment in countries ranging from Sweden and Italy to the Anglo-Saxon lands, such as Australia, the United States, and United Kingdom. Some of this is understandable concern about competition for scarce housing, for example, or pressure on health services and schools, or the impact on the native-born in low-skill jobs, and their wage levels. Few studies in key destination countries for international migration such as the United States, United Kingdom, Australia, and Ireland have found any large economic impacts from increased migration at all—the most frequent finding is that there is some small downward pressure on the wages (in real terms) of the native-born low skilled. In general the evidence doesn't indicate any other negative economic impacts of significant size. For example, migrants make a net contribution to government finances as they tend to be young and in work, and not entitled to claim any benefits. However, no amount of evidence will overturn the fear of adverse economic effects, as there is no social capital associated with newcomers to a society.

Many existing citizens also simply fear the effects of cultural difference—this is true whenever there has been a wave of immigration. It was true of the United States in the early twentieth century as poorer and foreign-speaking European immigrants took over from the earlier English-speaking waves. It was true of the United Kingdom when West Indians arrived during the 1960s to fill jobs, and of the south Asians who followed in the late 1970s onward. There will always be some alarm about how people with different cultural conventions and social norms will fit into society, and how they will affect the existing inhabitants, no matter how much experience we have now of the fact that they always do, and pretty much completely within one generation.

Diversity of another kind has been a source of tension, and that is the legally mandated diversity in the workplace and public institutions. Laws passed throughout the developed world since the pathbreaking civil rights legislation in the United States have increasingly required both public and private sector employers and civic institutions to ensure members of a range of social groups are not disadvantaged. The ebb and flow of the heated debate over affirmative action and the "political correctness" wars are testament to how divisive these laws are in fact. Again, liberal-minded people would prefer not to acknowledge that there is real opposition to mandatory diversity of this kind, but it certainly exists. Thomas Frank argues that the left's failure to take cultural concerns of a large group of Americans seriously led them to repeated electoral defeats, at least until Barack Obama's election as president in November 2008.[35] The weight this should be given in explaining the pattern of election results is debatable, given the range of other factors at play. But it's certainly the case that opinion on social diversity of this kind is quite polarized. In all Western societies, the center of gravity of popular opinion has definitely moved toward the tolerant since the 1970s, but there are wide differences of view.

Governance

Trust is essential for an economy to prosper. The new technologies have made the advanced economies even more dependent on trust, and high social capital. At work and in their daily contacts in the towns and cities in which most of us live, most people are engaged in more contacts that require them to trust a wider range of others than ever before. These will often be people outside their own company, even outside their own country. These structural shifts in the economy have contributed to a big increase in prosperity during the past few decades, thanks to the impact of ICTs on productivity. This includes the global reorganization of production, which has spread economic relationships over thousands of miles. The economic consequences of the new technologies have also brought about greater social tensions, cultural fears, a pervasive sense of anxiety and uncertainty. This is the "paradox of prosperity": that economic growth has come about through social disruptions, which are dramatic, given the radical and "general purpose" nature of the new technologies. These disruptions range from the inadequacies of social arrangements such as pensions and tax systems to the radical reorganization of the way businesses operate.

The financial crisis, and the consequent implosion in value in global financial markets in 2008, demonstrate this fragility. Repairing the current situation will be difficult. Andrew Haldane, a senior Bank of England official, has pointed out it is nothing like enough to restore market confidence. "A clean balance sheet might instil confidence, but it need not repair trust. Because it is a moral judgment, repairing trust can be a slow and painstaking business."[36] The sense that the institutions and arrangements for running society are failing is absolutely pervasive. We have been depleting social capital.[37] To ensure their continued success and social harmony, the leading economies will need appropriate institutions and governance.

There is certainly a vague awareness that governance—like the concept of social capital itself—is a more important issue than used to be the case. For example, it crops up frequently in discussion of the failure of poor countries to develop. The need for "good governance" has become a mantra among the aid-donor community. Poor economies have no chance of growth, according to the consensus, without good governance. No other policies will be effective without this foundation: the rule of law, protection for property rights, stable political institutions giving adequate voice to the needs of the people, and effective social institutions. Or, to put it another way, poor economies lack social capital. There is certainly strong evidence of a correlation between corruption and institutional failure on the one hand, and economic failure on the other.

However, the sense of failure is widespread too in the context of the rich economies. The financial crisis has reinforced the lack of trust, verging on contempt, for the political elite, the financial elite, and almost all forms of authority. The opinion poll evidence for this loss of deference in the Western democracies is startling. Moreover, the level of engagement with democratic institutions is diminishing almost everywhere. Over the last forty years, voter turnout has been steadily declining in established democracies, including the United States, Western Europe, Japan, and Latin America. In the United States, turnout has declined from 1960. In Europe, voter turnouts peaked in the mid to late 1960s, with declines since then. Globally, voter turnout has decreased by about 5 percentage points over the last four decades.

There is in many countries, as reflected in such polls, a disappointment in government. Many citizens believe their governments are failing them in important ways. Many of us have had to make big adjustments in our working lives. Old certainties known to our parents have gone. A lifelong career in one organization is unlikely. Companies have reorganized and downsized frequently. None provide a secure pension any longer. Big corporate names vanish overnight. Businesses are outsourced overseas, all too frequently it seems from the headlines. The fact that many of these changes affect a minority of the workforce is not relevant to their emotional impact. A great many people feel that they are on their own in a completely changed environment for work; and in that, they're correct. Individual capabilities and adaptability have become important.

This matters to government as well as private businesses because many government functions build around the private sector—employers collect income taxes, for example, and in many countries are involved in providing pensions or administering various benefits. Much of the welfare system is built on the assumption that people will stay with one employer, in full-time work, for long periods. The system of social support, which is one of the main functions of government in a modern economy, is built to a blueprint that has become obsolete. And the widespread sentiment that government is failing in its fundamental task of enhancing citizens' security in the widest sense is well-founded. So paradoxically, the cut and thrust private sector has done better than the public sector at increasing the levels of trust needed in the changed economy. The polls do suggest that people have greater trust in some private sector organizations than in the institutions of government.

It is not only at the level of national economies that governance has become a hot topic though. Corporate governance has been studied extensively for the past decade or so, and in a number of countries the law has been changed to try to improve corporate governance. Companies are urged to be transparent and accountable, and to take seriously a wider set of responsibilities than making a profit. Many commentators seem to believe companies have some quasi-governmental roles. Big corporations are certainly important social institutions.

At the same time, as described above, the spread of modern information and communication technologies has changed the structure of companies, making it harder for them to fill a social role in the way increasingly expected of them. Instead of the hub-and-spoke hierarchies, the structure best suited to an age when communication was costly, modern companies are much flatter and organized in a complex matrix or even in a loose network with other companies. Few last as long as the classic corporation of the 1950s and 1960s—the average independent life of a listed company has been in steady decline. This structure does not make it easy to offer stable employment and a pension, never mind more onerous social responsibilities. It is not even obvious that the most effective way for governments to collect taxes is via payroll deduction organized by companies, although most still do it that way.

And this is not the end of the contexts in which governance has become an issue. There has been a debate about the forms of international governance.[38] Should half-century old institutions like the UN, IMF, and World Bank be reformed? How can the emerging BRICs economies be given a voice in international debate, given that they are not in the G7? Is the G20 the best vehicle for international economic management? Should the EU continue to expand? Do Africa or the Americas need something equivalent to the EU? At what level do societies and economies need governing? Is there a need for more and better transnational governance? Or should it be more local, reflecting the aspirations of smaller units such as Catalonia or Scotland? In terms of geographic scope and institutional form this debate is wide open.

These multiple failures of governance have been emerging over at least a decade. There is ample evidence from opinion polls that around the developed world the degree of trust in politics and public organizations—and also big companies and many professions—has been in decline.

Conclusion

High trust is essential to the kind of economy we have now, but at the same time fragile. Building social capital needs more careful attention; future prosperity will depend on husbanding and strengthening it. We start in a weakened position, due to the financial and economic crisis, and the overhang of debt that will be its legacy. The decline of trust and depletion of social capital takes us right to the central issue for the second half of this book: What institutional and governance reforms can start to correct the unsustainable trends identified here in the way we organize our economies? The need for institutional change in response to the underlying structural and technological changes is pervasive. Private and public sector organizations, rich and poor countries, local and global agencies, all face their own challenges of trust and governance. This chapter has touched on some of the institutional challenges; the issue of institutional reform is center stage in the second half of this book.

PART TWO   Obstacles

SIX Measurement

THE FIRST HALF OF THIS BOOK has set out the central challenge of our times: economic growth is essential but the way it has been achieved for the past generation cannot continue. To argue, as has become fashionable, that Western economies should just stop growing is delusional. There is no quick fix to the challenge.

Growth offers material benefits and also, increasingly in the world's richest economies, offers people more potential to develop their capabilities and shape their lives in enjoyable and meaningful ways. Social welfare, to use the technical language of economics, is without doubt improved by economic growth. At low levels of income, growth is essential to prevent hunger, improve health, provide adequate housing and communications. At high levels of income—and contrary to some of the stronger claims of "happiness" gurus—more growth continues to improve our well-being. We value greatly the variety and opportunities it brings. The structure of the advanced economies has changed dramatically, and much of the growth taking place now involves services and intangibles. We value these services, experiences, and creativity. Although it's hard to visualize, this is still growth. Its absence makes us unhappy. So policy decisions will continue to need to deliver a growing economy.

Yet, as the previous chapters describe, the modern world has plunged into a crisis of growth. The nature and distribution of the economic growth experienced in the leading economies for the past generation has been unsustainably flawed. There has been an overconsumption of nonrenewable resources and natural wealth has been squandered; the amount and way we consume will need to change to avert climate and ecological catastrophes, although there is (forgive the pun) heated debate about the extent of the changes needed. The social structure of Western countries has allowed current generations to consume at the expense of an intolerable burden of debt on future generations, one which the workers and taxpayers of the future will reject, with the potential for socially and politically catastrophic consequences. The viability of some societies is threatened by their deep unfairness and by the gradual corrosion of trust between people who must nevertheless live together in an everyday miracle of mutual dependence for the economy and society to thrive. The sense of crisis is everywhere, reflected in public cynicism about politics and brought to a boil by a sense of urgency about the environment and the state of the economy after the financial crisis. The upward trend in the number of natural disasters around the world seems an apt reflection of the financial and economic crisis, and the sense of crisis so many people in many countries feel about their political and business elites.[1]

We've reached the point of Enough. The recent experience of economic growth is that it has destroyed opportunities, either for particular social groups or for future generations. Can it be reshaped in order to continue without incurring such untenable costs?

One possible conclusion would be that this point marks the end of the triumphant free market capitalism that has ruled economic policy since the fall of the Berlin Wall and collapse of communism. The financial crisis and subsequent recession have certainly made the role of government more prominent, but mainly as a result of crisis management. Many commentators have argued that the state should reenter economic management in a more deliberate way, given the staggering demonstrations of market failure we've experienced.[2] I will indeed go on in this part of the book to discuss the many ways in which markets fail, and the policy conclusions to which pervasive market failures point. But there are also many ways in which governments fail too. It was because these government failures were taken to extremes behind the Iron Curtain that communism collapsed so dramatically. The pendulum then swung, during the 1990s and 2000s, firmly toward the free market model, but sending it swinging right back to the starting point of 1970s style statism would be foolish. Markets have many virtues as well as flaws.[3]

In fact, there is a broad crisis of governance, encompassing both markets and governments. It is rooted in deep technological and social changes as well as in the dimensions of unsustainable choice described in the first half of the book. Growth, which dramatically improves social welfare, rests on innovation. We're in the habit of thinking of innovation simply as a matter of technology, new inventions such as computers and medicines. But the profound social impacts of fundamental technical change, whether it's steam or computing, mean that innovation must also include the social rules that organize the way we live together and cooperate. The rules haven't kept up with the technology. Now, just as in the early Victorian era, the mismatch between the underlying technological structure of the economy and the institutions governing the economy is the source of political and social upheaval.

Society is experiencing a broad crisis of governance—a jargon word which is nevertheless a useful shorthand for all the ways in which we cooperate to organize our lives together in society. In the wake of the financial crisis, attention has focused firmly on the shortcomings of markets. The solution to many people lies in a return to the kind of government intervention linked to the economics of John Maynard Keynes, who did so much to shape the postwar mixed economy. Yet the response to the crisis, including tackling levels of debt, will put the spotlight on the shortcomings of government. As James Piereson has put it: "The present financial slump represents both a crisis of free markets and of the mixed system that Keynes envisioned and did so much to bring into being. It is a system in which government plays a large role in the economy, but in many areas on the basis of decisions that are highly political in nature."[4] Solutions to the formidable problems set out in the first section of this book will lie in rethinking institutions and the rules by which they operate. This includes both private and public institutions; both formal—like companies and governments—and informal—social norms and habits. The question is how, in the context of both dramatic social and technological change and a crisis of sustainability in the economy and in nature, we can continue to thrive in large and complex societies. It's a difficult challenge, and this section of the book sets out in more detail why it is proving so hard to achieve necessary changes, by looking at some important obstacles.

This section of the book is thus about the institutions and rules according to which the economy operates, and in particular about why it seems to be so hard to respond to the many problems facing the leading economies.

This chapter will start with the question of measurement. It might seem an odd starting point, tangential to the serious issues needing to be addressed. But I share the Enlightenment belief that good information, based on careful quantification, is essential for making decisions that can change things for the better. All of the leading thinkers of that era regarded accurate measurement as fundamental to the advance of knowledge and progress of human kind and were greatly interested in the detail of measurement systems. (Thomas Jefferson, for example, tried to introduce the French system of metrification to the United States.)[5] Roy Porter, one of the leading historians of the Enlightenment, speaks of a "growing culture of quantification" that characterized and enabled the advancement of knowledge.

Why does measurement matter? Starting with measurement questions is a way of exposing some key conceptual gaps in how we think about the economy. The fact that the measurement framework no longer fits the shape of the economy is not a trivial issue. What and how we measure anything is shaped by and also shapes the concepts we use to try to understand what's happening. Measurements also carry a special weight in policymaking because they make it easier to justify decisions, even though many important considerations might not be at all easy to measure. Measuring those things that can be measured is essential but so is remembering that some things can't be measured.

This exploration of the gaps leads on to a discussion in the next chapter about the differences between what is measured and what is valued. Value has a moral as well as a practical dimension. But economists have for decades avoided discussing both the difference between value and prices, and the importance of values in the wider, moral sense in shaping the economy. This has only reentered economic debate quite recently. One example is the focus on "social capital," referred to in chapter 5. But more generally, the recent financial crisis means there has been a surge of interest in the question of whether markets go with the grain of moral values or against it. The next chapter argues that the benefits of markets in delivering good economic outcomes—the central claim of economics—depends on the values that structure those markets, because markets are social institutions that embody underlying values and cultural and social norms. One reason markets have come into question in the general debate is because the values embodied in the way they operate have departed from the values held by many citizens— not all markets are immoral, but the operation of markets in recent times has become in some respects immoral. Important as the measurement questions are for guiding policy, policies that are to enhance social welfare will also depend on making the right judgment about what society values.

There is also another important reason markets have become worse at reflecting values, which is again related to the structural, technical changes taking place in the leading economies. The nature of these changes means the extent of what economists call "market failures" has greatly increased. Many more of the things we want to buy, the services and goods shaping economic growth toward the weightless, have the features of "public goods." The outcomes of delivering them solely through private transactions in markets can diverge from those which would ensure the greatest possible social welfare.

One conclusion, which might seem to chime with the spirit of the times, would be to increase the scope of government activity. But government failure is just as extensive as market failure, and for similar reasons, as set out in chapter 8. Conventionally, market failure is presented as a rationale for government intervention in the economy; and conversely, many economists see government failure—as so clearly demonstrated by the communist countries but elsewhere too—as the justification for using markets to organize the economy. This "states versus markets" perspective is bogus, however. Debates about the *scope* of government intervention on close inspection turn out to be about the *nature* of government intervention.[6] Markets and governments are likely to fail in similar ways because the "failures" stem from inherent problems such as information asymmetries and spillovers between individual decisions. These make it hard for any institution, whether market or state or some other structure, to bring about an ideal outcome.

The deep changes in the structure of the economy have made current institutional and governance failures—in both markets and government—acute. The figures on the loss of trust in almost all institutions, described earlier, show that this is widely sensed. In contemplating how to respond to the challenges of Enough, we need to think about the whole array of economic institutions—markets, governments, firms, and households. Contrary to the way they are often discussed, they do not occupy mutually exclusive spheres of activity, but rather overlap with each other. What's more, each type of institution has shortcomings, and often in the same circumstances.

This discussion in the next three chapters will set the stage for the final section of the book, where I turn to the question of what processes and institutional frameworks might improve on the structures which have begun to fail us so badly. First, then, measurement.

What Should We Be Measuring?

Could there be anything less glamorous than statistics? Yet dull as questions of measurement might seem, how we measure things has a profound effect on the impact we have on the world. When we step outside the realm of things we can immediately perceive with our own senses, measurement is all we have to shape our knowledge and beliefs. The physicist Lord Kelvin put it like this in a famous comment: "When you can measure what you are speaking about, and express it in numbers, you know something about it; but when you cannot measure it, when you cannot express it in numbers, your knowledge of it is of a meager and unsatisfactory kind; it may be the beginning of knowledge, but you have scarcely, in your thoughts, advanced it to the stage of science." Science writer Steven Johnson notes that an improvement in the accuracy of measurement often leads to "a fundamental shift in the perception of the world."[7]

The emphasis on the importance of measurement can be overdone, especially if it leads to an underemphasis on the need for analysis and thinking as well. Some things can be important without being measurable, but the insistence in our modern scientific societies on being able to quantify everything sometimes makes us place too little weight on unmeasurable entities. Nevertheless, as we saw in earlier chapters of this book, the way we measure the economy does have a decisive effect on how governments shape policy and indeed on our own decisions about what to consume and what to save.

A clear conclusion is that economic policies should be based on a wider range of statistics than GDP alone, and in particular that measures of the economy's wealth in the widest sense—including natural and human resources—should also be monitored. GDP measures *flows* of goods and service each year, whereas we need also to take into account the *stock* of resources, which captures many years' worth of activity. Basing economic policy on GDP alone and not national wealth is like running a company with reference only to profit and loss accounts and not the balance sheet. One government, Australia's, already offers pointers to the use of economic statistics in ways that will help us to know when we have got to the point of Enough. More on this later.

But first, I want to spend some time on other profound measurement problems, which arise from the way the structure of the economy is changing. These present tougher measurement challenges than adding measures of economic, social, and natural wealth to the array of existing statistics that governments monitor in setting policy. For the problem is conceptual: it isn't immediately obvious what to start measuring. Why so?

An ever-increasing share of the advanced economies is made up of intangible activities—they are services such as health care or management consultancy or payroll services or acting, or they are servicelike aspects of goods such as research and design or marketing and after-sales service. For a number of reasons, these intangibles are not measured well in current economic statistics. What's more, increasing swaths of the economy have features that mean either that the price of the activity charged in a market transaction is not necessarily a true reflection of their value, or that the price that can be charged does not cover their costs. This has long been a problem affecting the way government services such as education and policing are measured in GDP. It is a growing problem as, due to technological change, a growing share of the economy consists of goods and services that cost a lot to create in the first place but then not much to reproduce or distribute—the fixed costs of producing them are high due to high up-front investment but the marginal cost of producing and selling an additional item is close to zero. These increasing returns activities are growing in their extent, as seen in the growth of goods and research-intensive goods as a share of the leading economies' annual output.

The more you think about the measurement problems, the more it becomes clear that the difficulty in measuring is a result not just of failing to collect the right statistics but is actually due to the way we think about such activities. The conceptual framework that lies behind existing economic statistics is a bad fit for an economy that is no longer mass-producing standardized manufactured goods. The structure of the economy is changing, and so is what people value. This is true both in the sense of what they'll spend their money on in the weightless economy and in the sense of a growing appreciation of the legacy of today's economy for tomorrow's society. Looking at dry statistics—Mr. Gradgrind's "Facts! Give me facts!"—is a path into deep questions about what society values.

This sounds rather cryptic. So I'm going to start this statistical expedition with teachers and then go on to tell a story about string quartets and the mega rock band U2.

WHAT'S A TEACHER WORTH?

The fact that some costs are rising faster than the general rate of inflation in the economy was first noted by William Baumol in a classic 1966 paper and in a 1993 follow-up.[8] He noted the same phenomenon in services such as health care and teaching, and in the performing arts, in several leading economies. It's widely known that health budgets for example grow at a consistently faster pace than the economy as a whole. The fact that the phenomenon has occurred in many different countries indicates it is not specific to the health or education systems of a particular nation. Baumol also noted that it had occurred over many decades, so could not be linked to a specific economic event. He concluded that these services, like the performing arts, have a "handicraft" aspect. They cannot be automated; on the contrary, their "production" involves the individual attention of the person delivering the service to its users. And their quality also depends on the amount of time and effort spent on their delivery. There is no or only limited scope for standardization and the use of technology to increase productivity. The increase in output is tightly limited by the amount of time spent by an individual performer—or teacher or nurse. If these workers are paid more as the years go by—just like everyone else in the economy thanks to economic growth and rising living standards—the cost consumers must pay for their services will rise relative to other prices.

Baumol wasn't alone in noting this phenomenon—a number of economists at that time, thirty or forty years ago, made the point in different ways. In his well-known book *The Social Limits to Growth*, Fred Hirsch diagnosed the problem as affluence allowing more and more people to demand "positional" goods whose output could not be expanded in line with incomes. His examples included classic public goods such as uncongested roads, definitionally scarce goods such as high-status houses, and also services similar to those explored by Baumol, such as medicine. John Kenneth Galbraith made a similar point in *The Affluent Society*—in turn citing Keynes. Galbraith wrote that consumer desires that result from efforts to keep up with others "may indeed be insatiable; for the higher the general level, the higher still they are." Emulation means that the satisfaction of some wishes creates new ones.[9]

As the fact that we've continued to afford health care and education over the intervening decades shows, we shouldn't thereby conclude that it will become ever harder to afford these "luxury" services. For one thing, there is some slow improvement in productivity in these services. For instance, new communications devices save health workers time—computers automate some record-keeping, and perhaps they can download the day's tasks on a mobile device rather than dealing with paperwork. There are thus incremental savings of time, freeing up a bit more time for the same individual to perform their core tasks.

More important, there has been and continues to be massive productivity growth in the rest of the economy. So we can afford more of the "luxury" services. Baumol writes: "To achieve such a goal—ever greater abundance of everything—society must change only the proportions of its income that it devotes to different products." The share of total incomes and GDP dedicated to spending on these services will rise over time. His back of the envelope calculations based on extrapolating then-current trends indicated that between 1990 and 2040 spending on education and health care could come to account for a half of GDP but even so American consumers would still have nearly quadrupled their consumption of all goods and services.

Yet there's still a challenge in this pattern.

In many countries—less in the United States than elsewhere but there too—many of the services characterized by this pattern are currently provided by the government. If that doesn't change, the trend implies that the government will account for a growing share of GDP. It seems unlikely that people will be happy for a rising share of their incomes to go in tax, even if they are also consuming more public services, at least without greater confidence that governments can spend well. But a debate about what services should be transferred from the public to the private sector will be politically contentious—especially in the context of a necessary and severe squeeze on government budgets in coming decades.

There is also a psychological difference in how people feel about different types of services. Going out to concerts or the theater feels like—it is—a completely discretionary activity. If we feel rich, we don't mind paying more. A rising share of household spending is already going on entertainment of various kinds—films, concerts, holidays, music—and it doesn't feel odd to describe this as a "luxury" that is one of the fruits of modern affluence. However, it does seem perverse to describe health and education as "luxuries." We know we're going to need more of them. The growing number of pensioners will need carers, nurses, and doctors. Advances in medical technology mean our expectations of health care are constantly on the increase, and we expect the health service to provide us with the latest techniques and drugs. Similarly, expectations of the education system are rising in what is so often described as the "knowledge economy." More young people are staying in higher education, and we expect standards to continue improving at every level. It doesn't feel like an option not to consume more and better health and education services as time goes by.

Figure 12. Who will care?

Yet one consequence of the way services like these are eating up a rising share of personal and government budgets is the employment of a growing army of low-paid and low-status workers in these sectors, sometimes illegal immigrants. At the same time that many people would insist on the intrinsic value of carers, teachers, and so on, they've grown increasingly reluctant to pay them higher wages. There's definitely a paradox in the willingness to pay for costly entertainment and consumer gadgets compared with the reluctance to pay for higher salaries in social care and teaching. The psychology of this difference would be well worth exploring.

It's a paradox we're all aware of, though. Particularly after the financial crisis, it's clear that the gap between private rewards and social value as between, say, investment banking and teaching, is untenable. Teachers contribute more socially than they are paid, especially in the public sector, whereas bankers' social contribution is greatly exceeded by their pay—especially with bonuses included. The existence of a gap between public and private value is well known, and indeed forms the basis of conventional welfare economics.[10] Rarely, however, has that gap appeared to be as much of a chasm as it does today.[11]

Will Baumol concludes:

> The same arguments apply to the live performing arts, to libraries, to police protection, to restaurants, to welfare support for the impoverished and to many other critical services. If we do not think through the complex problems just described, or fail to do so in short order, we face a society increasingly characterized, in the words of JK Galbraith, by private affluence and public squalor. Already, unmistakable and disquieting signs are available for all to see.[12]

He is right. The political rows about school or police budgets, about low pay in the caring services, about fair access to the best possible health care, are ubiquitous and intense. How should these services be valued and priced, and how paid for? And are there any clues in the way we think about "new economy" sectors that are starting to experience the same effects?

The Economics of Music

As Baumol pointed out, the same pattern applies to many services—his other example was the performing arts. Take a string quartet. They will sell some recordings but a high proportion of their income is likely to come from live performances. Of course, they will earn less than Bono of U2 or Madonna make from concert tours. But classical performers will still have to charge enough to pay themselves a living wage, and the level of a living wage will rise as living standards in the whole economy rise. While we might expect artists to be willing to suffer a bit for their art, and be a bit poorer than the rest of us, we don't insist that they are paupers. What they earn will not drift too far from earnings in other sectors of the economy—just as with teachers or nurses. At the same time, there is a limit to how many more performances and how many more audience members each performer can entertain. There are only 365 days in a year, and venue sizes can't realistically grow without limit. Air travel might speed up the time between concerts a bit but there is a tight limit to productivity growth.

Performers' earnings must therefore rise even though there is a limit on the size of the audience they can reach through live events. The upshot is that the cost of each concert ticket will climb relative to other prices in the economy. Attending string quartets playing Mozart concertos is therefore also what economists would call a luxury good: demand for such concerts will go up as incomes rise, and spending on the tickets will grow faster than the economy's average growth rate. An ever-higher share of income will go on concert tickets, whether for the Orchestra of the Age of Enlightenment or U2.

Music is an apt example because it also demonstrates a second effect, on top of the long-standing trend toward a ervice-based economy. That is the impact of information and communication technologies on the structure of the economy and the way we think about and measure productivity and growth.

Tastes differ but almost everybody loves some kind of music, and music has always found its way swiftly to new technologies. There are many music radio stations. Music is played in stores and subways. Now that we can, many of us carry our music round with us all the time, plugged into our own musical world via an iPod or other MP3 player. And lots of people too go to concerts of all kinds. Of course, in the pregadget past going to a concert—or making one's own music at home or with friends nearby—was the only way to hear music performed. It had to be live, and as a result the amount of time people could spend listening to music was limited. Technology changed this dramatically. The telephone was first envisioned as a technology for broadcasting music—users were supposed to dial in to a concert performance. The radio and the gramophone won out instead, although technology is coming full circle now as more and more people are listening to music over their mobile phones.

These new technologies—and Radio Corporation of America was the hot technology stock, the Google of its day—massively expanded the market for music. The life of a performer in the early twentieth century had been one of constant touring and live concerts; but performers could reach a much larger audience through these new technologies than they could by performing live. Their earnings were augmented by record contracts and rights payments by radio stations. The commercial music industry started to take its modern shape. Demand for records grew and grew. Artists innovated—there were more of them as a larger market can sustain many more producers and making music became a viable career for many more people than had been the case in the past. Different genres emerged, and record companies became big business.

The technology has moved on again. The Internet has made the cost of distributing music digitally essentially free. But artists still want to make a living—or preferably a fortune—and the record companies and some musicians are even more upset about being disintermediated. U2's lead singer Bono sounded off about it in the New York Times: "A decade's worth of music file-sharing and swiping has made clear that the people it hurts are the creators."[13]

Is this true? They (or their record companies) do have to cover some high upfront costs. Marketing to turn an artist into a big name and publicize new albums is expensive, and there are costs in the initial recording. On the other hand, the new technologies have dramatically reduced the cost of creating and publishing new music. As the purpose of copyright is to incentivize innovation, by creating a temporary monopoly for artists, there is a fraught policy debate at the moment about the extent to which governments need to use the power of the state, and the threat of jail, to enforce music copyright. Bono and others argue that the legal threat is too weak in the face of easy online copying. Critics respond that this simply aims to ensure that the current model by which commercial businesses extract money from consumers of music is preserved, to the detriment of both music lovers and new artists, who always borrow from older artists because that's the nature of creativity in the arts.

The debate is an empirical matter. Are music revenues rising or falling? As James Boyle has pointed out in his excellent book *The Public Domain*, there might be more to be earned in other ways in a market growing thanks to a new technology, just as videos grew revenues for the movie studios, when they were introduced, rather than—as the studios vehemently argued at first—decreasing them.[14] For example, free access to music online creates more fans from people who might never have heard the performer in the past if they had had to buy a CD for twenty-five dollars. Fans will buy some digital music. They'll also buy merchandise and attend concerts. Depending on how much the market for a performer's music grows, these new revenue sources could exceed the amount lost from not selling physical CDs and from the various ways consumers download the music for free online. Threatening to imprison music-loving customers for illegal downloading seems, in this wider perspective, wrongheaded.

There is evidence that the new technologies are indeed growing the music market, despite the extent of (illegal) free downloading. Economists Felix Oberholzer-Gee and Koleman Strumpf conclude in their work:

> Overall production figures for the creative industries appear to be consistent with this view that file sharing has not discouraged artists and publishers. While album sales have generally fallen since 2000, the number of albums being created has exploded. In 2000, 35,516 albums were released. Seven years later, 79,695 albums (including 25,159 digital albums) were published (Nielsen SoundScan, 2008). Even if file sharing were the reason that sales have fallen, the new technology does not appear to have exacted a toll on the quantity of music produced.[15]

They also conclude that "technology increased concert prices, enticing artists to tour more often and, ultimately, raising their overall income." Growing demand for live music on the part of increasingly affluent consumers who are spending a rising proportion of their income on entertainment in general and music in particular will keep concert prices high. In fact, it will keep concert prices rising relative to the general price level. For it's possible to charge very large sums for concert attendance. The most popular music festivals are big business. The United Kingdom's Glastonbury Festival took £24 million in ticket sales for four days of music in 2009. Mama Group's Live Music division, which includes the Mean Fiddler Group, a concert promoter, had revenues of £30 million that year. The Coachella Value Music Festival in Indio, California, took $15 million for three days of rock and alternative music in 2009; the three-day Lolapaloozza festival in Chicago took $17 million in 2008, and Stagecoach Festival in California took $6 million for two days in 2009. Live Nation, the world's largest promoter reported $2.5 billion in sales in 2009 from 41 million people attending 9,085 shows. AEG Live had $888 million from 2,531 shows and 12.9 million in attendance. U2's 360 degree tour in 2009 grossed over $311 million for forty-four shows. It is expected to achieve total gross ticket sales of $750 million by the end of 2010. Michael Jackson's final tour of the United Kingdom had originally been for ten concerts, but this was increased to fifty to meet demand. More than 1.5 million fans caused two sites offering presale tickets to crash within minutes of going oline. In two hours, 190,000 tickets were sold. Tickets appeared on eBay for as much as £10,000. There is a balance of costs and benefits to the producers of music from switches from one form of consumption to another, but there is still plenty of music consumption.[16]

By now you might be asking what this all has to do with the climate change debate and GDP statistics. The point is that the new technologies are changing feasible pricing strategies in a number of industries. This is a broader point than the inability of big record companies to update their business model. The combination of high upfront costs and close to zero distribution costs characterizes all digital industries, causing upheaval in music, film, the media, and publishing, and many other industries too—software, for one, teaching perhaps, and other knowledge-intensive businesses such as pharmaceuticals. There is a challenge for all these businesses in finding ways to make prices correspond to the values consumers place on the goods and services they are providing. The pattern makes them much more like public services—more like a park, which costs a lot in salaries and materials to create and maintain in the first place but almost nothing to allow one more person to walk in the park.

In the jargon, a large and growing segment of the economy consists of expansible and nonexcludable products. Additional consumers can be served at low or no cost, and it often proves difficult to prevent consumers from paying a zero price for them. Yet how much are such services worth to their consumers? More than the zero they cost, at the margin, to provide? If so, why do businesses struggle to charge their customers anything? The technology in music, as in other industries, changes what's valuable—or at least chargeable—by changing the pattern of costs and consumer demands.

Figure 13. Intangible and ephemeral.

In short, a large and growing share of the economy consists of activities with a lot of the economic features of public goods. This is an important phenomenon going to the heart of the question of what it is about the economy that matters.

VALUING INTANGIBLES

The underlying problem is not just a question of where the money will come from to pay for services with this central, inescapable element of personal effort. There is also a question about how to attach a value to work of this kind. How can we measure what it's worth?

In the economy of the 1960s, much of the output consisted of manufactured goods, and the commanding heights of the economy were held by automakers, steel mills, and chemicals plants. Improvements in mechanization and management meant that over time the productivity of production workers increased steadily—that is, the number of items made by each worker on average. Productivity gains meant more profits, and higher wages as well as higher dividends for investors in manufacturing firms. It was relatively straightforward to make the link between input—work effort—and output. But how can the productivity of a nurse of teacher or policeman be measured? For one thing, quality is more of an issue. Which nurse is more productive—the one who looks after twenty patients a day or the one who looks after ten, spending more time with each, so they leave hospital sooner and happier? Should we even think about the productivity of nurses separately from the people's health, for it would be better still if the number of sick people needing nursing care were to decline.

The more you think about it, the harder it is to understand what productivity means in great swaths of the economy. Is the worth of a trader in the financial markets best measured by his trading profits? A few years ago many people might have said yes, but there is some debate about that now. Is my productivity as an author and economist best measured by the number of words I write in books and reports, or by their innate quality, or just by how much I can persuade people to pay me? None of these seems right. Number of words ignores quality, as indeed does earnings per book or report, which depends more on what I can persuade people to pay. But using the innate quality would be hopeless for the purposes of measuring and analyzing the economy—we would have to use literary critics and other economists who could peer review my work in order to devise the statistics on my productivity. Is teaching more productive if class sizes are bigger (more pupils per teacher) or if they are smaller? Do we need a quality of learning per pupil per teacher measure and how would we calculate that? Productivity is a concept appropriate in industries producing products, but not for many of those delivering services. (The mismatch struck me when I visited a bank and was taken into the secure room holding the computer servers. My host patted one of the stacks and said: "And this is where we make the mortgages.")

The difficulties of measuring intangible output have been exercising statisticians for some years. Meanwhile, the intangible share of the economy has grown enormously. Around two-thirds of GDP in most OECD countries is accounted for by services, not amenable to easy measurement. Since 1980, although GDP in these economies has increased enormously, its (literal) weight has not, so broadly speaking all of the growth for the past thirty years has been weightless or intangible.[17] The proportion of stock market values of major companies accounted for by intangibles, or "goodwill," as accountants describe it, has grown to stand at about 75 percent of the S&P 500.[18] As described in chapter 1, it has been difficult enough to make any attempt at accounting for quality improvements in physical goods such as computers and cameras in GDP. The problems of accounting for intangibles in the GDP statistics are in a different league.

What's more, intangibles span a wide range of services from entertainment to nursing. These share some of the same economic characteristics. Although in the past services of the former type were protected by technology from the difficulty of measuring productivity and matching reward to value, that is changing rapidly. So, bizarrely, many previously highly profitable businesses are looking quite a lot like public services in some respects. The zero marginal cost of conveying the song or movie to another user makes it harder to charge anything, but that in turn is undermining the provision of the service. Many businesses are scrabbling to find what it is they can charge for in order to cover their costs and sustain profit margins.

This all points toward the conclusion that our conceptual framework for understanding economic value hasn't kept up with the way the economy has changed.

INNOVATION IN STATISTICS

Economists and statisticians certainly understand the problem. Questions of measurement have not only reached the public policy debate, they have been explored extensively within the profession.

One type of innovation has been the challenge to the monopoly of GDP over policy debates, and the development of either alternative or supplementary indicators. This was covered in chapter 1. The commission set up in France by President Sarkozy, chaired by Nobel laureates Amartya Sen and Joseph Stiglitz, has been perhaps the most high-profile and certainly the most recent detailed effort to set out a suite of indicators in addition to GDP. The final report called for a "dashboard" of indicators. This must be right. More governments should follow the example of the Australian government, which publishes each year an array of indicators—selected after a public consultation—including those favored by the Sen and Stiglitz Commission. (The Australian project is described in chapter 1.)[19]

The statistics the Sen and Stiglitz Commission advised governments to monitor—specifically including wealth of all types, financial, human, and natural, and the distribution of income and wealth—go some way toward measuring comprehensive wealth. As discussed earlier in the book, this is the measure necessary to ensure that we will pass onto later generations at least as many natural and human resources as we inherited from our predecessors. But although the commission emphasizes the importance of measuring balance sheets as well as flows of output and income, it underplays the need for policy to acknowledge what will be left of posterity. Responsibilities to future generations are implicit rather than explicit. The important aspect of the Economics of Enough is to find measurements that will focus policy choices on a longer time horizon and give the future its proper weight in the structures and institutions through which decisions are taken and the economy governed. The measurement part of this challenge requires the development of measures of comprehensive wealth, and although some researchers have made a start on this, the resources and weight of national statistical offices must now be brought to bear on it.

Measuring comprehensive wealth, including natural and human capital, will go a long way toward shaping policy around a longer time horizon. However, it will not be sufficient by itself. The short focus of policymaking was identified as the reason the future debt burden has been allowed to grow to unbearable proportions. Chapter 3 discussed the way the structure of pensions and social security, as well as other deficit spending, has allowed current and past generations to live off the earnings of future generations. The hidden burden has grown to such an extent that it is unlikely to be honored by those future workers. In addition to redesigning the structures of spending that created the problem in the first place, the element of time needs to be incorporated into the accounting system for government finances.

This could be done with the introduction of generational accounts. These are increasingly widely available, although typically as the work of think tanks and academic researchers rather than official statistical offices (although the UK's National Statistics and Treasury have in the past done some work of this kind). For the reasons set out in chapter 3, looking at the impact of current government spending patterns on future tax bills is a very bad news story, and it would take a brave politician to start publishing these as part of the standard official statistics. That courage is necessary, though, to make it possible for policy reforms that might avert the social and political catastrophe that is otherwise the only mechanism for enforcing fiscal sustainability. Again, official statisticians need to undertake this work.

However, measurements that will encourage decision-making over a longer time horizon don't by themselves address the challenge set out in this chapter. Economic growth in affluent societies like the United States and United Kingdom consists more and more of intangibles rather than physical stuff, and although GDP statistics do include services and other weightless attributes such as design and quality, they don't do it all that well. The problem, as the earlier description makes clear, is that the concepts suitable for measuring the number of very similar cars or refrigerators, and the metals and plastics used to make them, aren't right for measuring the care of a doctor or the attention of someone who's gone out to the movies.

For some years now, researchers have been puzzling about finding better ways to measure intangible value, a second area of important statistical innovation. Over the years there have been several research efforts on intangibles.[20] Early in 2009 the U.S. Bureau of Economic Analysis (BEA), which has often been at the forefront of practical statistical innovation, announced that it was exploring the feasibility of the experimental compilation of intangibles statistics in a "satellite account," which would offer a comprehensive framework for assessing this form of value in the economy. This satellite would include human capital, the knowledge captured in computer databases and creative property such as movies and music, brand values and "organizational capital" for example.[21] The aim of the work is to measure investment in intangible assets, but the BEA's report notes that the main barrier is the absence of the underlying measurements—for example, businesses don't record "investment in organizational capital" in their management accounts, so they can't answer questions about it in BEA surveys. And as the statisticians observe, the absence of measurements indicates that the concepts currently applied to the idea of intangible investment are fuzzy.

If measuring intangibles has a long way to go, one alternative way to think about the value being created in advanced economies now is to build statistics around the spending of time, as well as money. The use of time to capture value has long been appreciated—from the labor theory of value in classical economics to the old saying that "time is money." But one result of the impact of information technology has been that time has become quite explicitly a parallel currency. Time and attention are for many people a scarce resource, more in some cases than money and things (although these certainly remain the scarce resource for people on low incomes). For some of us, lack of time, not lack of money, is the constraint limiting what we do.

There are plenty of ways to describe the shortage of time and attention. One is the exponential growth of information.[22] Statisticians from the University of California Berkeley's School of Information Management and Systems found that worldwide production of original information stored digitally increased from around 3.2 million terabytes in 1999 to around 5.4 million terabytes by 2002, an increase of 69 percent in just over two years. Another is the constant innovation in labor-saving devices and methods, dating as far back as household electronics for busy housewives in the 1950s and 1960s, and now bringing us domestic robots and time management systems. Mobile communications and computers at home have brought the pressures of work into free time. The Blackberry is mocked—and resented—as the "Crackberry." Everybody, or at least everybody who works, is busy all the time. The pressure on our time has become one of the most familiar aspects of modern life. It's one of the motives behind the emergence of the Slow Movement, described in chapter 1.

An interesting aspect of the trend is the emergence of a gift economy online, with the gift consisting of the time spent contributing to online activities for no pay, a kind of digital volunteering. Much has been written about the prevalence of "free" content.[23] While traditional businesses such as record companies and newspaper publishers see their profitability under threat from the resistance of consumers to pay for digital content whose marginal cost is zero, a few novel online models depend entirely on the contribution of users' time for free so that other users in turn can access it for free. These are the open source activities such as Wikipedia and Linux.[24] The gift economy was prevalent before money; anthropologists have documented the cultural importance of giving gifts of food or pots or decorative items as a signal of social ties and status.[25] The gift economy is reemerging, at least in the online sector of society, as a postmoney measure of value. People now give time, and time contributed is a sign of status and social connection in online communities.

There is a telling contrast, however, between the high status of this kind of unpaid activity, and the traditional area of "non-market" activity such as domestic work and caring. Spending hours caring for children or disabled or older people is certainly a gift too. What's more, these activities overlap with the growing paid-for care sector, also low-status work that is often carried out by immigrants and typically characterized by low pay and poor conditions. With an aging population and shrinking public spending, the extent of paid-for care is bound to continue growing. For the reasons given by Will Baumol in his classic papers, it will grow as a share of the economy as well as in absolute terms. And there will be a shifting and blurred boundary between paid-for caring and other similar activities in the market economy and unpaid care in the domestic economy, with the time devoted to these activities the common standard of value.

In the world of Enough, in countries where the majority have ample food, clothing, and shelter, the choices people have to make about the allocation of scarce resources are increasingly about how they will spend their time. Time used is an increasingly important indicator of value. Time saved is an indicator of productivity. Of the huge increases in productivity attributed to information and communication technologies, a significant proportion has been due to improved logistics. In other words, due to the increased speed with which components and goods can be moved and the reduction in the time it takes to make things and deliver services.[26] Much of our economy now operates on a "just in time" system.

Although there is no systematic statistical approach to using time as a measure of value, a number of government statistics offices have introduced the innovation of time use surveys as a "satellite" to their conventional "national accounts" that form the basis of GDP.[27] Some of these—including Australia, the United Kingdom and United States—conduct and publish regular, albeit infrequent, surveys.[28] The United States started annual surveys in 2003, the United Kingdom five-yearly surveys in 2000. Australia conducts surveys at longer periods but the surveys date back to 1992. The Australian Bureau of Statistics sums up the purpose of time use surveys very neatly:

> The balance between paid work, unpaid work and leisure are important for a person's well-being and economic welfare. Patterns of time use have assumed increasing importance as a means to measure the productive value of households as economic units. The data collected by this latest survey will be used by the ABS to derive a monetary value for all forms of unpaid work to update measures that assist analysis of the national accounts for the household sector.[29]

The surveys ask respondents to explain how they spend a twenty-four-hour period, looking at the division of time between paid and unpaid work, the hours spent on leisure, personal care, sleep, travel, housework, child care, and so on. Averages can be calculated for different groups—men and women, people of different ages, and the unemployed, among others.

However, even these statistics, important as they are as a part of a full assessment of the shape of the economy, don't add up to a complete picture of the measurement of value.

THE CHASM BETWEEN PRICES AND VALUE

The blurring boundary between market and nonmarket activities goes beyond the traditional question of the contribution domestic activities make to measure of economic progress. As this chapter has set out, a rapidly growing share of the economy consists of activities that have "nonmarket" characteristics. This is partly because of the Baumol phenomenon: we are spending a rising share of income on activities with an intrinsic element of performance or experience, as our countries grow richer. These range from low-status care occupations through traditional professional occupations such as teaching and health care and law, to growing occupations such as the creative professions.

But it is also due to the changing structure of the economy, the fact that important growing industries, including the digital industries, have features that make them surprisingly like traditional public services, with upfront costs but (almost) zero marginal cost. There are many businesses complaining that they can't get consumers to pay for digital content, although it remains to be seen how far this is due to their reluctance to change what it is they charge for and how they do it; a few businesses and nonprofits are getting users to pay by contributing their time rather than money. There has been a vigorous debate about the challenge the presumption of "free" content poses to businesses in music, movies, and publishing. Less attention has been paid to the implications for measuring the economy, and yet conventional statistics do not capture at all well the shape or growth of the new economy taking shape.

There has been real progress in improving economic statistics: in the development of dashboards to supplement GDP; in the measurement of intangible value; and in looking at time use as an indicator of what people value. In each of these avenues, more progress is needed. GDP needs to be joined by a measure of comprehensive wealth; the role of intangibles needs to be better conceptualized in order to collect statistics; and time use surveys based on diaries are neither detailed nor frequent enough to give rich insights into what people do.

A more important point is that in spite of the many measurement avenues being pursued, there is an absence of a broad conceptual underpinning for thinking about the shape the economy is taking and should be taking. None of these statistical innovations, important as they are, will do enough to alter our mental model and the political dynamics. The evolution of existing statistics into the national income accounts, which still frame our assessment of the strength of the economy, came about in the 1930s as a response to the urgent challenges of the Great Depression. In the same way, we need to respond to today's crisis by shaping a new framework for understanding, measuring, and taking action.

SEVEN Values

THE THEME OF THE PREVIOUS CHAPTER was the need to measure better what we value. This chapter is about identifying what we value, in the context of an economy whose structure has been changing in fundamental ways, because better measurements in themselves won't improve social welfare. What's the right weight for policymakers to put on different indicators? How should they assess the metrics? One answer, the one many people would have given until recently, is that this challenge is best left to markets. Markets automatically reflect information widely dispersed through the economy and also the preferences of countless individuals, and aggregate all of that to match supply with demand, "as if by an invisible hand," to use Adam Smith's famous phrase.

For a generation—certainly for the twenty years after the end of the Cold War and fall of communism—relying on market mechanisms seemed the obvious way to ensure the economy delivered for all. Questions of value and values fell out of fashion. For obvious reasons, the earlier big ideological questions of communism versus capitalism seemed to have been settled by history. Political parties ran on their competence rather than ideology in most countries (at least outside the United States, where the culture wars took over from the Cold War as an ideological battleground). The economy was recession free for most of the period. Financial crises were isolated rather than systemic and typically occurred in distant countries where it was easy to imagine the people weren't really up to running a modern economy. In prosperous times, complacency isn't surprising. What's more, that prosperity seemed to validate the often-strident pro-free market views of the politicians who had "won" the battle with communism. Free markets seemed to be delivering all that was promised of them, such as growth, innovation, globalization, and the miracle of the Chinese economy.

Now, from the perspective of the most serious recession and biggest financial crisis since the 1930s, the benefits of markets are doubted and the question of values has come to the fore. This change in sentiment about markets as a means of organizing the economy builds on the earlier anticapitalism of those who protested about globalization. Many people now would probably agree that markets *can't* be relied on to deliver automatically what we value. In which case, the question is how can what society values be identified and achieved? After all, central planning is no more appealing today than it was in 1989. Are we really forced to choose between the inefficient (a government-run economy) and the immoral (a market-based one)?

In this chapter, I argue that this is a false dilemma. Markets are never value free, and so the abstract idea of a "free" market is not practically meaningful. That phrase disguises a particular value-laden version of how markets should operate. There are other sets of values that can and should shape markets in different ways. One reason that the financial crisis has thrown the merits of markets into such doubt in so many minds is that in the way they operated in many countries, especially financial markets, the values they embodied had drifted far away from the values widely shared in our society. If desired social values are reflected in actual market institutions, markets remain the most powerful mechanism for delivering socially and economically beneficial outcomes. So one challenge now is to ensure that the way markets operate reflect fundamental social norms and values—how to make markets moral.

A second reason that markets seem increasingly flawed now, as a social mechanism for matching money and values, follows from the discussion in the previous chapter of the way the structure of the economy has been changing. As discussed previously, more and more of the economy consists of intangible activities whose value is fragile and dependent on the social underpinnings of trust. What's more, many activities now exhibit some of the characteristics of public goods. The way markets are structured and managed (as they all are, by government regulation and laws) needs to reflect the increasing interdependence and complexity of the economy. "Free" market outcomes are unlikely to achieve the best outcomes in terms of social welfare when there are important externalities and a growing degree of mutual independence. So in this chapter I'll argue that markets remain a fundamentally important institution, but the next chapter will look at some of the new challenges of governance.

The Merits of Markets

The economic and financial crisis triggered by the collapse of Lehman Brothers in September 2008 prompted in its turn a wider questioning of the role of markets in the organization of the economy and society. In fact, the questioning of the priority given to markets by the dominant policies in most countries had been under way for some time. The high tide of what some would see as the fetishizing of markets came in the years of Ronald Reagan's presidency in the United States and Margaret Thatcher's premiership in the United Kingdom. The collapse of communism in 1989 cemented their ideological triumph. But successive governments in both countries (as well as international organizations such as the IMF and World Bank) continued to emphasize throughout the 1990s not just the practical merits of markets but their preeminence in society. However, as the decade progressed, and the process of globalization extended the reach of the market economy, dissent grew too. Starting with the "Battle for Seattle," a riot by demonstrators against the World Trade Organization meeting in that city in November 1999, the political movement against globalization and against capitalism grew ever more vocal. While it hasn't ever grown to the scale and significance of the demonstrations

Figure 14. Riot in Reykjavik against capitalism.

of 1968, the anticapitalism movement has had a growing impact on public debate for the past decade. The recent crisis has
reinforced the critique, and questioning the role and scope of
markets has become a mainstream issue. It would be widely accepted now that "market ideology" went too far, especially via
the financial markets.[1]

There's a paradox in this.[2] The steady ebbing of the influence of promarket ideology since the late 1980s has coincided
with a huge increase in global prosperity as the market economy
extended its reach to other countries such as India and China,
as well as the formerly communist nations of central and eastern Europe. In the advanced economies, too, GDP growth was
significantly higher from the mid-1980s on than it had been in
the sluggish years of the 1970s and early 1980s. The combined
impact of new technologies and the global policies of deregulation and privatization increased the rate of productivity growth
and the long-term potential of most of the OECD economies.
Unemployment fell almost everywhere and most of these coun-

tries enjoyed the longest economic boom on record. The recent recession has been severe but hasn't remotely reversed the gains in average per capita incomes recorded in the past decade or so.

Dramatic economic growth comes about when the structure of the economy changes—new technologies are introduced, existing businesses are severely disrupted as old working patterns and organizational structures change. The changes in the economy due to the spread of new information and communication technologies have been discussed at several points in this book. As this kind of restructuring involves changes in everyday social relationships and habits, great strides in economic potential often feel uncomfortable. There has been a long tradition of cultural and social opposition to these effects of capitalism, as described in chapter 1. The shape the opposition takes will change with the times. Certainly, the absence of communism and socialism as credible alternative systems makes current distaste for "market fundamentalism" very different in flavor compared with previous periods such as the 1930s and 1960s when the pendulum of opinion has swung that same way. Be that as it may, the crisis of recent years has certainly reinforced the view that markets have—in some way—gone too far.

But is the antimarket backlash any more than an emotional outburst before the bankers return to business as usual? After all, there were good reasons capitalism triumphed over communism in the Cold War. The alternative economic system of central planning was an utter failure in both economic and moral terms. It delivered neither economic results nor political legitimacy. Built on mass deaths inflicted by brutal dictators, it was morally bankrupt. Nostalgia for an ideology emphasizing social solidarity shouldn't be mistaken for practical politics.

The power of markets, on the other hand, is almost miraculous, as Paul Seabright so eloquently describes in *The Company of Strangers*. It is through markets that the massive complexity and variety of the modern global economy is coordinated. Only markets can convey the vast array of detailed information about preferences, incomes, the demands of buyers, and the costs of sellers. All of this is captured in the prices and quantities of goods and services exchanged, and the pressure for changes in prices and quantities whenever supply and demand are out of line. "The mutuality of advantage from voluntary exchange is . . . the most fundamental of all understandings in economics."[3]

Critics of economics are skeptical about the benefits of markets, arguing that economists have to make too many ridiculous assumptions for their conclusions to have any validity. For example, this line of argument goes, people don't have fixed preferences, don't necessarily know what their preferences are, certainly don't undertake any kind of rational calculations when they go shopping. On the contrary, people are irrational, impulsive, inconsistent. True, up to a point, but these arguments are often irrelevant. Many of the assumptions for which economists are mocked are made for the convenience of writing out mathematical versions of their theories. These mathematical models are useful for working out what will happen. Apart from anything else, mathematics is intolerant of internal contradictions and errors, and so a useful flashlight for exposing flawed theories. But they are only rarely essential to the fundamental insights. So, for instance, the key point about the economist's assumption of rational "selfishness" is not that people really are utterly selfish or that they do formal calculations before purchasing everything, but rather that it's entirely realistic to assume that people will act in their own self-interest on the basis of the information available to them. There is nothing in this that runs counter to human nature—on the contrary, it's in the genes. And the assumption of rational self-interest forms the basis of a powerful way to analyze situations where people do appear to be acting counter to their own interests—it can help identify the information asymmetry or the transaction cost or the psychological trait that would explain the divergence between actual behavior and rational calculation.

What's more, there is much empirical evidence that in many practical situations people with all their cognitive limitations and inconsistencies nevertheless do make choices leading to exactly the outcomes predicted by textbook economic theory. One of the pioneers of this research was Vernon Smith. He shared the 2002 Nobel Prize with Daniel Kahneman but popular attention has focused on Kahneman's experiments casting doubt on market efficiency rather than Smith's experiments demonstrating the validity of classical economic theory about markets. The dual award demonstrated precisely that both psychological frameworks, the rational and the "behavioral," work in certain circumstances—the trick is in applying the right framework in a particular set of circumstances, and I'm not aware of any systematic approach for deciding this. Smith and others have demonstrated that markets frequently do deliver the efficient outcomes predicted by the theory, in effect through a process of trial and error.[4] Participants do not consciously think of themselves as solving a theoretical economic model but nevertheless act as if they are following the laws of demand and supply—just as their physical movements show them acting as if they're following Newton's laws.

The experimental research has also shed much light on the way the rules of engagement in markets affect the prices and quantities. This literature has led to the creation of a discipline of market design. Governments have been able to sell assets for which it would once have been hard to conceive of a market—radio spectrum, for example, or permission to emit pollutants like sulphur dioxide or carbon. Market design can also improve the way government licenses are issued and sold, the way regulations are imposed, or even the way trading can occur on financial markets. In short, it acknowledges that markets *are* designed, and this can either be accidental or more deliberate. Given that government rules and laws set the framework in which all markets operate, how much better it is to think explicitly about their impact.

Markets are essential but flawed. They are essential for exactly the reason spelled out most clearly by Friedrich von Hayek, the conservative economist beloved of more recent free marketeers. That is that markets alone can encompass the masses of detailed information required to match demand and supply in an economy of any size and complexity, coordinating everyone's activities through the signals sent by prices and the impact prices have on people's decisions. In his 1945 article, *The Use of Knowledge in Society*, he wrote:

> The marvel is that in a case like that of a scarcity of one raw material, without an order being issued, without more than perhaps a handful of people knowing the cause, tens of thousands of people whose identity could not be ascertained by months of investigation, are made to use the material or its products more sparingly; that is, they move in the right direction.[5]

Hayek was highly influential in the move toward market-based approaches to economic policy in the 1980s and 1990s. The pendulum has swung decisively the other way, but it's essential to hold on to the effectiveness of markets in so many circumstances.

In sum, it is markets that can meet the huge variety of different demands and wishes people have, and do so astonishingly efficiently, giving people great choice. It's fashionable to say we have too much stuff, have become too materialistic. But markets don't only deliver "unnecessary" goods, whether you think that means designer handbags or tacky plastic toys. Markets bring us a huge array of services from haircuts to design, an ever-growing number of book titles and movies, astonishing scientific and technological innovations at prices that the great majority of people can ultimately afford. Markets consolidate a vast amount of information in the price—information about companies' costs, and about consumers' preferences and demands. The prices set in markets in turn create incentives for behavior that will enable demand and supply to be matched better in future. That's just as true of education, working through the labor market, and the incentives people have to study if wages for qualified workers are high, as it is of the shoe market. Without the market economy we'd be much poorer in every sense of the word. We'd have less money, less choice, less opportunity. One of the main reasons developing countries stay poor is that markets there can't develop, often due to government policies preventing them. Economic development *is* the spread of markets in place of the more ad hoc and personal economy of household production or barter.

SOCIAL MARKETS

Markets are therefore both essential and enhance our welfare, for all the reasons always given by conventional economics. But markets are not value free. On the contrary, actual markets in actual economies embody the social norms and underlying values of the societies in which they operate. It is also a mistake to think about markets and the state as opposites. Markets need an effective state to operate well, and a healthy state will in turn depend on a thriving market sector of the economy. One of the reasons global financial markets failed so catastrophically is because of a lack of effective governance. Financial markets were heavily but poorly regulated, in fact regulated to serve the interests of financiers.[6] This was possible partly because of the myth that markets operate in a vacuum, independent of society. The myth disguised the truth that no well-governed economy should have private businesses deemed by the government "too big too fail," as so many banks were regarded in 2008–9. The big banks had usurped political power. Effective regulation requires an acknowledgement of underlying political, social, and cultural values

So it's a mistake to demonize "markets" in an abstract way. Instead, what's needed now to help address the issues of Enough set out earlier in this book is an emphasis on the need for both markets and state interventions to embody shared values and social norms. Building from underlying values to social norms and shared beliefs will lay the foundations for building more effective formal economic institutions, as I will discuss in the next chapter.

Governments and markets are usually seen as mutually exclusive ways of organizing the economy. While it's understood that modern economies are mixed, with a significant government share in all the activities that add up to GDP, markets and public sector activities are thought of as occupying different and contrasting domains. After all, this was one of the main fault lines of the ideological battle between communism and capitalism. Under communism, the state planned economic activity, set targets for the output of different goods and services, and allocated materials to factories and people to work. Under capitalism, these decisions were decentralized and coordinated through markets and the price signals that emerged from the confrontation of demand and supply. This abstract perspective is all the sharper when we think about "free markets," the benchmark for policy reforms in many countries during the 1980s and beyond.

This opposition between government and markets is false. Both are a type of economic institution, designed to organize our life in large social groups. They are among an array of other types of institution, including households and businesses, and indeed there are different types of "government" organizations and "markets" too. None of these institutions could exist and function outside a basic political framework, usually the nation-state, which provides—with varying degrees of success—a legal framework, including the law of contract and employment laws, protection of property, policing and enforcement, security, standards for weights and measures and other technical features, and a monetary standard, and also sets the macroeconomic context. Indeed, the very concept of property, without which no economic activity from barter onward could occur, is shaped by the state—as Thomas Jefferson observed: "No individual has, of natural right, a separate property in an acre of land. . . . Stable ownership is the gift of social law, and is given late in the progress of society."[7]

"Government" in short is a phrase we use for the compulsory arrangements that make it possible for people to live in large societies. The nation-state is the predominant model of government, but there are supranational arrangements too—for example, the United Nations, the European Union, and a plethora of specialized bodies like the World Trade Organization and International Telecommunications Union.

There is vigorous disagreement about all aspects of these basic functions of government, about how they should be structured, about matters of detail. But even the most ardent "free marketeer" would accept the need for a minimum set of basic government functions. It's usually referred to as the "night watchman state." Many people, most probably, believe that rather more than the night watchman minimum is needed. In fact, once you get away from the extreme positions, there is wide spectrum of views about what the role of government should be.

All other economic institutions, including markets, exist within that context. The division of work within the household is shaped by the opportunities for paid work outside, and by laws such as those banning child labor. The activities of businesses—how many people they hire, the wages paid, the dividends they pay, features of the products or services they sell—are shaped by the law. Indeed, the boundary of a business—its decisions about what to produce in-house and what to buy in as supplies or outsource on the open market—depends on the costs and benefits of these different ways of transacting. Among the transactions costs will be laws and regulations, but there are others such as asymmetries of information. So, for example, tasks that are complicated or that can't be monitored easily because of an absence of information will tend to be carried out in-house.

The finer-grained one's focus is on an economy, the more apparent it becomes that the specifics of geography and history, culture and habit, shape a unique and intricate pattern of relationships. The boundary between a business and the markets in which it transacts will be fuzzy. Bits of businesses are bought and sold, supply chains shift around—and although this might be because a new road opens or a competitor launches a better product, it might equally well be because the purchasing manager of one company moves to another city because of his wife's job. Surprisingly often the people buying and selling in a market transaction will know each other.

This line of argument points to two conclusions. The first is that markets are social institutions. Few are completely anonymous—fully electronic markets on computer may be one example, and big stores in big cities another. Although they are much more anonymous than alternative types of economic transactions, markets still involve human relationships. James Buchanan, one of the originators of public choice theory, put it this way: he noted that the focus in economics tends to be on *choices* by individuals, whereas seeing the economy through the lens of *contracts* between people is equally illuminating.[8]

Another conclusion is therefore that the "market versus government" opposition is not a fruitful way to think about what institutional framework for the economy is best, and we should also consider households, firms, and perhaps other organizational types such as co-ops or residents' associations. Kenneth Arrow said: "Truly among man's innovations, the use of organization to accomplish his ends is among both his greatest and his earliest."[9] The literature of institutional economics is rich with examples of how collective arrangements of many kinds evolve in different contexts. Two key aspects of the context are the regulatory framework and the availability of information and in particular asymmetries of information—things that some people do know and others can't know. This is an area of research for which Oliver Williamson and Elinor Ostrom jointly won the 2009 Nobel Prize in economics. Besides, for the reasons discussed in chapter 3, governments simply don't have the financial scope to expand their activities in the decades ahead. We will have to ensure markets embody the values that matter to the societies in which they operate. Is this realistic, though, or a false hope?

CAN MARKETS BE MORAL?

Few people, even among the most ardent fans of market solutions, will disagree with the proposition that the financial markets have, from time to time, brought scandalous demonstrations of greed. While most traders earning multimillion bonuses no doubt think of themselves as upstanding citizens, the rest of us find it hard to find many shining examples of virtuous behavior on Wall Street or in the City of London. In the notorious words of cinema villain Gordon Gekko (Michael Douglas in *Wall Street*), "Greed is good" is the motto of the markets, but not of Main Street. Likewise, the cartoon "rational economic man" is a selfish being, whereas real people make choices motivated by the moral sentiments of Adam Smith and illuminated by modern evolutionary biology. But does the immorality of the financial markets and the all-out free market ideology they embody in fact corrupt the rest of the economy? Does the efficiency of market outcomes come at a price?

One researcher who thinks so is Donald Mackenzie, an Edinburgh University sociologist. He labels the effect "perfomativity."[10] By this he means that the theory of free markets—based on self-interested individualism—becomes the reality of behavior on the part of people engaged in those markets. He points out that economics is not just a research discipline that seeks to understand the world but also, to paraphrase Karl Marx, changes the world though its impact on policy and decisions. Financial economics has been particularly influential in this respect. Mackenzie and his coauthors single out the influence of Eugene Fama's efficient markets hypothesis, which says that stock market prices capture all available information about the value of the shares and investment managers can never consistently beat the market:

> The efficient market hypothesis is not simply an analysis of financial markets as "external" things but has become woven into market practices. Most important, it helped inspire the establishment of index tracking funds. Instead of seeking to "beat the market" (a goal that the hypothesis suggests is unlikely to be achieved except by chance), such funds invest in broad baskets of stocks and attempt to replicate the performance of market indexes such as the S&P 500. Such funds

have become major investment vehicles and their effects on prices can be detected when stocks are added to or removed from the indexes.[11]

Another example is the huge market for options (OTC derivatives), which were virtually nonexistent in 1990, small in 2000, and worth $604.6 trillion by the first half of 2009. Option pricing theory explains the growth—without the theory about what the prices of these derivative contracts ought to be, there could have been no trade in them. The theory created the reality of the market.

Needless to say, the financial crisis has severely undermined belief in the validity of the efficient markets hypothesis—although its creator, Eugene Fama, remains adamant that the theory is empirically correct. In a 2009 interview, he said:

> Prices are good estimates of the underlying value of the asset. There are real risks of volatility in stocks, and this current episode is a good example. . . . This is not a financial recession. The financial problems are an offshoot. But nobody wants to believe that markets are efficient—especially not investment managers who proclaim that they know better.[12]

A wider question is whether the theory of financial markets has affected not only the reality of those markets, but the wider economy. There are two related questions: One is whether theory directly changes the way the markets operate, the outcomes in terms of prices and quantities traded. The other is whether theory changes the norms of behavior and in this way affects market outcomes. The direct route might perhaps operate in financial markets but the indirect route almost certainly does, and not only in financial markets. The late nineties and noughties boom in financial markets affected social norms. The financial boom evidently led many participants to conclude that indeed, greed was good. Some justified their greed with the belief that the fortunes made by the few would trickle down to the many and increase overall prosperity.

What made this belief not just false but actively damaging was the way greed in finance spilled over as greed in other industries. Executives throughout business, and in the public sector too, came to believe that high pay and large bonuses were a reward for their talent. An industry of pay consultants came into being to dress up this contagious greed in terms of benchmarking against others—the argument was that it was essential to pay executives a salary and bonus comparable to what they could earn elsewhere. This was a self-fulfilling process, as jobs elsewhere were only paying so much because those other businesses had hired the same pay consultants, who told every client company that they should pay their executives enough to attract the best people, and therefore set off an ever-upward ratchet. All sense of due restraint seemed to vanish from the upper reaches of business, as executives came to misinterpret the rise in share prices due to a stock-market bubble as the result of their own talent, and worse, came to feel that extraordinarily high pay was their due because they saw so many other people among their social contacts and peer group making so much. Many bankers are still in this mindset, although executive pay outside the financial markets is gradually deflating.

The boom in the financial markets thus came to corrode social norms throughout the economy. In the countries where it went furthest—the United States and United Kingdom, the most promarket in terms of national political ideology and hosts of the world's major financial markets—the consequence can be seen in the increased inequality described in chapter 4. That chapter discussed the further consequences for the sense of fairness in society and for social capital and trust.

There is wider scope for a clash between markets and morals—it goes beyond the impact of social norms in the financial markets, spreading into society at large. Recent evidence suggests that the structure of the economy has moved voting patterns over time—economies based more on free markets have shifted the political center of gravity to the right over the years, whereas economies based on collective institutions such as union-employer bargaining tend to move toward the left: what voters believe about political choices is affected by the economic structure in which they live.[13] Danny Dorling of the University of Sheffield has argued that adherence to the view that markets are essential for an efficient economy leads people ultimately to believe that some aspects of markets such as the inequality described in chapter 4 are inevitable, and because "free" markets have brought about inequality in educational attainment and income, this must be the result of underlying differences in intelligence or effort.[14]

The issue of performativity is perhaps less significant than the existence of certain situations in which we believe a moral principle, often that of fairness, should trump the benefits of market outcomes. It should be said that economists tend to disagree with this proposition. Princeton economist Alan Blinder once surveyed users of a campus café where there were long queues at mealtimes to ask if there should be a separate till charging a higher price to people who didn't want to stand in line. The economists tended to say yes and others disagreed strongly. However, there are situations in which virtually everyone would agree that markets should be overridden.

On the heels of the latest financial crisis, Michael Sandel has made this point very forcefully. In his book *Justice*, he writes:

> One of the most striking tendencies of our time is the expansion of markets and market-oriented reasoning into spheres of life traditionally governed by non-market norms. . . . Since marketizing social practices may corrupt or degrade the norms that define them, we may need to ask what non-market norms we want to protect from market intrusion. . . . This is a question that requires public debate about competing conceptions of the right way of valuing goods. Markets are useful instruments for organizing productive activity. But unless we want to let the market rewrite the norms that govern social institutions, we need a public debate about the moral limits of markets.[15]

Sandel would draw those limits much more tightly than has been the case in the recent past. His book gives some examples from medicine, where the clash between morals and markets can appear acute. For example, should blood or human organs ever be bought and sold? Another example is provided by rationing in wartime. Conventional economics would appear to suggest that rationing is always a bad idea because by preventing the people who value a certain item the most from buying it, rationing creates inefficiency. Some people value the item less than others but all end up with the same amount. Besides, rationing encourages "black markets" to form, so there is unfairness anyway, as well as inefficiency. However, efficiency is trumped by wider considerations—longer-term ones—such as the greater importance of fairness and social capital when war puts a society under great strain.

What conclusions can we draw? That often efficiency will be the primary purpose of an economic institution or set of arrangements, and in that case a market mechanism is an unparalleled way of achieving it. This is especially true in the most advanced economies, which are large and complex, making markets not only the most efficient but the only viable way of organizing large swaths of the economy.

That market mechanisms are not abstractions, however, but living social institutions that can be better or worse designed to achieve desired outcomes. Governments set the rules shaping the way markets operate and can do so in ways which try to overcome market failures.

And that sometimes efficiency will not be the overriding social aim, in which case markets are not a sufficient mechanism for making and putting into effect social choices. But that raises the question of when efficiency and markets should rule, and when by contrast other considerations matter more. There is no definitive answer. It will depend on circumstances. However, the circumstances are changing. The changing structure of the economy is affecting the way markets should be organized.

How Markets Fail

Two decades after the crisis of communism, capitalism seems to be in crisis. Or so it is widely believed. To mark the twentieth anniversary of the fall of the Berlin Wall—and around the first anniversary of the onset of the massive financial crisis—the BBC's World Service commissioned a survey about capitalism covering more than twenty-nine thousand people in twenty-seven countries. Only in two countries—the United States and Pakistan—did more than a fifth of respondents agree that capitalism is working well. Across all twenty-seven countries, only 11 percent thought the system works well as it stands, while 23 percent said it is fatally flawed—rising to 43 percent in France and 38 percent in Mexico. Clear majorities everywhere except Turkey said they wanted government to be more active in regulating markets. In twenty-two countries large majorities said they wanted to see a redistribution of wealth, amounting to 67 percent of the whole sample.[16]

Whatever one's view on the causes of the financial and economic crisis, such a weight of popular opinion cannot be ignored. Even if you think capitalism is working pretty well despite the crisis—and after all, there have been many crises in financial markets over the centuries—it has to be acknowledged that there is at least a crisis of legitimacy. Majorities of people in many countries do not believe, at present, that markets are doing a good job of organizing the economy.

The immediate crisis is probably the least interesting way in which markets are failing at the moment, however. Financial crises do indeed recur in market economies, at least as far back as the tulip mania of the seventeenth century.[17] The economist Hyman Minsky has argued that there is an internal cycle of capitalism that guarantees there will be banking crises from time to time.[18] There have been a few in recent decades—in 1993–94, 1997–98, in 2001, as well as 2007–8. Each one is different, and the most recent crisis has been distinctive in involving the world's very biggest banks. So each carries new lessons, the les-

Figure 15. The symbolic capitalist bull isn't trusted.

son from the most recent being that regulators have allowed banks to grow too big. The full force of antitrust law now needs to be unleashed on the banking industry.[19]

But although the scale and seriousness of the recent financial crisis has been uniquely severe, it focuses attention on just one way of many ways that markets can fail, namely bubbles in financial markets. Other types of market failure deserve more scrutiny. They are unlikely to lead to headline-grabbing crises but nevertheless have profound implications for social welfare. It is worth underlining that markets even so are the best way of using the resources available to provide people with the goods and services they want. Markets are a uniquely efficient way of co-ordinating the separate decisions of many consumers and firms, reflecting in prices the masses of information needed about their preferences, about costs, about their budgets. According to Paul Seabright, after the collapse of the Soviet Union a Russian policymaker visited the United States and asked who was in charge of supplying bread to New York City.[20] This anecdote is funny precisely because we recognize the much greater effectiveness of the market for making sure people have the bread they need—in all the fantastic variety available in the city.

Having said that, it has to be recognized that *market failure* is widespread. Markets fail because, while they reflect individual preferences and valuations more effectively than any other mechanism, market prices do not take account of the impact individuals have on each other. There is a failure of the assumptions underpinning the conclusion that market prices truly reflect social value and therefore market provision is optimal. The most obvious type of market failure is an *externality*. These occur when the consequences of one person's or one firm's economic activity affect others who were not directly involved in the decision and whose interests were not taken into account. A classic example is the (negative) externality of pollution, such as when a factory pollutes the atmosphere to the detriment of all residents, without paying for clean-up or compensation. Externalities are often now referred to as *spillovers*. A particularly important kind of externality is the one discussed extensively in the first half of this book, the inability of future generations to participate in today's markets, even though they are affected by today's outcomes. Longer-lived institutions are needed for the future to be represented, and for decisions to be taken over a much longer time horizon. This is vital for decisions affecting the environment but also for investments such as large-scale infrastructure or policies that impinge on national assets and patrimony (the national heritage).

Other types of externality are also important. *Missing markets* arise when consumption is *nonrivalrous*, which means that consumption by one person does not prevent consumption by another, and/or *nonexcludable* in that it is not possible to exclude anyone from consuming the good or service. Products of this kind are also referred to as *public goods*, although some may be provided privately. Examples are parks or television programs (both nonrivalrous) and national defense and free-to-air public broadcasting (nonexcludable). If I walk in the park it does not stop others doing so too, and the additional cost of an extra visitor is zero. Covering fixed costs like buying flowers and paying a park keeper is most efficiently done through a fixed fee such as annual membership or a local tax. But determining what level that should be depends on the wishes of all potential park users. These circumstances mean there is often a role for the government to coordinate people's wishes. But note that—referring back to the previous chapter—a number of increasingly important sectors of the economy such as music and software also have these characteristics of nonrivalry and nonexcludability. Moreover, many goods and services are characterized by a lack of information about their quality. This can be either because of an *information asymmetry* between buyer and seller (the seller of a used car knows much more about it than the customer), or because it is an *experience good* which must be consumed to know what it's like, for example watching a movie. Information asymmetries and shortfalls are an important reason why markets might not work efficiently.

It will be apparent that there are many ways in which markets can "fail," more so than was the conventional wisdom in the 1980s and 1990s, and covering many more activities than those normally provided by the government. In fact, the changing structure of the economy means market failures are perhaps becoming more extensive. The share of experience goods has been increasing, and so has the share in the economy of industries with high upfront costs and "public good" characteristics.

A "TRILEMMA": CAPITALISM, DEMOCRACY, AND CULTURE

Why does market failure matter? The reason is that it introduces a gap between what society values and what the economy delivers. The scale of the recent economic crisis has opened many eyes to the shortcomings of capitalism, and in particular to what many would see as its ethical failings. Value is, of course, an ethical concept in addition to being an economic one. Market failure is the economic prism through which the gap between market prices and value can be viewed. There is a moral perspective as well.

A series of books published a generation ago forcefully made the point that capitalism only worked well thanks to the existence of moral values and social conventions that it gradually undermined.[21] Daniel Bell, in *The Cultural Contradictions of Capitalism* predicted that the "voracious sensation- and entitlement-seeking" that were products of capitalism would threaten the health of capitalism itself. He believed that the moral foundations of both communism and capitalism were shaky; that the efficiency of the American economy in delivering on its citizens' desires would threaten the ability to define a consensus on matters of public morality.

Galbraith, in one of his most famous works, *The Affluent Society* (1958), challenged the assumption that the continual increase in material production was a sign of economic and societal health. Because of this he is considered to be one of the first postmaterialists. Fred Hirsch, in *The Social Limits to Growth*, argued that Adam Smith's invisible hand was no longer operative in developed economies. He argued that the luxuries of one generation became necessities for the next as if society were a column moving steadily forward with the rich tasting the fruits that would eventually be conveyed to the rest of humanity. He predicted a future of increasing personal competition in an ever more vicious rat race and that such a process would have a detrimental impact on the moral fabric of society.

These authors were writing at a time when the social strains of the late 1960s and the oil shock of the early 1970s had clearly triggered a crisis of capitalism. The lesson is being painfully relearned by our generation. One example is an essay by Manhattan Institute scholar Jim Manzi, who writes of the "bifurcation of social norms in America," the chasm between patterns of life and behavior of the well-off and the poor. As a conservative writer, he blames welfare:

> A welfare state can best perform its basic function—buffering the human consequences of the market, without unduly hampering its effectiveness—where enough widely shared social capital exists to guide the behavior of most people in a bourgeois direction. But as it performs that function, the welfare state creates the incentives that push people toward short term indolence, free riding and self-absorption—thus undermining the very norms and consuming the kind of social capital it needs to operate.

But he is even handed in this critique:

> Wealthier and better-educated Americans have managed to recreate a great deal of the lifestyle of the old WASP ascendancy. . . . Political correctness serves the same basic function for this cohort that "good manners" did for an earlier elite; environmentalism increasingly stands in for the ethic of controlling impulses so as to live within limits. . . . Such behavior enables multigenerational success in a capitalist economy, and will serve the new elite well. But what remains to be seen is whether this new

upper class will have the nerve, wit and sense of purpose that led the old WASP elite to develop a social matrix that offered broadly shared prosperity to generations of Americans.[22]

Not surprisingly, writers on the left have made the same criticism of the loss of a sense of responsibility and propriety among the rich. In his essay "For Richer" (2002), Paul Krugman describes the root cause of these losses:

> The story of executive compensation is representative of a broader story. Much more than economists and free-market advocates like to imagine, wages—particularly at the top—are determined by social norms. What happened during the 1930s and 1940s was that new norms of equality were established, largely through the political process. What happened in the 1980s and 1990s was that those norms unravelled, replaced by an ethos of "anything goes." And a result was an explosion of income at the top of the scale.[23]

Why does capitalism seem to corrode its own moral and social foundations? Economic growth is a matter of efficiency, and if the rate of growth were all that mattered to us, question marks about the scope for market organization of social life like those just discussed would be an academic irrelevance. For maximum growth, a market framework would unquestionably be the most efficient. How well the economy does is a question of great importance to everyone. Economic growth is, contrary to the wishful thinking of happiness campaigners, important for social welfare. Even after people have a high enough income to meet their basic needs such as enough to eat and an adequate home, acquiring more goods but also importantly more services, more variety and greater quality, continues to increase well-being. The change in the character of the increases in GDP as economies grow rich is important—services of all kinds and features of products that depend on intellect or creativity account for a growing share of our increasingly weightless economies. People continue to want the economy to grow. No politicians will win elections by calling for the economy to shrink or even stand still.

However, it's widely believed that markets have made society worse, in a moral sense. What's more, as the first part of this book set out, we face the acute dilemmas posed by the fact that we've not reached a clear threshold at which we can say people have Enough. Increasing well-being by delivering continuing economic growth will require policymakers to ensure greater sustainability in many dimensions, environmental, of course, but also financial and social. The markets we have now have not achieved this. The boom of the early years of the twenty-first century revealed the limits, not to growth, but to politics in its broadest sense. The way we manage the economy, the institutions shaping who has what, the rules set by politicians—these are responsible for the dilemmas of Enough. The final part of this book will set out some priorities for institutional and political reforms that focus on combining democratic politics with a longer-term horizon so that choices made now take account of posterity.

There is a fundamental issue to address first, though, before turning to specifics. The priority given to economic growth in political debate is, as we've seen, perfectly valid; it's what voters want. However, it means the debate has come to be almost entirely about questions of *efficiency*. What works? This is the question asked by officials and politicians and in think tanks. "Evidence-based policy" is the mantra in Washington and Whitehall. And quite right too, surely. If policies have a specific economic aim, we don't want to select ones that don't work. For this reason, swaths of the political debate have become technocratic and managerial. This can be seen in the increasing influence of academic research on policy choices, and in the growing number of quasi-independent bodies composed of experts who make important decisions. Independent central banks are one example of this kind of body, but there are many others. There does indeed seem to be some evidence that removing certain decisions from the arena of day-to-day politics improves outcomes (although the boom and bust of this decade have certainly dented the claims of central banks to superior expertise). This shouldn't be surprising. Modern economies and societies are large and complex, presenting difficult problems some of which are indeed highly technical. In areas such as transport policy, energy, education, telecommunications, and many others, it is only sensible to use expertise and evidence to make decisions. Not only will there be a better chance that the decisions will be effective in achieving desired aims and boosting the economy, delegating decisions to bodies of experts might help focus choices on a longer time horizon than the few years at best that form the attention-span of politicians.

But, of course, efficiency isn't everything. The financial crisis has highlighted in many people's minds the need to keep other goals in mind. One of those, as described in chapter 4, is the unease about the unfairness of recent economic growth. The human sense of fairness runs deep. The extent of the inequality that will be tolerated politically can obviously differ in different eras, and the imperative toward greater equality is quite recent in historical terms. However, a desire for a minimum equality of either incomes or opportunities is part and parcel of democracy.

It's debatable whether or not a dynamic capitalist economy has to go hand in hand with democracy. Historically, the two have coevolved, and of course the collapse of the communist economies adds weight to the sense that there is a link between a successful and innovative economy and the demands of democratic politics. What happens in China as it continues on its capitalist path will test whether the link is inevitable. However, most of the leading economies are democracies, and democratic societies are populist societies. Fairness in a democracy where policy decisions are tested by popular vote requires not too much inequality, and it requires the provision of welfare and public services so that everyone (in principle) has a fair opportunity. Fairness is what makes the drive for an efficient economy politically legitimate. While fairness is essential in the Economy of Enough, there are some obvious trade-offs between the institutions democratic governments have created to deliver such demands and the financial sustainability addressed in chapter 3.

The trade-off between efficiency and equality is a familiar one. All economics textbooks note that there are circumstances when more unequal outcomes would generate faster growth. For example, progressive taxation helps equalize incomes but has an adverse impact on incentives to work harder. But this textbook trade-off simplifies reality too much. Not only do modern democracies have a commitment to a minimum degree of equality and entitlement, but also to individualism and self-expression. Given the complexity and scale of modern economies, and the diversity of the people living in them in today's globalized world, combining these separate desirable aims is challenging. In his 1976 book sociologist Daniel Bell labeled these separate social aims—efficient growth, equal entitlement, and individual choice—as *The Cultural Contradictions of Capitalism*. As the title implies, he argues that they conflict:

> The economic dilemmas facing western societies derive from the fact that we have sought to combine bourgeois appetites which resist curbs on acquisitiveness. . . .; a democratic polity which, increasingly and understandably, demands more and more social services as entitlements; and an individualistic ethos which at best defends the idea of personal liberty and at worst evades the necessary social responsibilities which a communal society demands.[24]

Is it impossible to achieve all the elements needed to enhance social welfare? Bell's book implies the existence of a "trilemma," in other words that it is possible to achieve only two out of the three aims simultaneously. In recent times Western economies have focused on growth and individualism but this has been achieved at the expense of equality. If equality is prioritized instead, as social chasms in some countries would seem to require, then in a diverse society with huge variation in incomes and capabilities it is hard to see how to avoid the kinds of inefficiencies that would reduce growth. If we did want instead to combine an efficient and dynamic economy with greater equality, Bell argues that individualism and self-realization would need to be sacrificed because those who earned the most would have to adopt a self-denying ethic. This was the case in the early years of capitalism, when what Max Weber called the Protestant work ethic led people to moderate their consumption and save for the future; status was linked not to conspicuous consumption but instead to hard work and civic virtue, even as that work contributed to the economic growth which made higher consumption possible. The ethic isn't unique to Protestantism; other traditions share the idea of the importance of the common good, outlasting the individual's interests. Indeed, there seems to be a pattern of swings from periods of inequality and social tension, coinciding with innovation and a dynamic economy (the 1870s, 1920s, 1960s) to periods of sobriety and cohesion (1890s, 1930s, 1970s).

If there is a "trilemma," which means only two of the three elements of social welfare are attainable at the same time, this chimes with a wider "impossibility theorem" in social welfare theory. Famously, in 1951 economist Kenneth Arrow asked whether individual tastes and preferences could be aggregated in a way that was logically consistent, obeying a set of seemingly innocuous conditions—and concluded that the answer was "no." Among the assumptions were that citizens had free choice and a range of credible alternatives before them. Each individual in the society (or equivalently, each "decision criterion") is assumed to assign a particular order of preferences to the set of possible outcomes. Arrow was in effect looking for a preferential voting system, a "social welfare function," which would transform the set of individuals' preferences into a single preference order for society as a whole.

Arrow's general theorem of possibility (commonly known as his "impossibility theorem" and for which he won the 1972 Nobel Prize for economics) says that if the decision-making body has at least two members and at least three options to decide among, then it is generally impossible (given his reasonable-looking set of logical assumptions) to design a social welfare function that implies an entirely free choice. Building on Arrow's work, Amartya Sen, another Nobel economist, has argued that one can make consistent and rational social choices from a range of options that is limited in sensible ways.[25] He writes that coming to terms with the impossibility problem in the case of social decision mechanisms "is largely a matter of give and take between different principles with different respective merits" (Sen 1995). This literature too points to the need to find ways to focus on certain elements of social welfare in decision-making rather than engaging in a futile effort to achieve everything.

A different take on the "impossibility theorem" of social welfare comes from Michael Sandel, the eminent Harvard philosopher. He sets out three fundamentally different approaches to the idea of justice. In his book *Justice* he describes approaches to ethical questions based on utilitarian principles, principles of liberty, and principles based on the idea of civic virtue. Utilitarianism asks what choices will add most to the well-being of the largest number of people. It underpins economics and has great power as a lens for making the kind of trade-offs that pervade economic decisions, but can ride roughshod over the rights and ethical claims of individuals who are not part of the majority. Philosophies of freedom have brought our modern focus on individual rights, and there's no doubt that the priority given to freedom and individual choice in modern political theory and practice has been hugely beneficial. Amartya Sen is one of the prominent advocates of this approach to social welfare. A third approach—and the one preferred by Sandel himself—emphasizes the role of civic virtues as a guide for social choices. Neither the greatest happiness of the greatest number nor personal liberties, he suggests, can deliver important aims that most people would consider to be socially important, including all the dimensions of sustainability discussed earlier in this book. For that, there is a need for societies to have a strong sense of the values and ambitions that matter.

Each of these approaches has clear merits, and it seems likely that each therefore has its place. In the realm of trade-offs and technical economic decision-making, the "what works" approach of economics and evidence-based policy must be the right one. But—as we saw very clearly in the debate among economists about how to address the challenge of climate change—some issues might take us outside the territory of choices at the margin. Yet there are equally obvious attractions in an emphasis on freedom and individual choice. Sen and other economists have amply documented the importance of freedom for the practical benefits a free society brings as well as the intrinsic merits and impact on people's well-being. One example is Sen's famous demonstration that famines do not occur when there is freedom of the press;[26] and other economists such as Tim Besley have also shown that there is a link between some of the classic political and social liberties and favorable economic outcomes.[27] Equally, though, the appeal of a shared set of collective values in societies that have become fragmented and dissonant is also clear. There may be no single framework that is right in all times and circumstances, but perhaps this is, as Sandel would argue, a time for rediscovering values that can be almost universally shared.

Few people would argue that policymaking has delivered everything we might desire in terms of social well-being in recent times—after all, this is why there's a need for the Economics of Enough. If aiming at everything means we simply miss the target, how should we set priorities or limits? If it is not possible to find a way of aggregating social welfare so as to achieve all the distinct aims people might have for their societies, then which aims actually matter? Selecting values is an important political choice, often submerged in economic policy debates but unavoidable now. The last chapter discussed the need for better information to guide policy, and this chapter has discussed the need for clarity about values if social welfare is to be well served by policymakers. The third leg of the Economy of Enough is a set of institutions that ensure that society is governed well, and this is the subject of the next chapter. How might we respond to a general crisis of governance?

EIGHT Institutions

THE RECENT ANNIVERSARY of the November 1989 fall of the
Berlin Wall brought back emotional memories for Europeans of
my generation. Like many children growing up in the Cold War
1960s, I had nuclear nightmares: grey landscapes of ash and
devastation with no one else left alive, and the ticking of Geiger
counters counting out the rest of eternity. The postwar division
of Europe dominated the cultural landscape too. Literature and
the arts were shaped by it, as much as politics and diplomacy.
The whole of 1989 had brought a succession of dramatic and
exciting events east of the Iron Curtain—the strikes in the port
of Gdansk and martial law in Poland; massive and near-silent
Czechoslovak crowds gathering in Prague's Wenceslas Square
in their Velvet Revolution; the opening of Hungary's border
with Austria leading to a quickly growing flood of people from
east to west. The marches in Leipzig in the GDR were part of
a half-continentwide phenomenon and led to the breach of
the symbolic Wall in East Germany's capital. I watched the
events, holding my breath in case it all went wrong at the last
minute, on an ancient small black-and-white television in the
depths of the English countryside. It couldn't have been more
exhilarating. Seeing the images again, twenty years on, was still
an emotional experience.

After the drama of the end of communism came the debate.
Even those who found Francis Fukuyama's famous and trium-
phal declaration of "The End of History" abrasive had to acknowledge that the philosophical basis of communism and economic planning was in tatters.[1] In the economic sphere, the first

chance people on each side of the divide had had for an honest look at each other's way of life made it clear that the capitalist economies had massively outperformed the centrally planned ones.[2] In the political sphere, there was no question about the huge costs imposed by repression, conformism, and the absence of civil liberties on countless individuals. For all the nostalgia now in the Eastern bloc countries for aspects of communism, including the social solidarity of those times, it was proved to be an overwhelming failure.

There is no doubt that the failure of communism and central planning gave enormous impetus to the West's decisive move toward a dogmatic free market version of capitalism, spearheaded by the governments of Ronald Reagan in the United States and Margaret Thatcher in the United Kingdom. The political dynamics and intellectual trends in the economics profession at the time were mutually reinforcing. This was the heyday of "new classical economics," which made much of the merits of markets and the failures of government intervention.

As discussed in the last chapter, the recent financial crisis has drawn attention to the failures of markets instead, especially the financial markets. The outcomes delivered by a market economy might not be those corresponding to the greatest social welfare, as there are values not well reflected in market prices. The experience of a generation's worth of policies emphasizing the role of markets in the economy has disappointed many people. More than that, I've been arguing that a sense of crisis in the order of the economy and society is both widespread and justified. But that doesn't mean, as many commentators have presumed, that fixing the economy just needs the government to take a more direct and active role.

Apart from anything else, governments will not be able to spend directly as much as they have in the past, as we saw from the earlier discussion of the unsustainable debt burdens in so many countries. This chapter discusses some "government failures" or limitations on the effectiveness of some types of policy, regardless of the budget situation. It then goes on to look at how

Figure 16. Economic planning collapsed with the Berlin Wall in 1989.

paying attention to a richer array of institutions and economic rules would improve the way our economies run, above all giving a longer-term focus to both individual decisions and policy-making. "Good governance" is the mantra in current discussions of economic development; it ought to be so for the advanced economies as well. As well as better measurement and clarity about values in society, better institutions are necessary too.

How Governments Fail

Oliver Williamson, one of the 2009 Nobel laureates in economics, pointed out in his acceptance lecture in Stockholm: "Because all feasible modes of organization are flawed, the observation of a 'market failure' does not. . . . warrant regulation (which also experiences failures)." It is a wise caution against the presumption, which has characterized much economic analysis since the pioneers of welfare economics first diagnosed market failure, that the government can always fix the problem.[3] Williamson draws our attention to the intractability of the problem of organizing the economy in some circumstances.

The diagnosis of how governments fail as economic managers starts with the theory of "public choice." Originating with James Buchanan and Gordon Tullock's pathbreaking book *The Calculus of Consent: Logical Foundations of Constitutional Democracy* (1962), this approach rightly gets away from the presumption that decision-makers in government, politicians and bureaucrats, always act in an impartial and objective way in order to improve the welfare of society. On the contrary, like everybody else, they will be inclined to act in their own self-interest, which will include being reappointed or reelected and promoted. The public choice approach was extended by Mancur Olson. He analyzed the way special interest groups can so effectively "capture" government decisions.[4] So government actions will often ignore the interests of other groups or—particularly relevant for my argument here—those who can't vote, including future generations. An economy in which the government plays a large role may well be short-termist and populist even in a broadly honest democracy. In authoritarian countries, or corrupt countries, or those without a vigorous free media, there is no reason at all to expect government intervention to enhance social welfare.

Of course, all Western countries, including the United States with its relatively small public sector, do have extensive government intervention in the economy. The most ardent free marketeers recognize that governments are needed to ensure the rule of law and uphold contracts, to build some parts of the country's infrastructure, to provide services especially at local level—policing, garbage removal, public schools, road maintenance, and so on—and to provide at least a minimal welfare safety net. As the size of government relative to the economy grew in the West during the postwar years, so did dissatisfaction with how well the public sector served citizens. This was voiced in different ways across the political spectrum. John Kenneth Galbraith struck a chord with his liberal political constituency when he wrote of "private affluence and public squalor," which was a call for better as well as more government services. By the time Ronald Reagan said in his first inaugural address, "Government is not the solution to our problem; government is the problem," his audiences were receptive.[5]

Why had government come to seem so ineffective by the 1980s? After all, the share of the economy accounted for by government had climbed from 24 percent in 1950 to 34 percent by 1980 in the United States, and to 43 percent on average in the OECD, so on the face of it, government should have been achieving more. What's more, it's hard to argue that any economy has become substantially less regulated in recent decades. There are several related reasons for the perception that government actions were becoming less and less effective.

First, a large part of the increase in expenditure was due to higher social spending, or in other words spending arising from social problems such as pensioners with inadequate incomes or single parents or unemployment. The share of social spending in total government expenditure has trended upward in most OECD countries, on average from 16 percent in 1980 to 21 percent in 2005.[6] That obviously does not feel like a success. It's also in large part the underlying reason for the unsustainability of government deficits and debts, as discussed in chapter 3.

Second, government regulation has become extensive, even intrusive, without most people seeing obvious benefits to it. After all, financial services were already heavily regulated before the 2008 crash. All kinds of products have safety rules and requirements but these add to the cost and inconvenience of life without preventing significant incidents such as oil spills or auto recalls. There are restrictions on people's freedoms, and the protections gained in return aren't obvious. One argument, with which I have great sympathy, is that regulation has on the whole served the powerful. Dean Baker, for example, argues that financial regulation has helped big banks, regulation of medicines has served big pharmaceuticals corporations, and new laws on copyright and patents are designed to protect the revenues of record companies against the interests of consumers.[7]

Third, and related to this, Western societies have become more complex and difficult to manage. Partly this is due to social change, the sources of the problems just mentioned. Partly, it is due to the continual innovation and specialization in the economy, the globalization of production, the development of new services, the innovation in financial markets. If bureaucrats and politicians were once able to direct the economy effectively from the center, it's hard to see how they could manage it now. It has become harder to identify the public interest as opposed to special interests.

For these reasons, the job of government has grown harder. In addition, while private businesses have on the whole made great strides in improving their productivity thanks to the use of new technologies, there has been little if any improvement in productivity in the public sector. People who are used to lots of choice and good service in their experiences as consumers are disappointed by the low quality of service and its lack of personalization in their experiences as citizens. During the decades that marked the start of large structural changes in the economy, driven by information and communication technologies, the structure of government has changed much less. Nor have governments begun to come to terms with the proliferation of information in the Internet age, and the ways that has changed their citizens' capabilities and demands.

At the same time, the provision of services in the public sector has not kept pace with the productivity changes in the private sector due to new technologies. This is partly a measurement problem, as statistics on public services often use the number of employees to calculate the level of output, making the figures on productivity flat by definition. But it's a real problem too. The adoption of technological tools has often been slow, due to anything from lack of investment to the opposition of strong public sector unions seeking to safeguard jobs and working practices. Strikes are far more likely in the public sector than the private.

The result has been a growing challenge to the authority and expertise of public service workers. By the 1980s, and drawing inspiration from the earlier public choice literature, it was a standard diagnosis that public services were being run by self-serving elites with insufficient attention to the real needs of their "customers," the taxpayers funding them. The reason *government failure* is widespread is essentially because of the shortcomings inherent in having public officials take decisions on behalf of other people while lacking the information they need or the incentives to reflect fully the preferences of those they are supposedly serving. In short, they were unresponsive, inefficient monopolies. One response was privatization, a central policy of the Thatcher government, which caught on around the world. In many countries the past thirty years, have seen large areas of economic activity—telecommunications, energy generation, postal services, transportation, water supply—sold by governments to private investors.

The decade saw too the start of a worldwide wave of reform often gathered under the heading "New Public Management."

The common theme of the reforms was to try to introduce mechanisms of the market into public services, sometimes by creating competition, sometimes through decentralization to more local level of decision-making, often by a focus on using targets to improve productivity and effectiveness. New Public Management aimed to constrain the bureaucrats by implementing some or all of the following features in government:

- Spreading the use of private sector management practices and technical expertise;
- Introducing measures of performance, and performance-related pay;
- Decentralization and downsizing of organizations in the public sector, including the spread of bodies with much greater autonomy from politics;
- Greater competition in the public sector;
- Tougher budget discipline.

The details vary from country to country, but the disappointment with reforms of government under this heading is pretty universal.[8] There is no evidence that efficiency in public services has improved, or that government activity is generating better outcomes. On the contrary, some would argue that the reforms have been counterproductive—competition has simply created gaming in public sector tendering, targets have distorted activity just as much as production targets used to do in the old Soviet Union. As John Kay has put it, "The reasons targets do not work are evident from any study of the failure of planned economies. You can require people to meet goals, but that is not at all the same as encouraging them to meet the objectives behind the goals. By emphasizing targets you undermine both their motivation and their ability to achieve these more fundamental underlying goals."[9]

One particularly strong criticism is that the introduction of values and habits from the private sector has undermined the ethos of public service.[10] As an OECD survey put it, the reforms "failed to understand that public management arrangements not only deliver public services, but also enshrine deeper governance values."[11] To put it starkly, we expect much more from our police service than from any private sector company—public services must also embody fairness, for example, along with all the other values we'd consider central to our ability to live together in society. Perhaps introducing some of the norms of private sector management into the public sector has been in fact counterproductive? The simple-minded application of New Public Management theory, introducing ideas such as performance-related pay from the private sector, might well have weakened public sector collegiality and ethos. The loss of confidence in the public sector has in turn led to the use of private sector consultancy to deliver public services, in many cases spectacularly expensive, wasteful, and vulnerable to lobbying interests.

At any rate, the result of two decades of government reform is that trust in the institutions of government and politics has continued to erode. People broadly speaking still trust doctors and teachers, but not politicians and bureaucrats, and not the institutions of government. In a 2003 Ipsos Mori British poll, 91 percent trusted doctors and 87 percent trusted teachers to tell the truth. The proportion saying they trusted politicians was 18 percent, journalists 18 percent, and government ministers 20 percent. In a 2008 survey, 50 percent of respondents said they trusted the BBC, and 47 percent trusted the British National Health Service. By contrast, 65 percent trusted the government least. The decline in trust began before the reforms introduced by President Reagan and Prime Minister Thatcher, and has continued since.[12]

Both Reagan and Thatcher ran campaigns in which government became an object of ridicule. Ronald Regan declared that he had come to Washington to "drain the swamp" and American culture picked up this antibureaucratic, antigovernment wave. Elaine Kamarck of the Kennedy School of Government found that "a careful examination of the data shows that the decline in trust persisted in the face of changing economic fortunes, it persisted in the face of real governmental accomplishments and it persisted in the face of changes in political parties and policies. And by overwhelming margins Americans attributed the lack of trust in government to the belief that the government itself was full of waste, fraud and abuse."[13]

A year before the election of Reagan and ten years before the fall of Berlin wall, Thatcher launched an attack against the bureaucratic state, referring to it as the "greedy and parasitic public sector." The result of these campaigns and the governments of these two leaders was an era of intense dissatisfaction with government bureaucracy.

The search for a more effective government continues, not least in the way the financial sector is regulated. The earlier discussion about the challenge of government debt, and the crises of fairness and trust, will make it plain that public sector reform remains an urgent issue. I'll return later to the question of what shape it might take, given the scale of interrelated crises of sustainability described in the first half of this book. For now, we should note that although there is a clear appetite for more active and effective government, the history of public service reform, and even more the dismal history of the government-run, centrally planned economy, is disappointing.

Government failure has been a widespread reality.

Indeed, governments fail in many of the same kinds of contexts in which markets fail, and for the same reasons. Neither form of organization can deliver good results in contexts where there is asymmetric information, meaning that one person knows something that others cannot monitor in any way—for example, how much effort they're putting in to their work, or how hard a task requiring certain skills actually is to carry out (think about calling a plumber to fix a leak—you have to trust his diagnosis; likewise with doctors or teachers). That asymmetry will often be linked to a principal-agent problem: public sector workers (agents) are carrying out tasks for citizens and taxpayers (principals), in the way that corporate managers are working for shareholders. The advantage in those relationships is on the side of the agents. Whether a certain task is in the public or private sector will not change the information structure. "Public goods" (in the economist's sense) retain their characteristics making them hard to price and manage no matter who is providing them.

In addition, in both markets and government activities, there may be transactions costs in conveying very detailed and specialist information. One branch of economics has long recognized that very many transactions cannot occur in a market because of the kinds of externalities and information asymmetries listed above. This is why institutions such as firms exist at all. The classic example in the literature of institutional economics[14] is a vertically integrated business that cannot rely on external suppliers because of inadequate information and/or a lack of trust in dealing with another business with its own incentives.[15]

A BROAD INSTITUTIONAL FRAMEWORK

There are problems or "failures," then, with the two approaches to managing the economy that are usually taken to be both the only alternatives and mutually exclusive: markets and governments. However, this is an impoverished view of how economies operate. The array of institutions and rules is much wider. Families, firms, unions, and voluntary organizations are types of economic institution as well. So are informal arrangements such as car-pooling, babysitting circles, PTAs, and so on—sometimes described as civic society. Some thinkers, especially on the right, argue that the growing role of government in the economy has suffocated too many alternative economic institutions.[16]

In a famous passage, Nobel laureate Herbert Simon imagined visitors from Mars looking at the social organization of humans on Earth:

> The firms reveal themselves, say, as solid green areas with faint interior contours marking out divisions and departments. Market transactions show as red lines connecting firms, forming a network in the spaces between them. . . . Organizations would

be the dominant feature of the landscape. A message sent back home, describing the scene, would speak of "large green areas interconnected by red lines." . . . When our visitor came to know the green masses were organizations and the red lines connecting them were market transactions, it might be surprised to hear the structure called a market economy. "Wouldn't 'organizational economy' be the more appropriate term?" it might ask.[17]

Institutional economics was recognized in the award of the 2009 Nobel Prize jointly to Elinor Ostrom and Oliver Williamson, the former a specialist in collective, social institutions and their boundary with markets, the latter in the economics of the firm, and the boundary between businesses and markets.[18] The central message in Williamson's work is that the more people depend on each other, perhaps because they have made specific investments to do business with each other, or perhaps because the business involved is complex and difficult to explain definitively in a written contract, the more likely it is that they will be inside the same firm rather than transacting via a market exchange. Ostrom's focus has been on a type of institution previously overlooked, collective institutions that are neither arms of government nor businesses, but provide effective ways of governing common property such as water rights. She identified, through extensive fieldwork, grassroots institutions that worked better than top-down government interventions based on inadequate local knowledge and detail. Her work helps to steer us even more firmly away from the tempting but bogus idea that we must choose between either "government" or "markets." The institutional canvas is much wider than these conventional tramlines suggest, and this is an important point when it comes to thinking about how, as nations and as a global society, we can design answers to the challenges and crises set out in the first half of this book.

Indeed, Ostrom has set out the central challenge in building the Economy of Enough:

Human societies endure across decades, centuries, and millennia. Citizens in democracies are mortal and endure only for a generation, so to speak. Memory, knowledge, and skills are erased with death. Open, democratic, self-governing societies face the challenge of transmitting information, knowledge, and skills from one generation to the next. Civic knowledge is necessary to sustain the continuity of civil relationships in the conduct of civic affairs by both drawing on past achievements and realizing new potentials. Human rationality is grounded in the condition of fallibility, with potentials for learning. How to realize such potentials will engage each of us in our quest for meaning about the conditions of life that we share with others.[19]

Setting out both the failures of government and the failures of markets is a useful corrective to the tendency to contrast sharply "markets" and "government." *Both* are vital economic institutions. Both are needed to find effective ways of coordinating our lives together in large and complex societies. The debate about whether "free markets" or "intervention" is best, which has so dominated politics and policy for decades, is pointless. Markets work well where governments work well. Governments can only deliver for their citizens if what they do is complemented by a thriving market economy, creating wealth.

In practice, there is a fuzzy boundary between organizational arrangements, and moreover different countries vary enormously in the forms of government intervention in the economy and in what activities take place in the public rather than the private sector. Both the United States and Sweden are very prosperous economies, despite their sharply contrasting arrangements for the boundary between market and government activity. What's more, this boundary changes over time. The public-private boundary reflects voter preferences, and the specifics of history and culture, not to mention changes in technology and the availability of resources—not an objective, once and for all assessment of the existence of certain market failures.

Clearly, there are also likely to be interactions between "market failures" and "government failures." We have seen this all too clearly recently in the heavily regulated financial sector where both market and regulatory failures ultimately led to many banks in many countries forcibly crossing the private-public border to become state-owned or state-controlled. Some problems of coordination are just hard, and any approach to them will be flawed.

That does not mean there are no economic principles to guide us in drawing the boundary. The long experiment in planned economies behind the Iron Curtain demonstrated comprehensively that the public sector is very bad at very many kinds of economic activity—such as producing the right number of pairs of shoes in the right sizes and colours, innovating in consumer electronics or creativity in popular culture, for example. On the other hand, the government can do well in providing public transport, education and health care, basic scientific research, and encouraging sophisticated arts like ballet and opera.

Democratic government is obviously the overarching mechanism for resolving social priorities in the face of market failures. But how to implement collective choices is a challenge given the reality of government failure too. What's more, new technologies are making the challenge even harder.

The Impact of New Technologies

Technological change alters the nature and scope of market failures, as discussed in the last chapter. For example, mobile telephones ended the natural monopoly in the fixed telephony network. This paved the way for the successful privatization of many former state-owned, fixed-line monopolies in many countries, as competition was available from new mobile operators. Similarly faxes and then e-mail have created new forms of competition with the old postal monopolies. Smart cards and electronic monitoring have made it feasible to exclude some drivers from the roads at certain times. In all of these examples, the role of government—the type of intervention needed—has changed.

The new information and communications technologies have had a more profound effect on market economies, however. They form what economists refer to as a "general purpose technology" because they affect the organization of the economy in a wide-ranging way, like steam or electricity or rail in the past.[20]

One widespread effect has been to increase the scope of economies of scale, as there are many industries in which it is now possible to reach a much larger number of consumers at very little additional cost, thanks to the possibilities of online marketing and distribution. Network effects have amplified this dynamic. So in many industries, the structure has evolved into a small number of very large firms competing across all products and services, and often globally, and a large number of small businesses supplying particular niches. Software is a clear example: it costs Microsoft almost nothing to supply one additional copy of its software, as almost all the cost is up-front development. And once enough people are using Word, or Windows, many other people will find it attractive to use the same software. The structure of the software industry is exactly that pattern of a few very large businesses indeed and a proliferation of small ones either selling compatible add-ons or serving niche markets.

That's not the only effect of the new technologies. A larger share of the richest economies is accounted for by "experience goods"—education, health, entertainment, leisure activities—as described earlier. As people grow richer they spend a growing share of their incomes on services of this kind, rather than on the material basics of life. This issue crops up again in the next chapter.

What's more, information itself is a public good. A quotation from Thomas Jefferson making this point has become well known:

If nature has made any one thing less susceptible than all others of exclusive property, it is the action of the thinking power called an idea, which an individual may exclusively possess as long as he keeps it to himself; but the moment it is divulged, it forces itself into the possession of everyone, and the receiver cannot dispossess himself of it. Its peculiar character, too, is that no one possesses the less, because every other possesses the whole of it. He who receives an idea from me, receives instruction himself without lessening mine; as he who lights his taper at mine, receives light without darkening me. That ideas should freely spread from one to another over the globe, for the moral and mutual instruction of man, and improvement of his condition, seems to have been peculiarly and benevolently designed by nature, when she made them, like fire, expansible over all space, without lessening their density at any point, and like the air in which we breathe, move, and have our physical being, incapable of confinement or exclusive appropriation.[21]

The extraordinary decline in the price of communicating information, and spread of access to information, has made this public good "problem" acute—as can be seen from the intense debates about the scope and enforcement of copyright in music and publishing. Consumers might not think about it in these terms, but "free" is the right price from the perspective of social efficiency given that the marginal cost of providing an extra copy of a song or album is zero.[22]

Taken together, these technological developments have altered somewhat the types of market failure that are most pressing. Some former natural monopolies have become much less relevant. On the other hand, in the weightless economy the scope of information asymmetries, consumption externalities, and economies of scale has become much greater. So the information revolution has contributed to the sense of government failure, has extended the scope of some important market failures—and has also posed new challenges for other institutions. As the work of Herbert Simon and Oliver Williamson highlights, businesses are important social institutions too.

The Wider Crisis of Governance

The impact of very low-cost information is visible in the organization of companies as well. During the past two decades there has been an upheaval in the way business is organized. One aspect is the spread of supply chains around the globe, in increasingly specialized activities, to take advantage of lower costs for some components, or specialist knowledge and expertise for others. Adam Smith's division of labor has become a global rather than a national phenomenon. Low-cost and efficient communications have made this possible by enabling the logistics and coordination needed.

Another aspect is the wave of restructuring in the corporate sector, the downsizing and "delayering" in some companies, the new mergers in other cases. The increased scope of economies of scale, described earlier, explains the merger wave that has occurred in each of the recent economic upswings. On the other hand, cheap information has changed the ideal corporate structure from the older model of a centralized hierarchy to the modern model of a networked or matrix organization. Why this should be so can be seen from a transport analogy: the costs of transportation explain why air travel follows a "hub and spoke" arrangement. Similarly, costly information processing made hierarchy the efficient corporate model. The radical reduction in those costs means companies are more efficient if decision-making is as decentralized as information.

The work of institutional economists explains the structure of organizations in terms of transactions costs. Relationships are brought within an institution when the costs of a transaction in a market would be too high. Information makes up one important element of transaction costs, and by decreasing them so much the information revolution has thus contributed to a widespread crisis of governance.[23]

Another important transaction cost is created by distrust. The corrosion of trust in Western societies, described earlier, has increased transaction costs at the same time that reductions in information and communication costs have worked in the other direction. It isn't at all clear what the combined implications for governance will be. What shape should institutions take in future? I'll end this book with some suggestions, but the answer will depend in part on whether the corrosion of trust in our societies continues or can be reversed.

However, it is clear that there is a widespread crisis of governance.

Market failures are pervasive, as we saw in the last chapter. Thanks to the financial crisis, many people have lost confidence in markets, even though over many decades markets have increased prosperity and deliver the everyday miracles of all the bread that's wanted in New York City and every other product and service, in all their variety, that people in the advanced economies want to buy.

Governments are failing too. Inadequate regulation played its part in the financial crisis. Indeed, I think there's a strong argument that the financial crisis was much more a failure of government and of politics than a failure of markets. For example, over the years governments permitted banks to reduce the amount of capital they held, and allowed ever-riskier types of lending and trading activity, and in the United States lifted the ban that used to exist on the same institution doing both commercial and investment banking. There may also be a deeper reason why governments' regulation of the financial sector was so lax. Simon Johnson, the former chief economist of the International Monetary Fund and currently a professor at MIT's Sloan School—not a natural radical—published an article called *The Quiet Coup* in which he argued:

> Elite business interests—financiers, in the case of the U.S.—played a central role in creating the crisis, making ever-larger gambles, with the implicit backing of the government, until the inevitable collapse. More alarming, they are now using their influence to prevent precisely the sorts of reforms that are needed, and fast, to pull the economy out of its nosedive. The government seems helpless, or unwilling, to act against them. . . . A whole generation

of policy makers has been mesmerized by Wall Street, always and utterly convinced that whatever the banks said was true.[24]

John Kay, another eminent economist, made a similar point about the UK government in a *Financial Times* column, "Investment bankers had become the most powerful political lobby in the country and there was no vestige of political support for action to restrain City excess. Light touch regulation was not just a matter of policy but a matter of pride. . . . Little has changed. The government continues to see financial services through the eyes of the financial services industry, for which the priority is to restore business as usual."[25]

The failures of government go wider, however. Public services are lagging in their productivity and failing to deliver what citizens want. The public sector faces a huge challenge in trying to improve when government budgets will have to be slashed by far, far more than any time since before the Second World War.

Other types of organization have also suffered an erosion of confidence. This is certainly true of big businesses. Although many of the critics of multinationals would lump them in the "markets" category, in fact businesses are a distinct category of social organization. And an important reason for the erosion of trust in business is that many—including business executives—have forgotten their social role and responsibilities. The changing norms of behavior in business have, as we've seen, played an important part in making some societies less fair and thus in corroding social capital.

In fact, the loss of trust and the impact of information and communication technologies have caused upheaval in all kinds of organizations in the modern economy, including companies. Some aspects of this are matters for the companies and their shareholders: if they are not as productive as their competitors, there is no wider social issue. Other aspects are matters of public concern, however. In particular, the drive to increase in size in order to take advantage of economies of scale is an issue. There has been a sharp divide among experts on competition policy between those who think that it's good for consumers that Microsoft is so big, because this means lower prices and the benefits of network effects, and those who think it's bad for consumers because it hasn't been possible for new or better operating systems and browsers to serve more consumers.[26]

There are merits in both sets of arguments. As someone who was a UK competition regulator for eight years in the 2000s, I've come to the conclusion that too many companies are simply too big and too similar. Innovation is being stifled. More important, there is a concentration of power in the hands of some big companies. The wider point here is that governance is a central issue in every quarter of the economy. Institutions of all kinds need reshaping if the challenges of Enough set out in the first half of this book are to be tackled.

Public Values and Public Deliberation

The scale of the problems facing Western societies now is so great that addressing them has to be a shared effort with shared values and ambitions. After the period of the 1990s and 2000s, when politicians and voters broadly accepted that economic growth was the top policy priority and the domain of markets in the way the economy is organized should expand, the pendulum has swung firmly in the opposite direction. But voters will still expect their elected representatives to deliver economic growth. What's more, the dire situation of most government budgets and the size of the debt burden mean that strong growth is an essential.

This burden will also call into question the assumption of ever-increasing entitlement, especially in societies as diverse and lacking in cohesion as the United States and United Kingdom. Governments will have to cut spending, not increase it. Yet, as we saw in chapter 3, as incomes grow, people's demand for the kinds of services that are often paid for through taxes, such as education and old age care, will steadily rise. It is difficult to know how these pressures will alter the landscape of politi-

Figure 17. Public space in the ancient agora.

cal choice. But whatever happens, the issue of how good a job governments do will be under the spotlight. The financial crisis made everyone very aware of the scope for markets to fail. We will soon be reminded about how much scope there is for governments to fail too.

Navigating through the multiple pressures of the years ahead is going to require debate about collective values. This has an old fashioned flavor, after decades in which the dimension of political debate was whether the state or markets were the best way to organize society. I think it is now clear that the "either-or" debate, corresponding to the old left-right divide in politics, is inadequate. States and markets need each other in order to be effective. Managerialism is not an adequate substitute, however. Although complicated modern societies do present many technical problems needing technocrats to solve them, benign experts cannot make the deeper choices involved in social welfare decisions. Also needed is a process of public debate about our underlying values, a forum for reaching something like a consensus about difficult choices—as in the idealized public space of ancient Greece.

There has been an active debate in political science about the scope new technologies offer for citizens to engage in decision-making. The possibilities canvassed range from specific deliberations about particular questions, citizens' juries, to the mass online organization of political campaigns as illustrated by Barack Obama in the 2008 U.S. presidential election campaign. But the reality is that most people are extremely uninterested and uninformed about the details of politics and don't want to spend their own time in active participation. After all, fewer and fewer even want the bother of voting in elections, even though some of the most recent (November 2008 in the United States and May 2010 in the United Kingdom) have seen increased turnout.

Still, a more realistic avenue for achieving wider participation will have to go with the grain of behavior. More likely to contribute to a new public space are the more motivated: political bloggers; activists organizing through social networks; participants in public consultations that now take place online and tend to attract therefore many more comments; individuals supplementing traditional media through the creation of what's known in the media business as "user-generated content," that is videos, pictures, and comments created by individuals and sent to social network sites and to the traditional media for onward broadcast. Although still a minority interest, all of these forms of engagement are made easier by the Internet, and so the sphere in which public debate occurs is far wider than was possible only ten or twenty years ago. The impact of the Internet and social networking on politics and voter engagement in general is limited still, but the technologies are making it easier for the interested and engaged to take part in a more active and deliberative political process. Without wanting to fall for any hype about the impact of the new technologies on politics, we can speculate that ultimately they will alter how people perceive and engage with the political and policymaking processes.

THE IMPORTANCE OF INSTITUTIONS

This chapter has argued that markets and governments alike, along with businesses and other organizations, should be considered as different kinds of economic institution, all of which are needed for an economy consisting of millions of individuals to function effectively and sustainably. The Nobel Committee's note on the 2009 prize to Ostrom and Williamson puts this concisely: "Institutions are sets of rules that govern human interaction." It continues:

> One important class of institutions is the legal rules and enforcement mechanisms that protect property rights and enable the trade of property, that is the rules of the market. Another class of institutions supports production and exchange outside markets. For example, many transactions take place inside business firms. Likewise governments frequently play a major role in funding pure public goods, such as national defense and the maintenance of public spaces. Key questions are therefore: which mode of governance is best suited for what type of transaction, and to what extent can the modes of governance that we observe be explained by their relative efficiency?[27]

The two economists were honored, in short, for spelling out that different kinds of transactions in the economy call for different kinds of institutions. If the basis of the transactions changes, so must the governance.

There is much research confirming the importance of good institutions for growth.[28] Earlier Nobel prizes were awarded to economists who had explored this, to Herbert Simon (in 1978) and Douglass North (in 1993), and the idea has been eagerly taken up by economists trying to explain why some developing countries seem to remained trapped in poverty. It is one thing to accept that good quality institutions matter, but another to describe what makes them "good."

What principles can guide us toward ways of organizing the economy to adjust to the deep structural changes under way due to new technologies and also help us address the challenges of Enough? What are the proper roles for markets, government, firms, and other collective institutions? I will save specific suggestions for the next chapter, but set out some general guidelines here.

First, and most important, there is no "right" place for the boundary between public and private sector, or between markets, firms, and other kinds of collective institutions. The types of institutional arrangements that are best for each country will depend on both the structure of the economy and on the preferences of the millions of people whose decisions constitute "the economy."

Because, second, institutions need public acceptance and consent to be effective. This might not amount to formal institutions of democracy—looking at China, for example, it's hard to be sure whether freedom in the political and freedom in the economic sphere have to go hand in hand. However, governance is more likely to be effective if those "governed" are not only willing but also able to modify and improve the institution. In markets, choices about what to buy and supply, and at what prices, provide ample feedback mechanisms. Their radical democracy is one of the many merits of markets. In other contexts, including business, good feedback mechanisms are important.

A third principle concerns the availability of information. As set out earlier, information asymmetries are a source of market failure and also explain many of the actual features of economic institutions. Of course, information has become much more widely available and we swim in a constant ocean of the stuff now, but there are some things that can't easily be known or observed. Ostrom gives an example of controlling a hunting ground: it will be much easier to prevent overhunting by setting seasons when it's permitted and others when it is banned rather than by setting quotas for hunters. It's easy to observe whether or not people are violating rules about closed seasons, but not easy to measure how many animals each hunter is killing. The design of rules is an important knack. The traffic light as an elegant self-enforcing mechanism, described earlier, is a good example.[29]

Finally, for all their merits, the institutional scaffolding for the economy needs to address important market failures. One of the central failures is the inability of markets and politics alike to make decisions with regard to a longer time horizon. In earlier chapters I wrote of the need for the pace of growth and the amount of consumption to ensure that we leave something for posterity—that the comprehensive measures of wealth we will bequeath are no lower than those we inherit. Only the right institutions can ensure that decisions taken today have a sufficiently long time horizon.

Institutional innovation will be vital in the Economy of Enough. Finding better institutional structures—using the new technologies—will be key to ensuring decisions about today's choices and activities give proper weight to the needs of the future. The right structures will involve a more productive and thoughtful interplay between markets and governments than we've typically had in the past, one taking account of the dramatic technological and structural change in the economy. There will need to be an acceptance of the reality that governments and markets will often "fail" in the same contexts because of transactions costs and information asymmetries, so neither one nor the other is likely to offer the best solution. And institutions will need to embody decision-making for a time horizon long enough to represent the interests of future generations.

The time has come to turn to some possible solutions or at least directions for the future.

PART THREE Manifesto

NINE The Manifesto of Enough

THE FIRST PART OF THIS BOOK set out the dimensions of the multiple challenges currently facing the leading industrial economies. It's mainly in the context of climate change that the wider public have become aware of looming crisis, and even in that context there is little sign of tremendous public appetite for changing behavior. But alongside the potential impact of climate change, we face a debt crisis, a result of untenable social security arrangements in aging societies as well as the impact of bailing out the banks that caused the financial crisis; a strong sense of unfairness caused by inequality and the failure of certain groups to benefit much or at all from greater prosperity; and the depletion of social capital against a background of declining trust in authority and institutions. All these intertwined problems add up to an extraordinary set of challenges.

And yet people still want the economy to grow. It is wishful thinking to claim that economic growth doesn't increase happiness. It would be dangerously complacent to plan policies on the basis that citizens won't mind sacrificing growth for the sake of the environment or social cohesion. To do so would be to sacrifice any hope of gaining political traction for change. What's more, poor countries need to continue growing to reduce poverty and satisfy natural aspirations to reach the living standards of the leading economies. Rich countries need economic growth because otherwise it won't be possible to avoid the debt trap and create the political conditions for a less unequal and higher trust society.

However, the nature of economic growth in the advanced economies is changing; new technologies have brought about significant structural change. There is an opportunity as well as a challenge in this. The increase in productivity due to the adoption of new technologies since the mid-1990s holds out the promise of the real benefits of growth—not so much additional material benefits any more, in the advanced economies, as the variety of experience and self-fulfillment. The weightless economy is becoming more interesting and satisfying than the material economy. More consumer spending goes on things that would in the past have been outside the formal economy, and more jobs consist of activities nobody would have defined as work a generation ago. Some critics of capitalism see this as regrettable, the commercialization of previously personal activities. An alternative view is that technology-driven affluence has increased the scope for more people to engage in meaningful and enjoyable work. This in itself will contribute to well-being, given the psychological importance of "flow."

So although the challenges governments—and people—will need to address in the next generation are enormous, the dynamism of economic growth in the Western democracies holds out some hope that they can be addressed successfully.

The second part of this book nevertheless set out some obstacles needing to be overcome on the path to addressing the difficult and interrelated policy challenges facing Western societies. Essential stepping stones for moving from the current sense of undifferentiated and impossible problems are a wider array of measurements including measures of wealth, in order to incorporate a longer time horizon for policy decisions; more thought about the nature of productivity in an economy where a rising proportion of activity consists of intangibles and the boundary between different types of activity is blurring, as productivity properly understood is the basis of value as measured by markets and an element of any wider sense of social value; and a profound rethinking of the types of institutional arrangements through which the economy—and our societies—are organized.

This final chapter focuses on practical steps, taking into account the realities of changing public policy.

Getting agreement on painful changes in policies and institutions could be the hardest part of the challenge. In addition to the difficulty of analyzing the problems, there are also difficulties in finding the processes that can bring about change—especially against a background of a loss of trust in traditional political institutions. As I have emphasized in this book, modern societies, modern economies, are miracles of collective organization. "Government" is the name we give to the formal part of the framework of rules within which we live together. Other institutions, including businesses and voluntary organizations, along with norms of behavior and cultural expectations, make up the less formal or informal part of the framework. The effectiveness of the rules, in this wide sense, will depend on their legitimacy. In the Western economies the institutions of democracy (elections, parties, the legislature) are usually the focus when it comes to considering legitimacy. However, the opinion poll figures cited earlier suggest this is not a good focus—the formal political institutions appear to have lost a great deal of legitimacy.[1] Collective assent to any policy reforms can't be assumed just because a law passes Congress or Parliament; and conversely, policies with wide appeal might never make it through the partisan political process. What's more, although many people share the sense of malaise about politics and the kind of society we have, they are unlikely to embrace some of the changes I've argued will be needed. It's hardly going to be popular when governments cut public spending and jobs, or start to reduce entitlements to pensions or old age healthcare. In many Western countries, the people don't think much of the politicians, but the politicians have a pretty low opinion of electors too, given the reluctance to face up to the need for difficult changes.

For this reason, the proposals below emphasize the importance of the mechanisms for generating public debate and consent. Even in a context of crisis, a change of direction in terms of behavior and policy by hundreds of millions of people is difficult to achieve. The last time the framework for governance and policymaking changed as much as it needs to now was in the decade after the Second World War. Today's Crisis of Enough is a slower burn than the massive trauma of a global war—thank goodness. There is enough of a breathing space that there's time to adapt. But this also means there's a huge challenge in engaging the public debate and winning consent for change.

MEASUREMENT

I make no apology for beginning with the question of measurement. Understanding begins with careful observation and measurement. This is just as true of human society as the natural world. The information technology revolution—computer processing power, online databases, social networks—mean there is a massive opportunity to collect much more and better data on our societies and economies, and then to analyze and act on it. Nobel laureate Herbert Simon once noted: "In the physical sciences, when errors of measurement and other noise are found to be of the same order of magnitude as the phenomena under study, the response is not to try to squeeze more information out of the data by statistical means; it is instead to find techniques for observing the phenomena at a higher level of resolution. The corresponding strategy for economics is obvious: to secure new kinds of data at the micro level."[2]

The measurement question has several aspects. One is supplementing GDP, the measure of the flow of income generated by the economy each year, with a wider array of statistics measuring social and economic progress. Growth is essential for social welfare but other things will also contribute and governments should certainly monitor them too. But in addition, the way GDP is measured has not kept up with the changing structure of the economy and the intangible nature of growth. A better measure should include activities outside the market economy such as caring within the household and other uses of time. And the measurement of wealth, in its different forms—natural capital, human and social capital—must urgently be added to the measurement of income; the balance sheet of the economy is just as important as the annual change.

Improving the statistics we use to steer the economy is in principle the easiest of the reforms I suggest here, but nevertheless hard enough in practice. In large part, the challenge is a question of research. Economists and statisticians need to work on the concept of comprehensive wealth and its components, in order to bring future impacts of current policies into decision-making; on generational accounting, so the future pension and welfare burden is made explicit; and on the concept of productivity in services and intangibles as a step toward a better assessment of value. They need to create the required statistical framework, develop new surveys in place of existing surveys of activity, and start to collect the figures.

What does this imply?

Switch resources in official statistical agencies away from the current focus on ever-more detailed aspects of the existing national accounts in order to:

- invest more in statistical research and innovation to address the conceptual gaps—in particular comprehensive wealth and measurement of intangibles;
- until comprehensive wealth accounts are available, develop a wider set of progress measures, drawing on an extensive public consultation on the Australian model;
- estimate and publish a thorough assessment of the true government debt burden, including correcting the frequently used accounting fudges and taking into account future implied pensions and welfare obligations;
- invest in new "satellite" accounts covering environmental impacts, household activities, and time use, and link them with conventional economic statistics;
- all of which will require ceasing collection and publication of decreasingly relevant statistics.

The last step alone will prove surprisingly hard, as it turns out that everything will have some users who'll complain if they lose "their" statistics. But stopping painting a statistical portrait of the economy the old way will be almost as important as finding a new description. Historical statistics show that each economic epoch has its own character. Late Victorian statistics have a mass of detail on agricultural products, the legacy of an economy until recently dominated by food production, and a few figures on indicators of the new industrial economy, the length of rail tracks laid, number of factories, and exports of coal. By the 1930s, statistics covering the mass production industrial activities had taken the place of this rural portrait, but it wasn't until the 1940s and 1950s that the current national accounts framework was put into place. This framework now needs to undergo a significant evolution again, and to release the resources to do this work, statistical agencies will need to cut some current areas of work to fund new ones.

As the historical experience shows, it takes some years, or even decades, for a new conceptual framework to replace an old one. The switch requires a transitional approach—the patterns revealed by partial new statistics will help the development of a new framework. The most important single contributory factor will be an acknowledgement on the part of governments and statisticians that the switch is needed, that the existing framework is no longer adequate for assessing the economy. While there is plenty of good work taking place in official statistical offices, there's an understandable reluctance to concede that what's in place now is no longer good enough. Much of the work needed—as, for example, on comprehensive wealth measurement, or obligations to future generations—is being undertaken by academic researchers. It will need the weight of officialdom behind it.

There's a much greater problem in developing adequate statistics for poor economies, which have neither the money nor expertise to do so. Existing statistics are pretty poor anyway.

Even where they exist, there's great uncertainty as to their accuracy, given the means of collecting data. The gap that matters most for developing economies is the absence of comprehensive wealth measures, in order to demonstrate the almost-certainly shocking erosion of natural capital and absence of human and social capital in very poor countries. Such measures would lead to a marked change of perspective in policy development. In order to tackle the gap, innovations in technology and software will be needed to collect the necessary raw data. There are exciting examples showing the potential for the mobile phones and Internet applications to aggregate user-generated information. Existing applications include election monitoring and conflict reporting, but this is a promising and realistic avenue for the collection of statistics relevant to comprehensive wealth measures.[3] The next step in advancing this is:

- shift some current aid funding (a relatively small amount will be sufficient) to finance R&D on mobile and web applications that will improve information flows in developing economies;
- and to finance the training of officials so that they can monitor and collate statistics.

In fact, user-generated statistics could be useful in Western economies too, although they will prove essential in poor economies. Conventional economic statistics in the OECD countries are collected by surveys of businesses or shops or individuals. It's an expensive process as the surveys need to be very large scale. The statisticians should look at using "user-generated content" and new technologies in order to cut costs and make the transition that's needed in the figures they collect.

There has already been significant innovation in measurement of the economy, as will be clear from some of the examples given in earlier chapters. This includes time use surveys, which I believe will need to be refined and more widely adopted to understand trends in both well-being and productivity in services. It includes also something like both the process and the outcome of the statistics in *Measuring Australia's Progress*. The indicators in this publication are selected via a public consultation and provide the wider array of measures of the economy indicated by the well-being debate. In addition, the OECD (in its "Measuring Society's Progress" project) and the Sen-Stiglitz Commission for President Sarkozy of France have made recent contributions to the debate about supplementing GDP with other indicators. So on this particular question there has been much research already, with a high degree of consensus as to how to go about it; and the issue now is putting the weight of resources and political will behind it. Involving the wider public in the selection of indicators seems to me essential, not only for its legitimacy but also because it's their well-being that is supposed to be the object of the exercise.

There has also been a good deal of work on improving current GDP statistics, measuring intangible value and productivity in services, as described in chapter 6, including by leading agencies such as the Bureau of Economic Analysis, the Australian Bureau of Statistics and the Office for National Statistics. This is a detailed and complicated area of research. It strikes me as increasingly Ptolemaic. The astronomer Ptolemy, making careful observations of the heavens in the first century AD, realized that the view of God's universe with the Earth at its center did not match the evidence. His response was to adapt the earthcentric view to what he saw in reality by adding complicated cycles and minicycles on to the supposed circuit of the sun around the earth; changing to a suncentric theory was a step too far. In the same way, the statistical framework is currently introducing complicated adjustments to the existing measurement of output and productivity. The action really is in the *adjustments*, such as the "hedonic" techniques used to adjust prices of items like computers for quality improvements. However, the key thing is again to put political weight and also resources into continuing this research, as there will be no shortcut to a new framework.

VALUES

This book has covered such a wide range of policies that it isn't possible to set out in any detail the responses needed across the board, from environmental policies to pensions and welfare to financial reform. The details will differ greatly from country to country anyway. Nevertheless, the diagnosis set out in this book points to some clear areas for reform and also some clear principles.

The first of these principles is *stewardship*, the need to ensure that future generations will have at least as much as our own. Lengthening the time horizon for policymaking, whether thinking about carbon emissions or government debt, is an urgent priority.

The second is *revalorization*, or in other words admitting that a market economy operates within a framework of values. If there is a "trilemma," we need to strengthen the leg representing the moral dimension of capitalism.

The third principle is *decentralization*, in the sense that the impact of massively cheaper information costs and the availability of information in the advanced economies make it highly unlikely that top-down decisions by governments will be the optimal way for solutions to the challenges of Enough to emerge. The implication of technology for governance structures will affect politics and the wider institutional shape of Western economies—a point picked up below.

How might these principles work in practice? Just in case anybody is underestimating the challenge, there's a cautionary tale in the lesson of the financial crisis for the prospects of achieving changes in the policy framework. Every commentator agreed that it has been the most serious crisis and recession since the 1930s, and that policy reform is essential. But that reform has moved at a snail's pace given the need to achieve international agreement on both the principles and the practical details of implementation. Two years from the collapse of Lehman Brothers, as I write, very little financial reform has yet been achieved, and indeed the financial crisis has moved into a new phase with the bailout of Greece and crisis of the euro. It will be another three or four years before relatively minor reforms are implemented.

With such difficulty on reforms about which there is such a consensus, but a powerful opposition lobby in the banking industry, how much harder will it be when it comes to far more divisive or political challenges? Chapter 4 of this book argued that the dramatic increase in inequality in some countries, notably the United States, would need to be reduced. The extremes of inequality prevailing today offend our innate moral sense of fairness and will not prove politically tolerable. But it is not just a question of morality but of practical consequences too. The chasms in society—and this is just as true of European and Asian countries as the United States—are corroding social capital to the point where it is undermining the foundations of future economic dynamism.

What will it take to start to narrow the extreme inequality of incomes and life chances? It would be easy to despair of the possibility of doing anything. Past experience suggests that governments can do quite a lot to redistribute incomes after tax and welfare benefits—and indeed they do. This postintervention distribution is less unequal than the pretax distribution of income. However, taxing the rich to give to the poor has its own practical limits, and the evidence suggests that a top marginal rate of income tax above about 50 percent is counterproductive. What's more, it goes against the strong sense in some polities, including the United States, that if people work hard and earn money, the government shouldn't take it away from them. This practical limit to redistribution sits on top of an underlying dispersion in earnings which, economists pretty much agree, comes from the impact of new technologies on the earnings potential of highly skilled people—the "superstar" or "winner takes all" effect described in chapter 4.

Yet it is too pessimistic to conclude that nothing can be done to reduce inequality, as a great deal could be done to change the prevailing social norms about income. And it's linked to the essential reforms of the financial system that are slowly under way. Organized crime aside (a boom industry since 1989), the most ostentatious flaunting of wealth has emanated from the banking sector. As it turns out, these vast earnings and bonuses were undeserved. The bankers ran up large losses, ruined their shareholders, and left taxpayers with the bill. It will be extraordinary if they turn out to have fooled, scared, or bullied politicians around the world into stepping back from fundamental reform of the banking sector. There is as close to consensus as I've ever experienced in the economics profession that the financial sector should not be allowed to retain the structure and behaviors that caused the crisis—although as yet politicians have done nothing fundamental.

The banks are too big, too connected to each other so that when one failed the whole system came tumbling down, and too similar so that each went awry in the same way. They have served low-income customers very poorly indeed. Plenty of reforms have been suggested. Through breakups enforced by antitrust agencies and through regulations such as higher capital requirements, banks should be made smaller. More effective competition is needed to ensure banks serve customers better. For example, the authorities need to encourage the entry of new competitors. These could be community banks. They could be completely new entrants using new technologies such as mobile phones, with low costs allowing them to offer a better deal to customers. The power of the big banks in the developed world means poorer people living in the United States and Europe now have less access to financial services than people in developing countries who can transact by mobile phone or access microfinance if their incomes are low.

However, the key point about the reform of big finance for my current argument is the impact such high incomes in banking have had on the rest of society. The bonuses far in excess of salaries, and the spending on big houses, fast cars, and designer clothes they funded, did create a climate of greed. People in other professions who are in reality in the top 1 percent or even 0.1 percent of the income distribution were made to feel poor by the bankers.[4] Banking bonus culture validated making a lot of money as a life and career goal. It made executives working in other jobs, including not only big corporations but the public sector too, believe that they deserved bonuses. Remuneration consultants, a small parasitic group providing a fig leaf justification for high salaries, helped ratchet up the pay and bonus levels throughout the economy. The whole merry-go-round of bonuses and performance-related pay is a sham. In almost every occupation and organization it is almost impossible to identify the contribution made by any individual to profits and performance—complicated modern organizations all depend on teamwork and collective contributions. Some individuals do stand out and can be rewarded in the traditional way with increases in basic pay and promotions from time to time.

The UK government introduced in late 2009 a penal tax on bonuses above £25,000 in banking (these are bonuses on top of large salaries, of course). The tax was criticized, not only by bankers but also by others who thought the measure impractical. But it was one of the few measures any government has so far taken to reform banking that was absolutely right. The symbolism is vital even if by itself the measure doesn't bring to an end the corrosive culture of greed. Whatever the practical limitations on their actions, governments can still achieve a lot in symbolic terms, which should never be underestimated when it comes to impact.

Governments could do a lot more to change the social norms that helped destroy the Western financial system. For example, they could halt bonus payments in the public sector altogether, or introduce a general additional tax on nonfixed parts of people's pay packages. I am not opposed to people making more money if they studied hard, or worked hard for it, or took the risk of setting up a successful new business—on the contrary, effort and entrepreneurship must be rewarded amply. Nevertheless, governments have to give a lead in restoring the sense of moral propriety and social connection between those people who are part of the extraordinarily wealthy global elite and the great majority of those with whom they share their own nation. Senior bankers should also contribute to this task of making greed and excess socially unacceptable once again. I know from personal conversations that many eminent bankers are ashamed of their industry, but they've been much lower profile (not least because they'd be accused of hypocrisy) than their colleagues who are completely unrepentant about what's happened in banking. One exception is Stephen Green, chief exec/chairman of HSBC: "The industry has done many things wrong. It is important to remember that many ordinary bankers have always sought to provide good service to their customers, but we must also recognise that there have been too many who have profoundly damaged the industry's reputation." Too many people, he continued, had "abandoned asking whether something was the right thing to do and focused only on whether it was legal and complied with the rules."[5]

Most, however, have focused their energy on threatening dire consequences if politicians should have the temerity to legislate to constrain the unfettered activities of banks, which almost destroyed the economy and will scar the public finances for a generation.

The financial sector is a good place to start when it comes to ensuring social values have their proper place in the management of the economy. But it also demonstrates the intractability of some of the challenges. Achieving change will require a combination of policy changes introduced by governments, new regulations, tax changes, and so on, and changed social norms. The formal rules set by governments interact with informal ones to shape the economy. The effect of the informal, the social norms, shouldn't be underestimated, as the example of the spread of greed in finance and big corporations and from there to the rest of society so clearly shows. Indeed economists have shown that there is a social contagion in many dimensions of life, such as obesity, crime, or suicide.[6]

Governments can influence social norms—examples of successful antismoking campaigns show how powerful government action can be. However, our own behavior as individuals, and our own social relationships, are important too. We can and should change our own patterns of spending.

One of my themes has been the need for the future to weigh more heavily in choices made now, choices by governments, companies, organizations, and individual consumers. In several ways, the past generation or two have been running down capital so much that the economy inherited by future generations will be poorer—perhaps catastrophically so, if climate change does indeed occur on the large scale of some predictions. Giving the future its due weight requires the current generation to invest more now.

Some forms of this investment will be nonfinancial. However, many will either directly or indirectly require people to save more for the future and spend less on current consumption.

This is a bit of a generalization as there are countries such as Japan and Germany where both businesses and individuals do save a high proportion of their incomes—although these examples are countries where the aging of the population has become so marked that even with high savings rates the implied pension debt burden on the future is still too high. There are also emerging countries, in particular China, where the savings rate is so high it could be considered excessive. Chinese savings have been allowing American consumers to enjoy their present level of spending and government services, but at some point Chinese consumers will want to enjoy the benefits of their thrift themselves.

In the United States and United Kingdom in particular, the level of savings has dropped much too far; in the boom times up to 2008 there should have been much more. The U.S. household savings rate declined from 9 percent in 1995 to 5.2 percent in 2007, though it had a surge in 2009 to 6.9 percent. For the United Kingdom, the ratio declined from 10.3 percent in 1995 to 2.2 percent in 2007, and rose sharply from a negative figure

(–1.1 percent) in the first quarter of 2008 to 8.6 percent in the third quarter of 2009. An increase in savings ratio is normally associated with an economic downturn, but the ratio is also boosted by the fall in interest rates that has reduced mortgage payments. For the period 1987–2007, the United Kingdom had the lowest mean saving rate as a proportion of GDP of OECD countries for which data exist. The savings rate of the United States was only slightly higher. The U.S. savings rate has been lower since 1980 than in the years after the Second World War. United States net national savings fell to –2.5 percent in the third quarter of 2009, the lowest level since the Great Depression. And whereas savings in the private sector has been on the rise, including both households and corporate savings, government deficits have swamped savings in the private sectors.[7]

Things that have to balance always, after the fact, do balance, and this includes the deficits and surpluses of the different groups in the economy—individual households and businesses, the government and foreigners. With a huge government budget deficit in both countries, and low savings on the part of the household sector, inflows of financing from foreign investors have been keeping the national financial accounts in balance. There is no chance of the government deficits vanishing quickly. Foreigners are losing their appetite for investing in the two countries, although not (yet) catastrophically quickly. How this rebalancing will come about is another matter. The most likely mechanism is that the dollar and pound will fall sharply in currency markets, causing inflationary pressures, which will lead the two central banks to increase interest rates. A more appealing mechanism is if the returns on investment opportunities such as equities and corporate bonds rise due to productivity gains and innovation, but it would be risky to count on that— and anyway, if that were to be the case the foreign investment would still be around too.

So increasing saving by the private sector is partly a question of macroeconomic adjustment in big deficit countries like the United States and United Kingdom. But there needs to be behavioral change on the part of individuals as well. Saving in order to invest in the future is an important characteristic of a healthy economy and society. The Nobel economist Paul Krugman (in one of his nonpolemical outings) wrote a profound paper about what it is about a society that delivers economic growth.[8] Why are some dynamic and others stagnant? He presented this as a formal endogenous growth model, in which the path the economy takes is described by a series of equations that capture the way inputs of capital, labor, and human capital (that is, people's intelligence, skills, and knowledge) are turned into outputs of goods and services, and the way investment in both physical and human capital comes about. Two parameters turn out to be decisive in determining whether the economy is trapped in a vicious cycle of stagnation or achieves a virtuous circle of investment and growth. The first reflects the shadow of the past—whether people's decisions are heavily affected by the weight they put on past experience. The second reflects their expectations for the future—are they confident about the likely returns on their current activities and do they think the future is important? Growth is in a sense self-fulfilling. An economy is dynamic if the people who constitute it think it will be.

In recent times, British and American consumers (as a whole) have demonstrated scant interest in the future. The bill for this irresponsibility is due. A change in expectations and attitudes is overdue.

People's behavior responds strongly to incentives. There are economic tools that can make a difference to saving rates. Higher interest rates are one, but so are sales taxes that make spending less attractive. Behavioral economists have identified a number of techniques for prompting people to save more—a simple and effective one is making people opt *out of* rather than opt *in to* retirement saving plans, or in other words have their contributions deducted automatically from their pay unless they choose *not* to do so, in contrast to the current convention that people make an active decision to join a saving plan and have deductions made from their paycheck.[9] Employers can set these up—it doesn't have to be a government policy. Financial regulators can insist that banks and finance companies play their part in the way they structure accounts. For example, do they make it more or less automatic that money in a checking account above a certain limit is "swept" into a savings account, where customer inertia is likely to leave it? The banks would rather have it sit in the checking account earning zero interest. But the way many banks exploit customer inertia at present—in exactly the opposite direction by requiring people to make an effort to get the best rate of interest available for them—is nothing short of scandalous. Is it too easy for people who cannot really afford the repayments to get credit cards and loans? The evidence of the boom and crash suggests it is.

Economic incentives can be strongly supplemented by other, social or behavioral, influences. During the Second World War governments turned to the power of advertising and appeals to patriotism to persuade citizens to save massively in the form of purchases of government bonds. The message would be different now but the scale of the challenges might well justify a similar technique. But it doesn't all have to be down to the government. When I was a child there was a savings club at my school, to teach us the habit; we all put in a penny or so each week (I think my parents gave me six old pennies as pocket money). Schools and places of worship could do the same now, under community banking legislation. Parents and older relatives have a massive influence on children's behavior; perhaps an online business could supplement their range of gift vouchers with savings vouchers for doting grandparents to give as birthday and holiday presents.

Some economists would argue that an increase in thrift shouldn't come too early, as the first priority is to make sure the economy pulls out of recession, especially when central banks have to stop printing money and raise interest rates, and when governments have to start cutting deficits and spending. For a year or two this is probably correct. Yet over the horizon of five to ten years, the people of a number of OECD countries, especially the United States and United Kingdom, will have to reverse the bad habits.

An increased amount of domestic savings will also be needed so companies can invest in future growth. The behavioral change needed on the part of business is to invest for the longer term. Many businesses (there are exceptions) currently demand that investment projects pay back in just two years; projects that would be profitable over the longer term are hard to get funded now. Of course this requires more financing but it's something to be encouraged (and the structure of tax incentives can help here). Businesses also need encouragement to look at the non-tangible aspects of investment returns as well as the financial returns, and a comparison of alternative plans should include the social and environmental impacts as well as the financial prospects, but also an assessment of *purpose*. What are we doing this for? There are many small ways in which governments can encourage businesses with a purpose in place of the blander and bigger businesses that have come to dominate the Western economies. They will differ from country to country. One example of a small measure that struck me as obviously sensible came from an article the novelist Jeanette Winterson wrote about her small community food store near London's historic Spitalfields Market. Why, she asked, couldn't the government encourage small enterprises with a lower tax rate on their premises? Why did she have to pay the same rate as a large supermarket chain?[10] Other countries will have different levers governments can use to indicate a sense of values and priorities: every tax code has its follies.

INSTITUTIONS

It will be clear from the example earlier of governments' impotence to respond to the financial crisis that there is a problem with politics. In fact, there are many examples of the ineffectiveness of conventional politics.

In the United States, President Obama was elected by 53 percent (with an increased voter turnout of 61.7 percent) on a platform including health reform. In opinion polls, 34 percent of Americans said they wanted him to go ahead—higher than the proportion of the population (15.8 percent) with no health insurance.[11] The reform bill struggled to pass Congress, and the president had to compromise on his plans. Normal enough, but conservative opponents of the president, both elected representatives and sections of the media, were unabashed about telling lies to try to kill the reforms—including some extraordinary inaccurate statements about the UK's National Health Service.[12] There's nothing at all wrong with partisanship per se as there are so often trade-offs and tensions in public decisions. But a country in which the public interest of extending health insurance coverage to all its citizens figures so little in the decisions made by politicians and in which the media have no sense of the obligation of impartiality is in a sorry state. Health reform was passed in the end, but American democracy looks much less inspiring than it did when I lived there twenty-five years ago.

The United States is certainly not alone in having a dysfunctional formal political system, though. The pervasive difficulties of all the advanced democracies involve the roles of elected politicians, the bureaucracy, the judiciary, and the media. Also in play is the vulnerability of decisions to lobbying by powerful interest groups and the use of legal challenges to political or official decisions, whether by businesses or campaign groups. In most Western countries, it is increasingly difficult for either bureaucrats or elected politicians to get *anything* done. Special interests have a stranglehold on many aspects of policy, all the more so in countries where fundraising for frequent elections is required. The heat of partisanship, of personal interests, of bitterness in politics, is torching the possibility of holding political or public office with an impartial, objective sense of public service. This is not necessarily the fault of the individuals taking part in the processes, most of whom certainly start out motivated by the idea of serving their fellow citizens. But the system is broken. Voters have no respect for politicians or the political system, bureaucracies are increasingly ineffective, the law seems progressively further removed from the administration of justice, and there is scant sense of responsibility in wide swaths of the media.

This is all reflected in the evidence, cited in chapter 5, of the loss of respect and trust people have for the formal institutions of politics and government, and for much of the media too. It is reflected in the cynicism of voters and political classes alike. On the whole, citizens ignore the political world as much as they can, and the political world ignores the citizenry as much as it dares. When 44 percent of members of Congress are millionaires, compared with an average income of $39,751 in the United States, the chasm is clear.[13] So too when Members of Parliament in the United Kingdom claim taxpayers' money for cleaning their moat or buying a second home far from their constituency, and are aggrieved at the subsequent public disgust because they all believe they're underpaid. Their salary (before expenses and allowances) is £64,766 compared with the national median of £20,801. Perhaps the job is worth more—but equally, perhaps too many MPs are benchmarking themselves against bankers and corporate lawyers rather than others working in the public service such as teachers or doctors.

The loss of political capacity is hardly a new complaint. But it matters for the Economics of Enough because not only are the current challenges huge, as will be clear from this book, but in addition the role of the state in the leading economies will be forced to change dramatically. Government budget deficits are already large, and in the short term big cuts in government spending will need to be introduced. Longer term, the provision of pensions, welfare benefits, and other government services will have to change. Taxpayers of the future will refuse to pay such large bills. Indeed, the crunch might come sooner than anybody imagined a short time ago: the investment funds that are among the biggest buyers in the world of government debt have indicated that it's becoming too risky for them to continue doing so. Greece has had to have an IMF bailout already, with Portugal and Spain also seen as vulnerable to defaulting on their government bonds. Bill Gross, managing director of Pimco, one of the world's largest bond funds, said that his firm would be a net seller of UK and U.S. government debt in 2010. He warned about the fragility of the UK government debt market, saying "the UK is a must avoid. Its gilts are resting on a bed of nitroglycerine. High debt with the potential to devalue its currency present high risks for bond investors."[14]

So a reduction in deficit spending and reshaping of public expenditure patterns is essential—and probably impossible, at least within current political structures. Government services will shrink from their current high point. Human needs will not shrink, however, and indeed will probably grow in the aging Western democracies. Something will fill the needs gap, perhaps private provision, perhaps more family care, perhaps voluntary organizations, or some mix of these.

On reflection, it shouldn't be surprising that a major restructuring of politics is necessary. The Western democracies have the political and bureaucratic structures of the mass-production hierarchical world of the late twentieth century, and that isn't a good way to run the twenty-first century economy. All of the private sector has undergone pretty dramatic change since the 1970s crisis—companies have innovated, reengineered, delayered, globalized, and outsourced. Yet the public sector has hardly changed. To give just one—telling—example, even in the United States, which is far ahead of most other OECD countries, it is still relatively difficult to access government services online. Meanwhile, in the sixteen years or so since web browsers and HTML made the Internet accessible to people in general, giant new online businesses have emerged, much of private business has used the technologies to boost productivity and serve customers better, and other businesses that ignored the forces for change are in the throes of an extinction crisis. Yet whether in the executive, legislature, or bureaucracy, the forces resistant to reform in government have largely proven stronger than the pressures to change.

It seems likely that many government organizations will face their own version of an extinction crisis before long. With such a record of resistance to change, self-reform seems unlikely. Public sector reformers have high hopes that widespread access to broadband and social networking technologies will at last do the trick. Certainly President Obama made effective use of them in his election campaign. In the United Kingdom then-opposition leader David Cameron made much of the scope for online engagement to empower citizens.[15]

There is some promise in the use of online technology. From my own involvement in a public sector organization seeking greater engagement with its users, as a BBC Trustee, I know that the technologies do make it easier for users' views to be known and taken into account, and do enforce a transparency that changes behavior. But the same experience indicates that the framework they are engaging with matters at least as much.[16] In the case of the BBC there was a new governance framework for the online consultation to feed into, one explicitly intended to alter the way decisions were made, to incorporate public views into the judgments made, and thereby change the organization.

In the public sector as a whole, technology alone will not achieve much change unless the governance framework changes too. The technology offers a means of gathering directly information about what citizens think, but it's still only a few people who engage even through online means; and besides governments have to use the information they get for anything to change. It is easy to overhype the scope for online technologies to change government. There is obviously some potential but much more thought will need to be given to how to use the technologies to improve engagement and accountability. Different media have in the past had different impacts on democratic engagement: the evidence for the United States is that radio and print enhanced political knowledge but that TV has reduced both knowledge and interest on the part of voters.[17] Online activity and social networks will have a bigger impact in the short term in the way they supplement and substitute for the traditional broadcast and print media. The media are part of the political system, an essential feature of democratic government.[18] The Internet has had a massively disruptive impact on existing news media, and perhaps offers a more direct channel through which politicians can engage with citizens, but it's still not clear what the impact will turn out to be on the politics of the future.[19]

Public sector reform is a huge subject with a huge academic literature, and a couple of decade's worth of failure pretty much everywhere in putting it into practice. We do not have governments engaging their citizens in an informed debate in order to take hard decisions about cutting pension entitlements, or raising taxes to pay for green energy investment incentives, or slicing 10 percent off total public spending every year for five years to keep the country from going bankrupt. I predict we will not get them. People don't really want to face hard choices. Instead, it's likely they will start to work around governments. In a transition from the old, twentieth-century traditional party politics to whatever new form politics will take, we're likely to see much experimentation—including using the online technologies—in creating new processes or institutions to tackle collective problems. Some of this will eventually change the way governments operate.

For example, deliberative processes in which groups of citizens take time to understand the complexities of an issue and debate it could become more widespread. Groups of individuals who are interested in a specific issue are already connecting via social networks such as Twitter and Facebook, debating the choices, and either acting directly or lobbying the officials or politicians involved in decisions. New media are taking shape and engaging the citizens who are most interested. Pretty much every issue can become a focus for this kind of active, informed citizenry; perhaps the official policy world could engage with it. Equally, though, it will require more of citizens—there is an onus on those who want to engage more directly with policymaking to ensure they are well-informed and motivated themselves by the public service ethos. So the technologies offer promising scope for political reform but not the certainty of improvement. We will need to see plenty of experimentation.

INSTITUTIONAL INNOVATION

One of the themes of this book has been the failure of the institutions and rules governing the economy to keep pace with the underlying technological and structural changes. This has been a constant theme of capitalism, given the driving role technological innovation plays in economic growth. So, for example, capturing the fruits of the innovation that we describe as the Industrial Revolution required social and institutional innovations ranging from limited liability legislation to enable the necessary accumulation and investment of financial capital via large businesses to the urbanization of the rural population to create the industrial workforce.[20]

One easy way to see what this means in today's context is to think about the traditional corporation of the 1960s and 1970s. These important social institutions were typically long-lived, certainly enough so for them to be made an important channel for collecting taxes, for running and delivering pensions and other welfare benefits such as health care or maternity pay, for training the workforce—and also, for that matter, for collecting statistics. They were hierarchical, and many workers would expect to spend years working their way up a single organization. As already pointed out, the new information and communication technologies have changed the optimal shape of organizations, and this has been reflected in more then twenty years' worth of corporate restructuring. Both the boundaries of businesses and their internal structure have changed. The wider social restructuring has yet to occur.

It will. People are using the access to information they've gained. For example, in the decade to 2009, the proportion of U.S. households with a broadband connection rose to 63 percent, ten times the proportion in 2000; 247 billion e-mails a day were being sent, compared with 12 billion in 2000. The number of pages indexed by Google rose from a billion to over a trillion; and the number of daily searches from 10 million to an estimated 300 million. The number of Wikipedia entries (in English) climbed from 20,000 in 2001 to 3.1 million in 2009. And with three hundred dollars, the amount of hard disk space someone could buy rose from 30 gigabytes to 2,000 gigabytes (2 terabytes) in 2009.[21] The United States has been at the forefront of the spread of access to the digital and online world, but the trend has been similarly dramatic in other OECD countries.

So individual citizens now swim in an ocean of information and access to communications, which they eagerly use. A number of authors such as Clay Shirky or Ori Brafman and Rod Beckstrom have written in some detail about what the implications of this distributed access to information and scope for decentralized coordination might mean in terms of organizations.[22] It's probably too early to be confident about any specific predictions, and one should be cautious about excessive techno-optimism, but nevertheless the lesson of previous waves of innovation in history is that institutions and society will be reshaped by new technologies. The incredible spread of access to information and communications today makes institutional innovation inevitable.

WHAT NEXT?

One of the contributions I hope this book makes to public debate about our economic future is to bring together in one framework of analysis several challenges. Each is serious enough in itself, but looking at them together makes it clear that the way the advanced economies have developed in the past generation cannot and will not continue. Looking at the problem as a whole, it is apparent that the way we individually and collectively respond to various challenges will change; and so the question to ask is how we can manage the change for the best, in order to avert the distress and disruption—perhaps even catastrophe—that would result from ignoring the need.

Managing change as a society, or indeed as a closely linked group of societies, will only happen if there is a shared analysis. The measurement questions I summarized earlier should be addressed urgently. But the failure of the Copenhagen climate change talks demonstrates clearly that even when there's ample statistical evidence of a problem, it can be too difficult to get the political consensus or momentum necessary. Likewise the inability of politicians to get a grip on the financial industry. Our existing political structures are not working well; neither elected politicians nor officials are easily able to implement any "difficult" policies. There are several reasons for this dysfunctionality, including the existence of some underlying social fractures that make consensus difficult to attain. One important reason is that the hierarchical governance structures we've inherited from the past are not appropriate or effective any longer.

Political leaders themselves recognize the need to find innovative ways of engaging with citizens, and are in various ways in various countries introducing some experimentation. However, it's up to us to engage with these efforts or to try other experiments ourselves. The political legitimacy of alternatives will build only slowly. Even though elected politicians are not held in high esteem, being elected remains an important source of legitimacy. But expertise and a clear sense of public purpose are sources of legitimacy too. After all, this is why some think tanks and academics already hold great sway over policy debates. Those of us who care about the challenges set out here can and will engage in the response. It will probably look messy, and it will be hard to identify a single "right" answer. In complicated modern economies, a wider portfolio of institutions is likely to be needed, and we should get out of our heads the few, simple categories of organization we're used to thinking about.

However, the most important changes will be the changes in our attitudes as individuals, and in the way we influence each other. The key attitudes will be acknowledging the future and acknowledging that our individual choices affect other people. In other words, we need to internalize a sense of responsibility to others, including those not yet born, in order to restore the moral fiber that is needed for market capitalism to deliver social well-being.

So, for example, each of us will need to combine our enjoyment of higher incomes and all that we can buy with them with the need to save more. Growth can and should continue but must be more sustainable. Higher savings are needed to fund greater investment in green technologies as well as continuing innovation in other industries. Innovation will help sustain a rate of growth sufficiently high to help ease some of the challenges of Enough. People in many OECD economies will also find that they need to save more to pay for some things their governments used to provide through the tax system, notably pensions. The scale of the implied public pension debt is too large for future taxpayers to finance it.

We will find ourselves rethinking the role played by the state in many cases too because of the rising share of our incomes that will need to go to services often provided by the government, including education and health. There isn't really a difference between buying education services and buying entertainment services in terms of the underlying economics. This means that people in some countries will probably have to discover a greater sense of self-reliance than they have been used to, and also points to the need for a debate about when the shared experience and opportunity arising from state provision is so important that a service ought to remain in the public sector. Education will through this lens look very different from old age care; it matters that everybody in a community has a similar knowledge base and set of attitudes and cultural values arising from similar educations, and investment in education is important for the whole economy, a public good in which people individually would not typically invest enough without public spending. Providing meals and nursing care for seniors is something any civilized and prosperous society will care about, but does not need for society's well-being to be a shared, common experience in the same way.

THE FIRST TEN STEPS

This book has had a large canvas, and the implications its conclusions have for policy decisions and the structures of government are wide. It's always easier to diagnose than prescribe when it comes to economic and social ills. So I want to end with some specific proposals for governments to help get started on the challenges of Enough.

1. Launch a Measuring Progress exercise, where none is yet carried out. Undertake extensive public consultation about what indicators the government should use to supplement GDP statistics. Commit to annual publication of the selected indicators, and a high-profile occasion on which the government will comment on the results, such as the presentation of the government's annual budget.
2. Ensure official statistical agencies have the resources and make the commitment to developing and publishing statistics on intergenerational accounts, so the extent of the true government debt burden is known and published; and to developing new statistics on intangible value, household activities, and time use.
3. Introduce policy measures to encourage increased savings by individuals. One important kind of measure would encourage saving directly. The details of how these might work will be specific to each country, but they could range from "opt out" schemes for retirement saving and additional tax incentives for long-term savings to the encouragement of cultural change—for example, by including the importance of saving in the school citizenship curriculum. Another kind of measure

would discourage spending, via taxes on consumption and specifically high-carbon consumption. Many countries have preferred to tax income because it is easier to make this a progressive system, taxing the well-off relatively more heavily. However, income tax systems have become complex with many distinctions and loopholes. A consumption tax approach could be much simpler, with some scope for progressivity, and could also readily be used to discourage high-carbon products and services. It always used to be commentators on the right who favored a consumption tax, but the increased concern about over-consumption has also swung some left-of-center commentators behind the idea.[23]

4. Ensure that tax systems encourage businesses to invest, and to do so over a longer time period than the two-year payback period that characterizes much current business planning. Again, the practical details will differ in different countries. But to give some examples, the tax treatment of dividends versus debt will affect companies' financial time horizon; the tax treatment of acquisitions as opposed to investment in organic growth likewise.

5. Make the old-fashioned virtue of public service a priority in implementing the inevitable cuts in public expenditure and reforming the provision of services. The process of cutting spending on services is bound to be painful, as the early experience of Greece shows, and is bound to be affected by compromises and deals. Still, it's essential that electorates have a sense that reforms are driven by more than financial necessity, and there are important principles and values involved as well.

6. Governments should address the extremes of income inequality. There needs to be a three-pronged attack. The first prong is the use of the moral scope for governments to influence behavior and norms through public comment. The second prong is using the tax system and the law to drive out the excessive use of bonuses; for example, the tax law might state that bonuses should not exceed base salaries. The third prong

is tackling legal and regulatory structures that give some professions market power allowing them to charge high fees and salaries, such as undue restrictions on entry into professions such as law and banking.[24] These steps should come on top of the government's normal use of the tax and welfare system to support society's poorest and most vulnerable members.

7. We need experiments in the use of the Internet to engage citizens more directly in public policy. Even if relatively few people take part, methods such as deliberative consultations on important decisions might prove an effective way of improving transparency and legitimacy in decision-making, and offer a defense of policy decisions against lobbying and legal gaming. Some political scientists are skeptical about the role online engagement can play in political processes, especially given some evidence that it can polarize opinion rather than achieving greater consensus.[25] But even if these skeptics are right about its direct impact, the Internet will indirectly affect the important role of the media in democracy and the provision of information to citizens.

8. Governments should consider also introducing or making greater use of institutions with an explicit duty to take account of the long-term and future generations. For example, one idea that emerged from the two opposition parties in the United Kingdom's 2010 general election and was implemented by them in the coalition government is a body responsible for long-term fiscal stability, as a counterweight to the short-term political pressures inevitably reflected by government decisions. The new body, the Office for Budget Responsibility, is required to comment on the impact of aging on the government's tax and spending plans. Some countries will have some existing institutions whose role is to act as guardians of posterity, but all countries need to pay more careful attention to their institutional framework.

9. This goes too for the world as a whole. I've spent little time in this book discussing the international economic institutions, as that's such a huge subject in its own right. However, they

clearly need reform. Their problem isn't just an insufficiently long time horizon but also their lack of legitimacy. From the European Commission, through the proliferation of UN agencies such as the IPCC, to the IMF and WTO, they are remote from voters, and sometimes even from member governments. The required reforms will be varied, but the common themes should be the clear embrace of a public service mission, openness, and greater direct engagement with the members of the public whose lives they will ultimately affect.

10. Each country should pursue its own policies to address the risk and likely degree of climate change, absent international agreement. Different populations will make different assessments, but it's vital to recognize that given the scientific uncertainties and moral judgements, there is no "right" answer as to what policies to introduce. This is properly a matter for democratic debate, and the debate therefore has to occur at the national level. There is no international agency with the credibility to tell national governments what they should do. But even without international consensus, any individual country can introduce a measure such as a carbon tax, to nurture new technologies and clean energy investment.

The success of any of these ten steps, whether these are measures to reduce income inequality, get citizens more engaged in policy deliberations, or persuade a nation to develop a long time horizon, depends on education. This hasn't been a book about education reform either, but ensuring people have the education they need to earn, participate in policy debates, and develop strong shared values is the central task of governments in running the economy as if the future matters.

Two centuries ago, in the early stages of the Industrial Revolution, and again just over one century ago in the high Victorian era, the restless dynamism of capitalism and the upheaval caused by new technologies presented our forebears with similar challenges to the ones we in the West face now. We still rely on some of the investments they made in response to the challenges of their times, and on the institutions they created. To look at some of the masterpieces of late-nineteenth- and early twentieth-century architecture or engineering, for example, is to be awed by the confidence those responsible were expressing in the future, and by the commitment they made to it. Less visible but no less important are the political, legal, and social institutions they bequeathed their successor generations. What is our legacy going to be?

ACKNOWLEDGMENTS

This book is dedicated to Kathleen Coyle, 1922–2010, who taught me everything that's important.

I have ranged widely, and I'm grateful to many people for their assistance and comments.

My heartfelt thanks to Ed Glaeser, Paul Seabright, Peter Sinclair, Gerry Stoker, and an anonymous referee for their helpful advice and comments on early drafts, and also to Peter Dougherty of Princeton University Press and my agent Sara Menguc for their constant encouragement. To Lindsay Fraser and Mary Beth Sutter for research assistance and helpful comments. To the following for their input on different parts of the book during its creation: Richard Baggaley, Tim Besley, Dave Birch, Philip Blond, Richard Bronk, Madeleine Bunting, David Fell, Ann Graham, Bob Hahn, Andrew Haldane, Jonathan Haskel, Will Hutton, John Kay, Stephen King, Adam Lent, Thomas Levenson, Janet Lewis-Jones, Michael Lyons, Ed Mayo, Bethan Marshall, Richard Marshall, Vincent de Rivaz, Mark Vernon, Danielle Walker-Palmour, David Wolman.

Above all, my love and thanks to my family, Rory, Adam, and Rufus, for putting up with me during the inevitable ups and downs of writing.

Responsibility for any errors and omissions rests with me.

NOTES

Notes to Overview

[1] See for example Chancellor (2000) for a history of speculative bubbles and Reinhardt and Rogoff (2010) for more recent experience.
[2] For a brilliant analysis of the epidemic nature of financial shocks, see Haldane (2009a).
[3] See for example Nordhaus (1997), Crafts (2010).
[4] Coyle (2003).
[5] Barber (2009).
[6] Schwartz (2004).
[7] For example, Trajtenberg (1989), Hausman (1997, 1999).
[8] Thomas Schelling (1978).
[9] Sen (2009b).

Notes to Chapter One

[1] *Metamorphoses*, Book 11.
[2] Frank (1999).
[3] Ramsey (1928), Dasgupta (2004).
[4] Crafts (2004), Nordhaus (2001).
[5] See my earlier books *The Weightless World* (1996) and *Paradoxes of Prosperity* (2001) for more on technology-induced structural change.
[6] Meek (2009).
[7] Ruskin (1860), 41–42.
[8] Bronk (2009), 4.
[9] Stern (2009), 12.
[10] For example, Frank (1999), Layard (2005), James (2007).
[11] Mill (1863).
[12] For example, Blanchflower and Oswald (2004), Easterlin (1974), Easterlin and Nagelescu (2009), Frey and Stultzer (2002), Layard (2005), Stevenson and Wolfers (2008).
[13] Trollope (1875), Fitzgerald (1925).
[14] Collier (2007), Pralahad (2004).

[15] Klein (2000).

[16] The details can be found on the Friends of the Earth website. See for example http:// www.foe.co.uk/community/tools/isew/templates/storyintro.html; accessed 17 June 2009.

[17] http://www.grossnationalhappiness.com/.

[18] http://www.neweconomics.org/gen/z_sys_publicationdetail.aspx?pid=289.

[19] http://www.ssa.gov/history/reports/boskinrpt.html; accessed 6 April 2010. For a detailed discussion of these indicators, see Coyle (2001), 11–17, and Coyle (2009), 103–9.

[20] Nordhaus (2002).

[21] Sen, Stiglitz, and Fitoussi (2009).

22 OECD World Forum, http://www.oecworldforum2009.org/,http://www.beyond -gdp.eu/download/bgdp-summary-notes.pdf.

[23] http://www.oecd.org/document/53/0,3343,en_40033426_40037349_43963509 _1_1_1_1,00.html. Accessed 31 March 2010.

[24] See for example Kropp (2009).

[25] Australian Bureau of Statistics, Mapping Australia's Progress, http://www.abs.gov .au/AUSSTATS/abs@.nsf/mf/1383.0.55.001?opendocument#from-banner=LN.

[26] Layard (2005), 33.

[27] The term was coined by Phillip Brickman and D. T. Campbell (1971).

[28] Layard (2005), 48.

[29] Haidt (2006).

[30] Crafts (1999).

[31] Johns and Ormerod (2007).

[32] For example, Angus Deaton (2008); Betsey Stevenson and Juston Wolfers (2008).

[33] Stevenson and Wolfers (2008), 3.

[34] Inglehart et al. (2008).

[35] Helliwell et al. (2010).

[36] See Blanchflower and Oswald (2004), Frey and Stutzer (2002), Van Praag and Ferer-i-Carbonell (2004), Inglehart et al. (2008).

[37] Sen (2009a).

[38] Ibid., 275–76.

[39] See Gilles Saint-Paul (2010) on the authoritarianism of the utilitarian-based approach to "happiness."

[40] Layard (2005), Wilkinson (2007).

[41] Including Mihaly Csikszentmilhalyi (1990), Ed Diener and Robert Biswas-Diener (2008), Jonathan Haidt (2006) and Martin Seligman (2002).

[42] Csikszentmilhalyi (1990), 9.

[43] Diner and Biswas-Diener (2008), 131.

[44] Ibid., 154.

[45] Haidt (2006), 96.

[46] Haidt (2006), 91.

[47] The drugs are the selective serotonin reuptake inhibitors such as Prozac. Haidt writes: "Prozac is a way to compensate for the unfairness of the cortical lottery" (ibid., 43). He does not condemn the use of this class of drugs to tackle depression, although he points out that there are side-effects.

[48] Ibid., 91–93.

[49] Csikszentmilhalyi (1990), 11.

[50] Haidt (2006), 175–76.

[51] Positive psychologists Chris Peterson and Martin Seligman have listed the character strengths whose cultivation promotes virtue in this sense on the website authentichappiness.org.

[52] Diener and Biswas-Diener (2008), 224.

[53] Csikszentmilhalyi, 160.

[54] Haidt (2006), 177.

[55] Barrington-Leigh et al. (2010).

[56] Frey and Stutzer (2007) and Saint-Paul (2011).

[57] See also Sen (1999a).

Notes to Chapter Two

[1] Orwell (1937), part I, section 6. "Dripping" is the fat collected from meat as it cooks.

[2] IPCC (2009).

[3] http://nobelprize.org/nobel_prizes/peace/laureates/2007/gore-lecture_en.html.

[4] Buckley and Mityakoff (2009).

[5] Surveys are included in Stern (2007) and Stern (2009).

[6] Stern (2009), 13.

[7] This inability is well-demonstrated in a China Daily assessment, "Blame Failure of Copenhagen Summit on Denmark, not China," Martin Khor (2010).

[8] "India Opts for Voluntary Cuts on Emissions," *Financial Times*, 4 December 2009.

[9] http://www.pollingreport.com/enviro.htm, accessed 7 April 2010.

[10] http://www.ipsos-mori.com/researchpublications/researcharchive/poll.aspx?oItemId=2552.

[11] Listed in letter from David Henderson to *Financial Times*, 7 April 2010.

[12] http://www.guardian.co.uk/environment/2010/jan/20/ipcc-himalayan-glaciers-mistake. See also http://www.interacademycouncil.net/?id=12852. Submissions were provided to the author by David Henderson, Gordon Hughes, and Ross McKitrick.

[13] http://www.guardian.co.uk/environment/georgemonbiot/2010/feb/02/climate-change-hacked-emails.

[14] I. Castles and P. D. Henderson (2003 a, b).

[15] McKitrick (2007).

[16] Nordhaus (2007).

[17] Nordhaus (2007).

[18] Conference on Global Climate Change, (2007) Robert Mendelsohn, "Climate Policy: Minimizing the Present Value of the Sum of the Abatement Costs and Climate Change Damages for All Time"; Gilbert Metcalf, "Distributional Consequences of Policies to Mitigate Warming Effects by Excise Taxes for Carbon Dioxide Emissions in the United States"; Peter Wilcoxen, "Economic Analysis of

Policy Choices for Dealing with Climate Change"; Ross McKitrick, "Response to David Henderson's 'Governments and Climate Change Issues: The Flawed Consensus.'" http://www.aier.org/research/conferences/climate-change.

[19] McKitrick (2007).

[20] Nordhaus (2007), 21.

[21] Dasgupta (2006), 8.

[22] Stern (2009), 71.

[23] See for example Hepburn and Klemperer (2006).

[24] Brundtlandt (1987).

[25] Dasgupta (2009a), 28.

[26] Solow (1992).

[27] Collier (2010).

[28] See http://www.teebweb.org/; accessed 10 May 2010; and also http://news.bbc.co.uk/1/hi/science_and_environment/10103179.stm; accessed 10 May 2010.

[29] Sen (2009a), 251.

[30] Dasgupta (2010), Diamond (2005); Homer-Dixon (1999); Collier (2010).

[31] Partha Dasgupta (2010), 7.

[32] See Hamilton and Clemens (1999), Dasgupta and Mäler (2000), Arrow et al. (2003, 2004), Dasgupta (2009b) for increasingly general treatments.

[33] Dasgupta (2009a), 42.

[34] Report by the Commission on the Measurement of Economic Performance and Social Progress (Sen et al. [2009], 67).

NOTES TO CHAPTER THREE

[1] Quoted by Achenbach (2010).

[2] http://www.whitehouse.gov/the_press_office/Remarks-by-the-President-on-Financial-Rescue-and-Reform-at-Federal-Hall.

[3] It is a textbook example of the collapse of a market due to asymmetric information set out in a classic article by George Akerlof (1970).

[4] IMF, *World Economic Outlook*, (April 2009), 203.

[5] See also IMF http://www.imf.org/external/np/speeches/2010/032110.htm; accessed 14 April 2010.

[6] Gokhale and Smetters (2003); accessed 1 April 2010.

[7] United Nations Population Division , "Completing the Fertility Transition," 2002 conference, http://www.un.org/esa/population/publications/completingfertility/completingfertility.htm, containing the following papers: "The Future of Fertility in Intermediate-Fertility Countries," http://www.un.org/esa/population/publications/completingfertility/RevisedPEPSPOPDIVpaper.PDF, also "Eamining Changes in the Status of Women and Gender as Predictors of Fertility Change Issues in Intermediate-Fertility Countries." http://www.un.org/esa/population/publications/completingfertility/RevisedCosio-Zavalapaper.PDF.

[8] Sen (1990).

[9] OECD (2006b), 42.

[10] Willetts (2010), 253.

[11] OECD (2006a), EU Projections European Economy: "The 2005 Projections of Age-related Expenditure" (2005). http://ec.europa.eu/economy_finance/publications/publication6502_en.pdf . Page 11 of the latter gives a good schematic of inputs to future age-related obligations.

[12] Speaking at the Global Economic Symposium, Ploen Castle, Schleswig-Holstein, 10 September 2009.

[13] In Q2 they were $80 billion, in Q3 $15 billion, Q4 -$2.7 billion, and Q109 $9.5 billion. See http://fpc.state.gov/documents/organization/99496.pdf and http://www.fas.org/sgp/crs/row/RL34314.pdf.

[14] Spilimbergo et al. (2009).

[15] Lipsky (2010), Speech by First Deputy Managing Director, International Monetary Fund, at the China Development Forum.

[16] Kobayashi (2009).

[17] This will occur as long as the inflation is either partly unexpected, so savers and investors haven't been able to safeguard against it, or there is incomplete indexation of wages, interest rates, etc. to inflation.

[18] Napier (2009).

[19] Jorgenson and Stiroh (2000).

[20] Olson (1996).

[21] UN (2006).

[22] Reinhardt and Rogoff (2010).

[23] http://www.imf.org/external/np/speeches/2010/032110.htm.

[24] See data at http://laborsta.ilo.org.

NOTES TO CHAPTER FOUR

[1] Hobbes (1651), Rousseau (1754).

[2] See for example Camerer et al. (2003) for a scholarly survey, or Ariely (2008) for a popular introduction.

[3] See Smith (1982) and papers in Bardsley et al. (2009), for example.

[4] Levitt and List (2009). See also Levitt and Dubner's *Superfreakonomics* (2009). Besides, as Steven Pinker has written: "When psychologists say 'most people' they usually mean 'most of the two dozen sophomores who filled out a questionnaire for beer money.'" Pinker (2008).

[5] List (2008).

[6] Haidt (2006).

[7] Trivers (1971).

[8] Dawkins (1976).

[9] Pinker (2008).

[10] De Waal (2008), 18.

[11] Ibid., 162.

[12] Sigmund et al. (2002).

[13] Hume (1739).

[14] Sala-i-Martin (2002a, b).

[15] Heshmati (2006).

[16] Milanovic (2005).

[17] Bourguignon and Coyle (2003).

[18] Milanovic (2005).

[19] These updated figures convert local currencies to dollars (so they can be compared) at purchasing power parity exchange rates, which differ significantly from earlier estimates, and the effect is to reduce the figures in "PPP dollars" for incomes in countries such as India and China. So whereas earlier figures suggested global income distribution had changed little in the late twentieth century, they now point to increasing inequality. This doesn't mean the massive gains in income and reductions in poverty in these Asian economies are illusory. It does affect the comparisons of "between country" inequality.

[20] Anand and Segal (2008).

[21] ILO (2008).

[22] A further complication in presenting the evidence is that income distribution can differ a lot when considered before and after the effect of taxes and benefits. Countries differ quite a lot in the extent to which government actions are redistributive and change the after-tax and benefit income distribution. It is also important to be consistent about comparing individual or household incomes— using household incomes avoids having to consider men's and women's earnings separately, because these differ everywhere, but in that case the household income figures should be divided by the number of people in the household as household sizes can differ from country to country.

[23] See for example NEP (National Equality Panel) (2010) for UK figures, Piketty (2010) for France, Wolff (2007) for U.S. estimates.

[24] Piketty and Saez (2006).

[25] Alesina, Glaeser, and Sacerdote (2001); and Alesina and Glaeser (2006).

[26] Krugman (2007).

[27] Krugman (2002).

[28] Testimony before U.S. Senate Committee on Banking, Housing and Urban Affairs, 16 July 2002. http://www.federalreserve.gov/BoardDocs/HH/2002/july/testimony.htm; accessed 22 October 2009.

[29] ILO (2008).

[30] Piketty and Saez (2006).

[31] Bhagwati and Blinder (2009), Blinder (2009), Blinder (2006), Becker et al. (2009).

[32] Kostas (2008).

[33] Blackburn and Bloom (1989), Acemoglu (2002), Saint-Paul (2008).

[34] Rosen (1981).

[35] Frank and Cook (1995).

[36] Coyle (1996), 115–17.

[37] See Saint-Paul (2008), Goldin and Katz (2008).

[38] Alesina and Rodrik (1994), Persson and Tabellini (1994).

[39] Barro (2000), Knowles (2001).

[40] In *Faultlines*, 9.

[41] Wilkinson and Pickett (2009), 3, 5.

[42] James (2007, 2008), Offer (2006), Henwood (2003), Atwood (2008).

[43] Coyle (1996), 2–7; Sheerin (2002).

[44] See Glaeser, Cutler and Shapiro 2003; also Glaeser and Cutler 2005.

[45] Cited in Wilkinson and Pickett (2009), 80.

[46] Kay (2009a).

[47] See for example Donovan et al. (2005), Smith (2008), Pew (2010).

[48] Putnam (2002).

[49] Pew (2007).

[50] Robinson and Jackson (2002).

[51] E. Cox in Putnam (2002).

[52] P. Hall, in ibid.

[53] B. Rothstein, in ibid.

[54] T. Inoguchi, in ibid.

[55] Putnam (2000), 27.

[56] Through what sociologists would describe as "weak ties." See Granovetter (1973).

[57] See for example the survey of this literature in Black and Devereux (2010).

[58] See for example Danny Dorling (2010) on the geographic expression of economic inequality.

[59] Groysberg (2010), 323.

Notes to Chapter Five

[1] "Ugandan Shock as Bank Disappears," http://news.bbc.co.uk/1/hi/world/africa/8164842.stm.

[2] Seabright (2010), 1–2.

[3] Ibid. See also Rivoli (2005).

[4] Sen (2009b), section 3.

[5] See Coyle (1996), chaps. 3–4.

[6] Putnam (1993).

[7] Putnam (2000). See also the website http://www.bettertogether.org.

[8] Dasgupta (2009c) (paper prepared for presentation at the Annual Bank Conference on Development Economics, Seoul June 2009).

[9] Keefer and Knack (1997).

[10] For a survey of the empirical findings on social capital, see Bowles and Gintis (2002).

[11] Nannicini et al. (2010).

[12] Coyle (2007).

[13] The original article and others are available on Intel's website, http://www.intel.com/museum/archives/history_docs/mooreslaw.htm.

[14] Nordhaus (2001).

[15] David and Wright (2005).

[16] Crafts (2004).

[17] Coyle (1996).

[18] Sheerin (2002).

[19] Brynjolofsson and Saunders (2009).

[20] Levy and Murnane (2005).

[21] OECD and UN World Economic and Social Survey (2005).

[22] I can't possibly do it justice here but good overviews of the issues can be found in Held et al. (1999); Woods (2000); Mattl and Woods (2009); Held, Kaldor, and Quah (2010).

[23] http://data.worldbank.org.

[24] Bobbitt (2002).

[25] Hosted by Warwick University, see http://www2.warwick.ac.uk/research/warwickcommission/.

[26] Although the 1997 book of the same name by Frances Cairncross did not make simplistic predictions of that kind.

[27] These reasons were originally set out in a famous passage by Alfred Marshall (1890)

[28] Glaeser (2008), Sassen (2002).

[29] Insight into these areas can be found in Davis (2006) and Mehta (2004), in the context of very different cities. See also the classic description of city economies by Jane Jacobs (1961).

[30] The term is the one used in official forms such as the census and statistics.

[31] See for example Glaeser et al. (1995).

[32] Page (2007).

[33] Alesina and Glaeser (2006).

[34] See also Dorling (2010), who argues that social inequality interacts with beliefs about the nature of society to increase divisions and reduce trust.

[35] Frank (2004).

[36] Haldane (2009b).

[37] Seabright (2010), chap. 1, Coyle (2003).

[38] Archibugi (2008), Siebert (2009).

Notes to Chapter Six

[1] See Annual Disaster Statistical Review, CRED, http://www.cred.be/publications, accessed 30 April 2010.

[2] See for example Roach (2009), Kaletsky (2010), King (2010).

[3] See Rajan and Zingales (2004).

[4] Piereson (2009).

[5] Linklater (2002).

[6] This is well demonstrated by Baker (2010).

[7] Johnson (2008).

[8] Baumol and Bowen (1966) and Baumol (1993).

[9] Hirsch (1976), Galbraith (1958).

[10] Musgrave and Musgrave (1973).

[11] New Economics Foundation (2009).

[12] Baumol (1993).

[13] http://www.nytimes.com/2010/01/03/opinion/03bono.html?pagewanted=all. It seems Bono himself has not been too badly hurt: he is managing director and cofounder of Elevation Partners, a private equity firm investing in the media and entertainment sectors. http://www.elevation.com/index.html; accessed 30 April 2010

[14] Boyle (2008).

[15] Oberholzer-Gee and Strumpf (2009).

[16] Eggar (2009), Arlidge (2009).

[17] Coyle (1996).

[18] The figure is from Ocean Tomo, http://www.oceantomo.com/productsand services/investments/indexes/ot300value.

[19] Measures of Australia's Progress, http://www.abs.gov.au/AUSSTATS/abs@.nsf/mf/13 83.0.55.001?opendocument#from-banner=LN.

[20] See overview in http://www.athenaalliance.org/apapers/MeasuringIntangibles.htm and Corrado et al. (2006); Haltiwanger, Haskel and Robb (2009).

[21] http://www.bea.gov/scb/pdf/2009/01%20January/0109_innovation.pdf. Accessed 10 December 2009.

[22] http://www2.sims.berkeley.edu/research/projects/how-much-info-2003.

[23] Andersen (2009).

[24] Shirky (2008).

[25] Sahlins (1972) and Hyde (1983).

[26] "U.S. Productivity Growth, 1995–2000," McKinsey Global Institute, October 2001.

[27] http://unstats.un.org/unsd/demographic/sconcerns/tuse.

[28] http://www.bls.gov/tus/ for the United States, http://www.statistics.gov.uk/ statbase/Product.asp?vlnk=9326 for the United Kingdom, and http://www.abs .gov.au/Ausstats/abs@.nsf/70e266437a51906dca256820001438b9/bc152d785dd4 b24fca256888001e548c!OpenDocument for Australia.

[29] Australian Bureau of Statistics.

Notes to Chapter Seven

[1] See for example Krugman (2009), Fox (2010).

[2] See Coyle (2001).

[3] Buchanan (2001).

[4] Smith (1982), Plott (2001).

[5] Hayek (1945).

[6] Johnson and Kwak (2010), Baker (2010), Beck et al. (2010).

[7] Letter to Isaac McPherson, 13 August 1813, quoted in Boyle (2009), 19.

[8] Buchanan (1975).

[9] Arrow (1971).

[10] Mackenzie et al. (2007).

[11] Ibid., 13.

[12] Coyle (2009).

[13] De Neve (2009).

[14] Sandel (2009).

[15] Ibid., 265.

[16] http://news.bbc.co.uk/1/hi/in_depth/8347409.stm and http://www.globescan.com/ news_archives/bbc2009_berlin_wall. Accessed 10 November 2009.

[17] Peter M. Garber (1989, 1990, 2000).

[18] Minsky (1992), 6–8.

[19] See Beck et al. (2010).

[20] This anecdote can be found in Seabright (2004, 2010) and is based on its author's personal experience, but has attained the status of urban myth and can be found unattributed in many places online.

[21] Bell (1976), Galbraith (1952, 1958), Hirsch (1976).

[22] Manzi (2010).

[23] Krugman (2002).

[24] Bell (1976), 248.

[25] The assumption of "unrestricted domain" in Arrow's original formulation drives the "impossibility" result, so Sen's contribution was to point out that aggregating social welfare requires the introduction of appropriate restrictions to the questions being debated.

[26] Sen (1999 a, b).

[27] Besley (2005).

NOTES TO CHAPTER EIGHT

[1] Fukuyama (1992).

[2] Spufford (2010).

[3] Medema (2009).

[4] Olson (1965).

[5] The address continued: "From time to time we've been tempted to believe that society has become too complex to be managed by self-rule, that government by an elite group is superior to government for, by, and of the people. Well, if no one among us is capable of governing himself, then who among us has the capacity to govern someone else? All of us together, in and out of government, must bear the burden."

[6] OECD (2009).

[7] Baker (2010).

[8] Dunleavy and Hood (1994), World Bank (2000), Dunleavy et al. (2006); "The New Public Management and its Legacy," The World Bank, (2000), http://www.mh-lectures.co.uk/npm_2.htm

[9] Kay (2010).

[10] Surveys of this literature include O'Flynn (2007), OECD (2001, 2003).

[11] OECD (2003), 3.

[12] Kamarck (2003).

[13] Ibid., 7.

[14] The study of the role, nature, and evolution of institutions in economic growth and economic behaviour.

[15] The well-known difficulty of establishing correct transfer prices within big organizations illustrates how hard it would be for the transactions concerned to involve explicit prices in an external market.

[16] For recent examples see Sowell (2007, 2008), Blond (2010).

[17] Simon (1991).

[18] An overview of their work is available in the 2009 Nobel citation and background paper   http://nobelprize.org/nobel_prizes/economics/laureates/2009/sci.html.   Accessed 8 June 2010.

[19] Ostrom and Ostrom (2004).

[20] Helpman (2004).

[21] Thomas Jefferson, letter to Isaac McPherson, 13 August 1813, http://press-pubs .uchicago.edu/founders/documents/a1_8_8s12.html.

[22] Andersen (2009).

[23] Coyle (2003).

[24] Johnson (2009); see also Johnson and Kwak (2010).

[25] Kay (2009).

[26] European Committee for Interoperable Systems, "The Court of First Instance's Judgement in Case T-201/04, *Microsoft v. Commission.* http://www.ecis.eu/issues/ CFI_Microsoft.htm.

[27] Kungl. Vetenskaps-Akademien, "Economic Governance," 12 October 2009, compiled by the Economic Sciences Prize Committee of the Royal Swedish Academy of Sciences. http://nobelprize.org/nobel_prizes/economics/laureates/2009/ ecoadv09.pdf.

[28] Acemoglu and Robinson (2008).

[29] Schelling (1978).

Notes to Chapter Nine

[1] Stoker (2006).

[2] Simon (1984), 40.

[3] Coyle and Meier (2009).

[4] See for example www.ifs.org/wheredoyoufitin for UK figures: a childless couple earning just £25,000 each have a higher income than 87 percent of the population.

[5] "HSBC's Stephen Green Finds It's not Easy to Attack Bonuses," *Times Online*, 3 March 2009.

[6] Cutler, Glaeser, and Norberg (2000).

[7] Weale (2009).

[8] Coyle (2007).

[9] Thaler and Sunstein (2008), Ariely (2008).

[10] Winterson (2010).

[11] Pew (2009).

[12] See for example, "How the House Bill Runs over Grandma," *Investors Business Daily,* July 2009. http://www.investors.com/NewsAndAnalysis/Article .aspx?id=503058, accessed 11 January 2010; and "Palin Paints Picture of Obama Death Panel," ABC News, 7 August 2009, http://blogs.abcnews.com/ politicalpunch/2009/08/palin-paints-picture-of-obama-death-panel-giving-thumbs- down-to-trig.html. Accessed 11 January 2010.

[13] Center for Responsive Politics, http://www.opensecrets.org/pfds/index.php#avg; http://www.cbsnews.com/blogs/2009/11/06/politics/politicalhotsheet/ entry5553408.shtml.

[14] "UK Crawls out of Recession," *Financial Times*, 27 January 2010.

[15] See for example http://www.spectator.co.uk/politics/all/5686658/little-platoons -online.thtml.

[16] Coyle and Woolard (2010).

[17] Gentzkow (2006).

[18] Sen (1999b), Besley et al. (2002).

[19] A good source for research is the Internet and Democracy Project at Harvard's Berman Center, http://cyber.law.harvard.edu/research/internetdemocracy.

[20] Miles et al. (2009), Landes (1969).

[21] Figures from http://www.forbes.com/2009/12/27/broadband-text-messages-technology-cio-network-data.html. Accessed 11 January 2010.

[22] Shirky (2008), Brafman and Beckstrom (2006).

[23] See for example Frank (2007).

[24] Baker (2010).

[25] See for example Sunstein (2007).

REFERENCES

Acemoglu, Daron. 2002. "Technical Change, Inequality, and the Labor Market." *Journal of Economic Literature* 40:1, pp. 7–72.

Acemoglu, Daron, and James Robinson. 2008. "The Role of Institutions in Growth and Development." Working Paper No. 10. Washington, DC: Commission on Growth and Development.

Achenbach, Joel. 2010. "The National Debt and Washington's Deficit of Will." *Washington Post*, 15 April.

Akerlof, George. 1970. "The Market for 'Lemons': Quality Uncertainty and the Market Mechanism." *Quarterly Journal of Economics* 84:3, pp. 488–500.

Alesina, Alberto, and Edward Glaeser. 2006. *Fighting Poverty in the US and Europe: A World of Difference*. Oxford: Oxford University Press.

Alesina, Alberto, Edward Glaeser, and Bruce Sacerdote. 2001. "Why Doesn't the US Have a European-style Welfare State?" Discussion Paper No. 1933. Cambridge, MA: Harvard Institute for Economic Research.

Alesina, Alberto, and Dani Rodrik. 1994. "Distributive Politics and Economic Growth." *Quarterly Journal of Economics* 109:2, pp. 465–90.

Anand, Sudhir, and Paul Segal. 2008. "What Do We Know about Global Income Inequality." *Journal of Economic Literature* 46:1, pp. 57–94.

Andersen, Chris. 2009. *Free: The Future of a Radical Price*: New York: Hyperion.

Andre, Carl. 2004. *In Praise of Slowness: How a Worldwide Movement Is Challenging the Cult of Speed*. New York: HarperOne.

Archibugi, Daniele. 2008. *The Global Commonwealth of Citizens: Toward Cosmopolitan Democracy*. Princeton: Princeton University Press.

Ariely, Dan. 2008. *Predictably Irrational: The Hidden Forces that Shape Our Decisions*. New York: HarperCollins.

Arlidge, John. 2009. "Mariah Carey, the Gloves Are Off." *Sunday Times* (London), 19 November.

Arrow, Kenneth. 1971. *Essays in the Theory of Risk-Bearing*. Chicago: Markham.

Arrow, Kenneth, Partha Dasgupta, Lawrence Goulder, P. R. Ehrlich, G. M. Heal, S. Levin, K.-G. Mäler, S. Schneider, D. A. Starrett, and B. Walker. 2004. "Are We Consuming Too Much?" *Journal of Economic Perspectives* 18:1, pp. 147–72.

Arrow, Kenneth, Partha Dasgupta, Lawrence Goulder, Kevin Mumford, and Kirsten Oleson. 2007. "China, the U.S., and Sustainability: Perspectives

Based on Comprehensive Wealth." Stanford Center for Sustainable Development Working Paper No. 313. Stanford, CA: Stanford Center for Sustainable Development.

Arrow, Kenneth, Partha Dasgupta, and K.-G. Mäler. 2003. "The Genuine Savings Criterion and the Value of Population." *Economic Theory* 21:2, pp. 217–25.

Atwood, Margaret. 2008. *Payback: Debt and the Shadow Side of Wealth*. London: Bloomsbury.

Baker, Dean. 2010. *Taking Economics Seriously*. Cambridge, MA: MIT Press.

Barber, Benjamin R. 2009. "A Revolution in Spirit." *The Nation*, 22 January.

Bardsley, Nicholas, Robin Cubitt, Graham Loomes, Peter Moffatt, Chris Starmer, and Robert Sugden, eds. 2009. *Experimental Economics: Rethinking the Rules*. Princeton: Princeton University Press.

Barrington-Leigh, Christopher, Anthony Harris, John Haltiwanger, and Haifang Huang. 2010. "International Evidence on the Social Context of Well-being." VoxEU, 24 April, http//www.voxeu.org.

Barro, Robert J. 2000. "Inequality and Growth in a Panel of Countries." *Journal of Economic Growth* 5, pp. 87–120.

Baumol, William. 1993. "Social Wants and Dismal Science: The Curious Case of the Climbing Costs of Health and Teaching." *Proceedings of the American Philosophical Society* 137:4, pp. 419–40.

Baumol, William, with William Bowen. 1966. *Performing Arts: The Economic Dilemma*. Cambridge, MA: MIT Press and the Twentieth Century Fund.

Beck, Thorsten, Diane Coyle, Mathias Dewatripont, Xavier Freizas, and Paul Seabright. 2010. "Bailing out the Banks: Reconciling Stability and Competition." London: Centre for Economic Policy Research.

Becker, Sasha, Karolina Ekholm, and Marc-Andreas Muendler. 2009. "Offshoring and the Onshore Composition of Tasks and Skills." Discussion Paper No. 7391. London: CEPR.

Bell, Daniel. 1976. *The Cultural Contradictions of Capitalism*. Oxford: Pergamon Press.

Besley, Timothy. 2005. "From Micro to Macro: Public Policies and Aggregate Economic Performance." *Fiscal Studies* 22:3, pp. 357–74.

Besley, Timothy, Robin Burgess, and Andrea Prat. 2002. "Mass Media and Political Accountability." London: London School of Economics.

Bhagwati, Jagdish, and Alan S. Blinder. 2009. *Offshoring of American Jobs: What Response from U.S. Economic Policy*. Cambridge, MA: MIT Press.

Black, Sandra, and Paul J. Devereux. 2010. "Recent Developments in Intergenerational Mobility." CEPR Discussion Paper No. 7786. London: Centre for Economic Policy Research.

Blackburn, McKinley, and David Bloom. 1989. "The Effects of Technological Change on Earnings and Income Inequality in the United States." Working Paper No. 2337. Cambridge, MA: National Bureau of Economic Research.

Blanchflower, David, and Andrew Oswald. 2004. "Well-being over Time in Britain and the USA." *Journal of Public Economics* 88, pp. 1359–86.

Blinder, Alan S. 2006. "Offshoring: The Next Industrial Revolution?" *Foreign Affairs* 85:2, pp. 113–25.

————. 2009. "How Many U.S. Jobs Might Be Offshorable." *World Economics* 10:2, pp. 41–78.

Blond, Philip. 2010. *Red Tory*. London: Faber.

Bobbitt, Philip. 2002. *The Shield of Achilles: War, Peace, and the Course of History*. New York: Knopf.

Bourguignon, Francois, and Diane Coyle. 2003. "Inequality, Public Perception, and the Institutional Responses to Globalization." *Mondea y Cridito* 216, pp. 211–50.

Bowles, Samuel, and Herbert Gintis. 2002. "Social Capital and Community Governance." *Economic Journal* 112, pp. 419–36.

Boyle, James. 2008. *The Public Domain: Enclosing the Commons of the Mind*. New Haven, CT: Yale University Press.

Brafman, Ori, and Rod Beckstrom. 2006. *The Starfish and the Spider*. New York: Penguin Portfolio.

Brickman, Phillip, and D. T. Campbell. 1971. "Hedonic Relativism and Planning the Good Society." In *Adaptation Level Theory: A Symposium*, ed. M. H. Appley. New York: Academic Press.

Bronk, Richard. 2009. *The Romantic Economist: Imagination in Economics*. Cambridge: Cambridge University Press.

Brundtlandt, Gro Harlem. 1987. "Our Common Future." *Brundtlandt Commission Report*. Oxford: Oxford University Press.

Brynjolofsson, Erik, and Adam Saunders. 2009. *Wired for Innovation: How Information Technology Is Reshaping the Economy*. Cambridge, MA: MIT Press.

Buchanan, James. 1975. *The Limits of Liberty: Between Anarchy and Leviathan*. Indianapolis, IN: Liberty Funds.

————. 2001. "Game Theory, Mathematics, and Economics." *Journal of Economic Methodology* 8:1, pp. 27–32.

Buchanan, James, and Gordon Tullock. 1962. *The Calculus of Consent: Logical Foundations of Constitutional Democracy*. Ann Arbor: University of Michigan Press.

Buckley, Bryan, and Sergey Mityakov. 2009. "The Cost of Climate Regulation for American Households." Arlington, VA: The Marshall Fund.

Cairncross, Frances. 1997. *The Death of Distance*. Cambridge, MA: Harvard Business Press.

Camerer, Colin, George Loewenstein, and Matthew Rabin. 2003. *Advances in Behavioral Economics*. Princeton: Princeton University Press.

Castles, I. and P. D. Henderson. 2003a. "The IPCC Emissions Scenarios: An Economic-Statistical Critique." *Energy and Environment* 14:2, pp. 159–86.

————. 2003b. "Economics, Emissions Scenarios, and the Work of the IPCC." *Energy and Environment* 14:4, pp. 415–35.

Chancellor, Edward. 2000. *Devil Take the Hindmost*. New York: Penguin.

Collier, Paul. 2007. *The Bottom Billion*. New York: Oxford University Press.

————. 2010. *The Plundered Planet*. New York: Oxford University Press.

Corrado, Carol, Charles Hulten, and Daniel Sichel. 2006. "Intangible Capital and Economic Growth." Working Paper No. 11948. Cambridge, MA: National Bureau of Economic Research.

Cosmides, Leda, and John Tooby. 1994. " Better than Rational: Evolutionary Psychology and the Invisible Hand." *The American Economic Review* 84:2, pp. 327–32.

Coyle, Diane. 1996. *The Weightless World*. Oxford: Capstone.

———. 2001. *Paradoxes of Prosperity*. New York: Texere.

———. 2003. "Corporate Governance, Public Governance, and Global Governance: The Common Thread." Manchester, UK: University of Manchester, Institute of Political and Economic Governance.

———. 2007. *The Soulful Science: What Economists Really Do and Why It Matters*. Princeton: Princeton University Press.

———. 2009. "Scholar Goes Online to Differ with the Obama Government." *Times* (London), 5 May.

Coyle, Diane, and Patrick Meier. 2009. "New Technologies in Emergencies and Conflicts: The Role of Information and Social Networks." Washington, DC: UN Foundation/Vodafone Foundation.

Coyle, Diane, and Christopher Woolard. 2010. "Public Value in Practice: Restoring the Ethos of Public Service." London: BBC Trust.

Crafts, Nicholas. 1999. "Economic Growth in the Twentieth Century." *Oxford Review of Economic Policy* 15, pp. 18–34.

———. 2004. "Steam as a General Purpose Technology." *Economic Journal* 114:495 (April), pp. 338–51.

———. 2010. "The Contribution of New Technology to Economic Growth: Lessons from Economic History." *Revista de Historia Económica/Journal of Iberian and Latin American Economic History* (Second Series) 28, pp. 409–40.

Csikszentmilhalyi, Mihaly. 1990. *Flow: The Psychology of Optimal Experience*. New York: HarperCollins.

Cutler, David, Edward Glaeser, and Karen Norberg. 2000. "Explaining the Rise in Youth Suicide." Working Paper No. W7713. Cambridge, MA: National Bureau of Economic Research.

Daly, Herman E., and John B. Cobb. 1989. *For the Common Good: Redirecting the Economy toward Community, the Environment, and a Sustainable Future*. London: Green Print.

Dasgupta, Partha. 2004. "Three Conceptions of Intergenerational Justice." In *Ramsey's Legacy,* ed. H. Lillehammer and D. H. Mellor. Oxford: Clarendon Press.

———. 2006. "Comments on the Stern Review's Economics of Climate Change." Online working paper. Cambridge: University of Cambridge.

———. 2009a. "The Place of Nature in Economic Development." In *Handbook of Development Economics*, ed. Dani Rodrik and Mark Rosenzweig. Amsterdam: North Holland.

———. 2009b. "The Welfare Economic Theory of Green National Accounts." *Environmental and Resource Economics* 42:1, pp. 3–38.

———. 2009c. "A Matter of Trust: Social Capital and Economic Development." *Annual Bank Conference on Development Economics.* Washington, DC: World Bank.

————. 2010. "The Place of Nature in Economic Development." In *Handbook of Development Economics*, ed. Rodrik and Rosenzweig.

Dasgupta, Partha, and K.-G. Mäler. 2000. "Net National Product, Wealth, and Social Well-Being." *Environment and Development Economics* 5:69, pp. 69–93.

David, Paul, and Gavin Wright. 2005. "General Purpose Technologies and Productivity Surges: Historical Reflections on the Future of the ICT Revolution." *Economic History*, EconWPA, online Working Paper No. 0502002.

Davis, Mike. 2006. *Planet of Slums*. London: Verso.

Dawkins, Richard. 1976. *The Selfish Gene*. New York: Oxford University Press.

Deaton, Angus. 2008. "Income, Health and Well-Being around the World: Evidence from the Gallup World Poll." *Journal of Economic Perspectives* 22:2, pp. 53–72.

Diamond, Jared. 2005. *Collapse: How Societies Choose to Fail or Succeed*. New York: Viking.

Diener, Ed, and Robert Biswas-Diener. 2008. *Happiness: Unlocking the Mysteries of Psychological Wealth*. London: Blackwell.

Donovan, Todd, David Denemark, and Shaun Bowler. 2005. "Trust in Government: The United States in Comparative Perspective." Mimeo, Western Washington University.

Dorling, Danny. 2010. *Injustice: Why Social Inequality Persists*. Bristol, UK: Policy Press.

Dunleavy, Patrick, and C. Hood. 1994. "From Old Public Administration to New Public Management." *Public Money and Management* (July–September), pp. 9–16.

Dunleavy, Patrick, Helen Margetts, Simon Bastow, and Jane Tinkler. 2006. "New Public Management Is Dead: Long Live Digital Era Governance." *Journal of Public Administration Research and Theory* 16:3 (July), pp. 467–94.

Easterlin, Richard, and Laura Nagelescu. 2009. "Happiness and Growth the World Over: Time Series Evidence on the Happiness-Income Paradox." IZA Discussion Paper No. 4060. Bonn, Germany: IZA.

Easterlin, Richard A. 1974. "Does Economic Growth Improve the Human Lot?" In *Nations and Households in Economic Growth: Essays in Honor of Moses Abramowitz*, ed. Paul A. David and Melvin W. Reder. New York: Academic Press.

Eggar, Robin. 2009. "You Don't Need to Sell a Million to Make a Mint." *Sunday Times* (London), 8 November.

Ehrlich, Paul. 1968. *The Population Bomb*. New York: Ballantine.

Financial Times. 2009. "India Opts for Voluntary Cuts on Emissions."

Fitzgerald, F. Scott. 1925. *The Great Gatsby*. New York, Scribner's.

Fox, Justin. 2010. *The Myth of the Rational Market: A History of Risk, Reward, and Delusion on Wall Street*. New York: HarperCollins.

Frank, Robert. 1999. *Luxury Fever: Money and Happiness in an Era of Excess*. New York: Free Press.

Frank, Robert. 2007. "Why Not Shift the Burden to Big Spenders?" *New York Times,* 7 October.

Frank, Robert, and Philip Cook. 1995. *The Winner Takes All Society.* New York: Free Press.

Frank, Thomas. 2004. *What's the Matter with Kansas? How Conservatives Won the Heart of America.* New York: Henry Holt.

Frey, Bruno S., and Alois Stutzer. 2002. *Happiness and Economics: How the Economy and Institutions Affect Human Well-Being.* Princeton: Princeton University Press.

———. 2007. "Should National Happiness Be Maximized?" Working Paper No. 306. Zurich: University of Zurich, Institute for Empirical Research in Economics.

Fukuyama, Francis. 1992. *The End of History and the Last Man.* New York: Free Press.

Galbraith, John Kenneth. 1952. *American Capitalism—The Concept of Countervailing Power.* Boston: Houghton Mifflin.

———. 1958. *The Affluent Society.* New York: Penguin.

Garber, Peter. 1989. "Tulipmania." *Journal of Political Economy* 97:3, pp. 535–60.

———. 1990. "Famous First Bubbles." *Journal of Economic Perspectives* 4:2, pp. 35–54.

———. 2000. *Famous First Bubbles: The Fundamentals of Early Manias.* Cambridge, MA: MIT Press.

Gentzkow, Matthew. 2006. "Television and Voter Turnout." *Quarterly Journal of Economics.* 121:3 (August), pp. 931–72.

Glaeser, Edward. 2008. *Cities, Agglomeration, and Spatial Equilibrium.* New York: Oxford University Press.

Glaeser, Edward, and David Cutler. 2005. "What Explains Differences in Smoking, Drinking, and Other Health-Related Behaviors?" Working Paper No. 2060 (February). Cambridge, MA: Harvard Institute of Economic Research.

Glaeser, Edward, David Cutler, and Jesse Shapiro. 2003. "Why Have Americans Become More Obese?" Working Paper No. 1994 (January). Cambridge, MA: Harvard Institute of Economic Research.

Glaeser, Edward, Bruce Sacerdote, and Jose A. Scheinkman. 1995. "Crime and Social Interactions." Working Paper No. 5026. Cambridge, MA: National Bureau of Economic Research.

Gokhale, Jagadeesh, and Kent Smetters. 2003. *Fiscal and Generational Imbalances: New Budget Measures for New Budget Priorities.* Jackson, TN: AIE Press.

Goldin, Claudia, and Lawrence Katz. 2008. *The Race between Education and Technology.* Cambridge, MA: Harvard University Press.

Granovetter, Mark. 1973. "The Strength of Weak Ties." *American Journal of Sociology* 78:1, pp. 1360–80.

Groysberg, Boris. 2010. *Chasing Stars: The Myth of Talent and the Portability of Performance.* Princeton: Princeton University Press.

Haidt, Jonathan. 2006. *The Happiness Hypothesis: Putting Ancient Wisdom and Philosophy to the Test of Modern Science*. New York: Arrow Books.

Haldane, Andrew. 2009a. "Rethinking the Financial Network." Speech at the Association of Corporate Treasurers, Leeds, April.

———. 2009b. "Credit Is Trust." Speech at the Financial Student Association, Amsterdam, 14 September.

Haltiwanger, John, Jonathan Haskel, and Alicia Robb. 2010. "Extending Firm Surveys to Measure Intangibles: Evidence from the United Kingdom and United States." American Economics Association Annual Meeting, January.

Hamilton, Kirk, and Michael A. Clemens. 1999. "Genuine Savings Rates in Developing Countries." *World Bank Economic Review* 13:2, pp. 335–56.

Hausman, Jerry A. 1997. "Valuation of New Goods under Perfect and Imperfect Competition." In *The Economics of New Goods*, ed. Timothy Bresnahan and Robert J. Gordon. Chicago: University of Chicago Press.

———. 1999. "Cellular Telephones, New Products, and the CPI." *Journal of Business and Economic Statistics* 17:2, pp. 188–94.

Hayek, Friedrich von. 1945. "The Use of Knowledge in Society." *American Economic Review* 35:4, pp. 519–30.

Held, David, Mary Kaldor, and Danny Quah. 2010. "The Hydra-Headed Crisis." Pamphlet. London: London School of Economics, Global Governance Centre.

Held, David, Anthony McGrew, David Goldblatt, and Jonathan Perraton. 1999. *Global Transformations*. New York: Wiley.

Helliwell, J., C. Barrington-Leigh, A. Harris, and H. Huang. 2010. "International Evidence on the Social Context of Well-being." In *International Differences in Well-being*, ed. Ed Diener, J. F. Helliwell, and D. Kahneman. New York: Oxford University Press.

Helpman, Elhanan. 2004. *The Mystery of Economic Growth*. Cambridge, MA: Harvard University Press.

Henwood, Doug. 2003. *After the New Economy*. New York: New Press.

Hepburn, Cameron, and Paul Klemperer. 2006. "Discounting Climate Change Damages: Working Note for the Stern Review." London, UK.

Heshmati, Almas. 2006. "The World Distribution of Income and Income Inequality: A Review of the Economics Literature." *Journal of World-Systems Research* 12:1, pp. 60–107.

Hirsch, Fred. 1976. *Social Limits to Growth*. Cambridge, MA: Harvard University Press.

Hobbes, Thomas. 1651. *Leviathan or The Matter, Forme and Power of a Common Wealth Ecclesiasticall and Civil*.

Homer-Dixon, Thomas. 1999. *Environment, Scarcity, and Violence*. Princeton: Princeton University Press.

Hume, David. 1739. *A Treatise of Human Nature*.

Hyde, Lewis. 1983. *The Gift: Imagination and the Erotic Life of Property*. New York: Vintage.

ILO. 2008. "World of Work." Geneva: International Labor Organization.

IMF. 2009. "World Economic Outlook." April. Washington, DC: International Monetary Fund.

Inglehart, Ronald, R. Foa, C. Peterson, and C. Weizel. 2008. "Development, Freedom, and Rising Happiness: A Global Perspective (1981–2007)." *Perspectives on Psychological Science* 3:4, pp. 264–85.

IPCC. 2009. "Climate Change Science Compendium." New York: UNEP.

Jacobs, Jane. 1961. *The Life and Death of Great American Cities*. New York: Random House.

James, Oliver. 2007. *Affluenza*. London: Vermilion.

———. 2008. *The Selfish Capitalist*. London: Vermilion.

Johns, Helen, and Paul Ormerod. 2007. "Happiness, Economics and Public Policy." London: Institute of Economic Affairs.

Johnson, Steven. 2008. *The Invention of Air: A Story of Science, Faith, Revolution, and the Birth of America*. New York: Riverhead.

Johnson, Simon. 2009. "The Quiet Coup." *The Atlantic* (May).

Johnson, Simon, and James Kwak. 2010. *13 Bankers*. New York: Pantheon.

Jorgenson, Dale W., and Kevin J. Stiroh. 2000. "Raising the Speed Limit: U.S. Economic Growth in the Information Age." *Brookings Papers on Economic Activity* 1, pp. 125–211.

Kaletsky, Anatole. 2010. *Capitalism 4.0*. London: Bloomsbury.

Kamarck, Elaine. 2003. "Government Innovation around the World." Cambridge, MA: John F Kennedy School of Government, Harvard University.

Kay, John. 2009a. "Review of *The Spirit Level*." *Financial Times*, 23 March 2009.

———. 2009b. "Labour's Love Affair with Bankers Is to Blame for This Sorry State." *Financial Times*, 25 April 2009.

———. 2010. *Obliquity*. London: Profile.

Keefer, P., and S. Knack. 1997. "Does Social Capital Have An Economic Payoff? A Cross-Country Investigation." *Quarterly Journal of Economics* 112, pp. 1251–88.

Khor, Martin. 2010. "Blame Failure of Copenhagen Summit on Denmark, not China," *China Daily*, 2 January.

King, Stephen D. 2010. *Losing Control: Why the West's Economic Prosperity Can No Longer be Taken for Granted*. New Haven, CT: Yale University Press.

Klein, Naomi. 2000. *No Logo*. New York: Knopf.

Knowles, Stephen. 2005. "Inequality and Economic Growth: The Empirical Relationship Reconsidered in the Light of Comparable Data." *Journal of Development Studies* 41:1, pp. 135–59.

Kobayashi, Keiichiro. 2009. "Fiscal Policy Again? A Rebuttal to Mr. Krugman." VoxEU, 27 April, http//www.voxeu.org.

Kosteas, Vasilios. 2008. "Manufacturing Wages and Imports: Evidence from the NLSY." *Economica* 75:298, pp. 259–79.

Kropp, Manuela. 2009. "Background Paper for the Second Session of the Trade Union-related Research Institutes' Network (TURI) Seminar 'European Responses to the Crisis and Alternatives to GDP as an Element of a Paradigm Shift.'" Brussels, 29 June.

Krugman, Paul. 2002. "For Richer." *New York Times Magazine*, 20 October.

———. 2007. *The Conscience of a Liberal*. New York: W. W. Norton.

———. 2009. "How Did Economists Get It So Wrong?" *New York Times*, 20 September.

Landes, David. 1969. *The Unbound Prometheus*. Cambridge: Cambridge University Press.

Layard, Richard. 2005. *Happiness: Lessons from a New Science*. London: Penguin.

Levitt, Steven D., and Stephen J. Dubner. 2009. *SuperFreakonomics: Global Cooling, Patriotic Prostitutes, and Why Suicide Bombers Should Buy Life Insurance*. London: Allen Lane.

Levitt, Steven D., and John List. 2009. "Field Experiments in Economics: The Past, the Present, and the Future." *European Economic Review* 53:1 (January), pp. 1–18.

Levy, Frank, and Richard J. Murnane. 2005. *The New Division of Labor: How Computers Are Creating the Next Job Market*. Princeton: Princeton University Press.

Linklater, Andro. 2002. *Measuring America: How the United States Was Shaped by the Greatest Land Sale in History*. New York: Penguin.

Lipsky, John. 2010. "Fiscal Policy Challenges in the Post-Crisis World." Speech by first deputy managing director, International Monetary Fund, at the China Development Forum. Washington, DC.

List, John. 2008. "Using Field Experiments in the Economics of Charity." *NBER Reporter*, Issue 4.

Mackenzie, Donald, Fabian Muniesa, and Lucia Siu, eds. 2007. *Do Economists Make Markets? On the Performativity of Economics*. Princeton: Princeton University Press.

Manzi, Jim. 2010. "Keeping America's Edge." *National Affairs* (January).

Marshall, Alfred. 1890. *Principles of Economics*.

Mattl, W. and N. Woods. 2009. *The Politics of Global Regulation*. Princeton: Princeton University Press

McKitrick, M. Ross. 2007. "Response to Henderson's 'Government and Climate Change: A Flawed Consensus.'" *American Institute of Economic Research Economic Education Bulletin* 48:5 (May Special Issue: "The Global Warming Debate: Science, Economics and Policy"), pp. 83–104.

Medema, Steven G. 2009. *The Hesitant Hand: Taming Self-Interest in the History of Economic Ideas*. Princeton: Princeton University Press.

Meek, James. 2009. "To Live in Remarkable Times." *The Guardian*, 5 January.

Mehta, Suketu. 2004. *Maximum City: Bombay Lost and Found*. New York: Knopf.

Milanovic, Branko. 2005. *Worlds Apart: Measuring International and Global Economy*. Princeton: Princeton University Press.

Miles, Nicholas, Charu Wilkinson, Jakob Edler, Mercedes Bleda, Paul Simmonds, and John Clark. 2009. "Wider Conditions for Innovation." Pamphlet. London: National Endowment for Science, Technology and the Arts.

Mill, J. S. 1863. *Utilitarianism*.

Minsky, Hyman P. 1992. "The Financial Instability Hypothesis." Working Paper No. 74 (May). Annandale on Hudson, NY: Jerome Levy Economics Institute, Bard College.

Musgrave, Richard A., and Peggy B. Musgrave. 1973. *Public Finance in Theory and Practice*. New York: McGraw Hill.

Nannicini, Tommaso, Andrea Stella, Guido Tabellini, and Ugo Troiano. 2010. "Social Capital and Political Accountability." Discussion Paper No. 7782. London: Centre for Economic Policy Research.

Napier, Russell. 2009. "Capital Behaving Badly Tries the Patience of Powers-that-Be." *Financial Times*, 10 August.

NEP. 2010. "An Anatomy of Economic Inequality in the UK: Report of the National Equality Panel." National Equality Panel. LSE Centre for the Analysis of Social Exclusion.

Neve, Jan-Emanuel de. 2009. "Endogenous Preferences: The Political Consequences of Economic Institutions." Political Science and Political Economy Working Paper No. 04/2009. London: London School of Economics.

New Economics Foundation. 2009. "A Bit Rich: Calculating the Real Value to Society of Different Professions." London: NEF.

Nordhaus, William. 1997. "Do Real Output and Real Wage Measures Capture Reality? The History of Light Suggests Not." In *The Economics of New Goods*, ed. Robert J. Gordon and Timothy F. Bresnahan. University of Chicago Press.

———. 2001. "The Progress of Computing." Cowles Foundation Discussion Paper No. 1324. New Haven, CT: Cowles Foundation.

———. 2002. "Productivity Growth and the New Economy." *Brookings Papers on Economic Activity* 2, pp. 211–44.

———. 2007. "A Review of the Stern Review on the Economics of Climate Change." *Journal of Economic Literature* 45 (September), pp. 686–702.

Oberholzer-Gee, Felix, and Koleman Strumpf. 2009. "File Sharing and Copyright." Working Paper No. 09/32. Cambridge, MA: Harvard Business School.

OECD. 2001. "Public Sector Leadership for the 21st Century." OECD: Paris.

———. 2003. "Public Sector Modernization." OECD: Paris.

———. 2006a. "Society at a Glance." OECD: Paris.

———. 2006b. "Live Longer, Work Longer: Aging and Employment Policies." OECD: Paris.

———. 2009. "How Expensive Is the Welfare State." OECD: Paris.

Offer, Avner. 2006. *The Challenge of Affluence*. New York: Oxford University Press.

O'Flynn, Janine. 2007. "From New Public Management to Public Value: Paradigmatic Change and Managerial Implication." *Australian Journal of Public Administration* 66:3, pp. 353–66.

Olson, Mancur. 1965. *The Logic of Collective Action: Public Goods and the Theory of Groups*. Cambridge, MA: Harvard University Press.

———. 1996. "Big Bills Left on the Sidewalk: Why Some Nations Are Rich, and Others Poor." *Journal of Economic Perspectives* 10:2, pp. 3–24.

Orwell, George. 1937. *The Road to Wigan Pier*.

Ostrom, Elinor, and Vincent Ostrom. 2004. "The Quest for Meaning in Public Choice." *American Journal of Economics and Sociology* 63:1, pp. 105–47.

Ovid. "Midas and the Golden Touch." *Metamorphoses*, Book XI: 85–145.

Page, Scott. 2007. *The Difference: How the Power of Diversity Creates Better Groups, Firms, Schools, and Societies*. Princeton: Princeton University Press.

Persson, Thorsten, and Guido Tabellini. 1994. "Is Inequality Harmful for Growth? Theory and Evidence." *American Economic Review* 84, pp. 600–21.

Pew. 2007. "Americans and Social Trust: Who, Where, and Why." Washington, DC: Pew Research Center for the People and the Press.

———. 2009. "Mixed Views of Economic Policies and Health Care Reform Persist." Washington, DC: Pew Research Center for the People and the Press.

———. 2010. "Distrust, Discontent, Anger, and Partisan Rancor: The People and Their Government." Washington, DC: Pew Research Center for the People and the Press.

Piereson, James. 2009. "The Cultural Contradictions of J. M. Keynes." *New Criterion* (May).

Piketty, Thomas. 2010. "On the Long-Run Evolution of Inheritance: France, 1820–2050." Working paper, Ecole D'Economie de Paris.

Piketty, Thomas, and Emmanuel Saez. 2006. "The Evolution of Top Incomes: A Historical and International Perspective." Working Paper No. 11955. Cambridge MA: National Bureau of Economic Research.

Pinker, Steven. 2008. "The Moral Instinct." *New York Times Magazine*, 13 January.

Plott, Charles. 2001. *Market Institutions and Price Discovery. Collected Papers on the Experimental Foundations of Economics and Political Science*. Cheltenham, UK: Edward Elgar.

Praag, Bernard M. S. van, and Ada Ferrer-i-Carbonell. 2004. *Happiness Quantified: A Satisfaction Calculus Approach*. New York: Oxford University Press.

Pralahad, C. K. 2004. *The Fortune at the Bottom of the Pyramid: Eradicating Poverty through Profits*. Pittsburgh, PA: Wharton Business School.

Putnam, Robert. 1993. *Making Democracy Work: Civic Traditions in Modern Italy*. Princeton: Princeton University Press.

———. 2000. *Bowling Alone*. New York: Simon & Schuster.

———, ed. 2002. *Democracies in Flux: The Evolution of Social Capital in Contemporary Society*. New York: Oxford University Press.

Rajan, Raghuram G. 2010. *Faultlines: How Hidden Fractures Still Threaten the World Economy*. Princeton: Princeton University Press.

Rajan, Raghuram G., and Luigi Zingales. 2004. *Saving Capitalism from the Capitalists: Unleashing the Power of Financial Markets to Create Wealth and Spread Opportunity.* Princeton: Princeton University Press.

Ramsey, Frank P. 1928. "A Mathematical Theory of Saving." *Economic Journal* 38:4, pp 543–49.

Reinhardt, Carmen M., and Kenneth Rogoff. 2010. *This Time Is Different: Eight Centuries of Financial Folly.* Princeton: Princeton University Press.

Rivoli, Pietra. 2005. *The Travels of a T-Shirt in the Global Economy: An Economist Examines the Markets, Power, and Politics of World Trade.* New York: Wiley.

Roach, Stephen S. 2009. "Whither Capitalism?" *The Globalist,* 5 March.

Robinson, Robert, and Elton Jackson. 2002. "Is Trust in Others Declining in America? An Age-Period-Cohort Analysis." Bloomington: Department of Sociology, Indiana University.

Rosen, Sherwin. 1981. "The Economics of Superstars." *American Economic Review* 71:5, pp. 845–58.

Rousseau, Jean-Jacques. 1754. "Discourse on the Origin and Basis of Inequality among Men."

Ruskin, John. 1860. *Unto This Last.* Nelson, Lancashire: Hendon.

Sahlins, Marshall. 1972. *Stone Age Economics.* London: Aldine Transaction

Saint-Paul, Gilles. 2008. *Innovation and Inequality: How Does Technical Progress Affect Workers?* Princeton: Princeton University Press.

———. 2011. *The Rise of Paternalism.* Princeton: Princeton University Press.

Sala-i-Martin, Xavier. 2002a. "The Disturbing 'Rise' of Global Income Inequality." Working Paper No. 8904. Cambridge MA: National Bureau of Economic Research.

———. 2002b. "The World Distribution of Income (Estimated from Individual Country Distributions)." Working Paper No. 8933. Cambridge MA: National Bureau of Economic Research.

Sandel, Michael. 2009. *Justice: What's the Right Thing to Do?* London: Allen Lane.

Sassen, Saskia. 2002. *Global Networks, Linked Cities.* London: Routledge.

Schelling, Thomas. 1978. *Micromotives and Macrobehavior.* New York: Norton.

Schwartz, Barry. 2004. *The Paradox of Choice: Why More Is Less.* New York: HarperCollins.

Seabright, Paul. 2010. *The Company of Strangers: A Natural History of Economic Life.* Princeton: Princeton University Press.

Seligman, Martin. 2002. *Authentic Happiness.* New York: Free Press.

Sen, Amartya. 1990. "More than 100 Million Women Are Missing." *New York Review of Books,* 37:20.

———. 1999a. *Development as Freedom.* New York: Oxford University Press.

———. 1999b. "Democracy as a Universal Value." *Journal of Democracy* 10:3, pp. 3–17.

———. 2009a. *The Idea of Justice.* Cambridge, MA: Harvard University Press.

———. 2009b. "Capitalism beyond the Crisis." *New York Review of Books* 56:5, 26 March.

Sen, Amartya, Joseph Stiglitz, and Jean Fitoussi. 2009. "Report by the Commission on the Measurement of Economic Performance and Social Progress." Paris.

Sheerin, Caroline. 2002. "UK Material Flow Accounting." *Economic Trends* (June), pp. 53–61.

Shirky, Clay. 2008. *Here Comes Everybody: The Power of Organizing without Organizations.* New York: Penguin.

Siebert, Horst. 2009. *Rules for the Global Economy.* Princeton: Princeton University Press.

Sigmund, Karl, Ernst Fehr, and Martin A Nowak. 2002. "The Economics of Fair Play." *Scientific American* 286:1 (January), pp. 82–87.

Simon, Herbert. 1984. "On the Behavioral and Rational Foundations of Economic Dynamics." *Journal of Economic Behavior and Organization* 5, pp. 35–56.

———. 1991. "Organizations and Markets." *Journal of Economic Perspectives* 5:2, pp. 25–44.

Simon, Julian L. 1996. *The Ultimate Resource.* Princeton: Princeton University Press.

Smith, Tom W. 2008. "Trends in Confidence in Institutions, 1973–2006." Paper No. SC54. Chicago: National Opinion Research Center.

Smith, Vernon L. 1982. "Microeconomic Systems as an Experimental Science." *American Economic Review* 72:5, pp. 923–55.

Solow, Robert M. 1992. "An Almost Practical Step toward Sustainability." London: RFF Press.

Sowell, Thomas. 2008. *Applied Economics: Thinking Beyond Stage One.* New York: Basic Books.

———. 2007. *Basic Economics: A Common Sense Guide to the Economy* Cambridge, MA: Perseus Books.

Spilimbergo, Antonio, Steven Symansky, Olivier Blanchard, and Carlo Cottarelli. 2009. "Fiscal Policy for the Crisis." IMF Staff Position Note, 29 September. Washington DC.

Spufford, Francis. 2010. *Red Plenty.* London: Faber.

Stern, Nicholas. 2007. *The Economics of Climate Change: The Stern Review.* Cambridge: Cambridge University Press.

———. 2009. *Blueprint for a Safer Planet: How to Manage Climate Change and Create a New Era of Progress and Prosperity.* London: The Bodley Head.

Stevenson, Betsey, and Justin Wolfers. 2008. "Economic Growth and Subjective Well-Being: Reassessing the Easterlin Paradox." *Brookings Papers on Economic Activity* 1 (spring), pp. 1–102.

Stoker, Gerry. 2006. *Why Politics Matters.* London: Palgrave Macmillan.

Sunstein, Cass R. 2007. *Republic.com 2.0.* Princeton: Princeton University Press.

Thaler, Richard, and Cass Sunstein. 2008. *Nudge: Improving Decisions about Health, Wealth and Happiness.* New York: Penguin.

Trajtenberg, Manuel. 1989. "Welfare Analysis of Product Innovations, with an Application to Computed Tomography Scanners." *Journal of Political Economy* 97:2, pp. 444–79.

Trivers, Robert L. 1971. "The Evolution of Reciprocal Altruism." *Quarterly Review of Biology* 46 (March), pp. 35–57.

Trollope, Anthony. 1875. *The Way We Live Now*.

UN. 2006. "International Migration Report." New York: Department of Economic and Social Affairs/Population Division, United Nations.

Waal, Frans de. 2008. *Primates and Philosophers: How Morality Evolved*. Princeton: Princeton University Press.

Weale, Martin. 2009. "Saving and the National Economy." Discussion Paper No. 340. London: National Institute of Economic and Social Research.

Wilkinson, Richard, and Kate Pickett. 2009. *The Spirit Level: Why More Equal Societies Almost Always Do Better*. London: Allen Lane.

Wilkinson, Will. 2007. "In Pursuit of Happiness Research: Is it Reliable? What Does It Imply for Policy." *Policy Analysis*, No. 590, 11 April 2007, Washington DC: Cato Institute.

Willetts, David. 2010. *The Pinch*. London: Atlantic Books.

Winterson, Jeanette. 2010. "Once upon a Life." *Observer Magazine*, 13 June, pp. 7–10.

Wolff, Edward N. 2007. "Recent Trends in Household Wealth in the United States: Rising Debt and the Middle-Class Squeeze." Working Paper No. 502. Annandale on Hudson, NY: The Levy Economics Institute of Bard College.

Woods, Ngaire, ed. 2000. *The Political Economy of Globalization*. Basingstoke, UK: Macmillan.

World Bank. 2000. "The New Public Management and its Legacy." Washington, DC: World Bank.

ILLUSTRATION CREDITS

Figure 1. Lazy Summer Afternoon. Copyright © Dhannte. Courtesy of Shutterstock. 21

Figure 2. Water-carrier in front of a grocery shop in Luxor, Egypt. Copyright © Vladimir Wrangel. Courtesy of Shutterstock. 34

Figure 3. Beijing traffic jam. Copyright © Michel Stevelmans. Courtesy of Shutterstock. 64

Figure 4. Flood water in the Ironbridge Gorge, Shropshire, England. Copyright © Christopher Elwell. Courtesy of Shutterstock. 75

Figure 5. Little girl coloring. Copyright © jcjgphotography. Courtesy of Shutterstock. 96

Figure 6. African child locked behind a metallic gate. Copyright © Lucian Coman. Courtesy of Shutterstock. 110

Figure 7. Two orangutans grooming each other. Copyright © Norma Cornes. Courtesy of Shutterstock. 120

Figure 8. Migrant agricultural worker's family. Seven hungry children. Mother aged thirty-two. Father is native Californian. Photo by Dorothea Lange. 128

Figure 9. Pyramid of Capitalist System, issued by Nedeljkovich, Brashich, and Kuharich in 1911. Published by International Publishing, Cleveland, OH. 132

Figure 10. A view of Checkpoint Charlie, the crossing point for foreigners visiting East Berlin. Photo by Helga T. H. Mellmann. 148

Figure 11. *Babel Revisited.* Copyright © 2004 Julee Holcombe. 167

Figure 12. Elderly man walking in park. Copyright © Dariush M. Courtesy of Shutterstock. 192

Figure 13. Green field with tree and double rainbow. Copyright © Ozerov Alexander. Courtesy of Shutterstock. 199

Figure 14. Reykjavik, Iceland, January 21, 2009: Protesters with flares at riots during protests against the Icelandic government's handling of the economy. Copyright © Johann Helgason. Courtesy of Shutterstock. 212

Figure 15. Gold Bull. Photographed on the streets of Chicago. Copyright © Kushch Dmitry. Courtesy of Shutterstock. 227

Figure 16. People atop the Berlin Wall near the Brandenburg Gate on November 9, 1989. Copyright © Sue Ream. 241

Figure 17. The Hephaisteion Temple (Theseion) atop Agoraios Kolonos hill, Athens, Greece. Copyright © Galina Mikhalishina. Courtesy of Shutterstock. 259

INDEX